Fluency in Distance Learning

A Companion Website for this volume is available at:
http://www.infoagepub.com/fenton-dlfluency

Fluency in Distance Learning

Celeste Fenton
Hillsborough Community College and
Training and Development Solutions, LLC

Brenda Ward Watkins
Hillsborough Community College and
Training and Development Solutions, LLC

INFORMATION AGE PUBLISHING, INC.
Charlotte, NC • www.infoagepub.com

Library of Congress Cataloging-in-Publication Data

Fenton, Celeste.
  Fluency in distance learning / Celeste Fenton, Brenda Ward Watkins.
     p. cm.
  Includes bibliographical references.
  ISBN 978-1-61735-000-9 (pbk.) – ISBN 978-1-61735-001-6 (hardcover) –
ISBN 978-1-61735-002-3 (e-book)
  1. Web-based instruction. 2. Internet in education. 3. Computer network
resources. 4. Internet in education. I. Watkins, Brenda Ward. II. Title.
  LB1044.87.F46 2010
  371.35'8–dc22

                                                        2010006703

Printed in the United States of America

Contents

Teaching Online

Insights into Distance Learning

Cyber Classroom. Virtual Classroom. Web learning. eLearning. Online Learning. eInstruction. Of all of the synonyms used to distinguish courses or degrees offered online through the Internet, *distance learning* is probably the most common. Distance Learning is defined by the United States Distance Learning Association (USDLA, 2009) as

> The acquisition of knowledge and skills through mediated information and instruction, encompassing all technologies and other forms of learning at a distance. (USDLA, 2009)

Distance learning involves the delivery of resources to sites remote from the point of origin of instruction. The receiving site may be another classroom, building, or home in the same city or different city, state, or country. The delivery mechanisms utilized could be multimedia, such as video and audio, computer, Internet, or some combination of these mediums. Distance learning can be referred to by a variety of terms, such as distance education, online learning, eLearning, e-instruction, and web-based instruction (WBI), which are commonly accepted in the United States; while the expressions *open learning* and *Open University* are also popular in Europe. Computer-based instruction (CBI) is a phrase sometimes used to

Fluency in Distance Learning, pages vii–xxii
Copyright © 2010 by Information Age Publishing
vii

depict distance learning, but this is a less accurate term, as CBI can also involve students receiving instruction on a computer via CDs or DVDs that does not involve accessing instruction from a remote location.

There are a variety of models for delivering instruction at a distance. In a report for The Sloan Consortium, Allen and Seaman (2008) organize course delivery into four separate classifications:

1. *Traditional*: zero percent online technology resources utilized to deliver content or engage learners
2. *Web Facilitated*: course is delivered primarily face-to-face, with one to twenty-nine percent usage of online technologies, such as utilizing a learning management system or website to present syllabus and assignment information
3. *Blended/Hybrid*: facilitation of course is a combination of online and face-to-face methods, with thirty to seventy-nine percent delivery conducted via online resources; examples of online activities include online discussions, posting and submission of assignments online, and multimedia lecture content available online.
4. *Online*: the primary facilitation of the course is online, usually with no face-to-face meetings and eighty percent or greater of teaching and learning activities conducted online.

In addition to the distance learning options outlined above, instruction may be delivered synchronously (teaching/learning events occur within the same time frame) or asynchronously (teaching/learning engagement takes place at different times). Further, while synchronous learning occurs at the same time, instructors and learners can participate in the instructional event at the same or different locations. The United States Distance Learning Association (USDLA, 2005) explains the diversity of alternatives available in distance education in the following way:

> Programming for distance learning provides the receiver many options both in technical configurations and content design. Educational materials are delivered primarily through live and interactive classes. The intent of these programs is not necessarily to replicate face-to-face instruction. Interactivity is accomplished via telephone (one-way video and two-way audio), two-way video or graphics interactivity, two-way computer hookups, or response terminals. (USDLA, 2005)

According to the USDLA, distance learning is utilized across the spectrum of educational platforms, from pre-K through higher education, continuing education, corporate professional development, and military and government training. Allen and Seaman (2008), in their annual report on distance education in the United States, reported that:

1. Over 3.9 million students were taking at least one online course during the fall 2007 term; a 12 percent increase over the number reported the previous year.
2. The 12.9 percent growth rate for online enrollments far exceeds the 1.2 percent growth of the overall higher education student population.
3. Over 20 percent of all U.S. higher education students were taking at least one online course in the fall of 2007.
4. Approximately one-third of baccalaureate institutions consider online to be critical to their long-term strategy
5. Enrollment in distance education increased from 1.98 million in 2003 to 3.9 million in 2007
6. In the fall of 2007 online enrollments represented approximately 22 percent of total enrollment, an increase from 11.7 percent in 2003.
7. The U.S. Department of Education reports that 76% of community colleges are actively involved in distance-learning programs in Career and Technical Education. (p. 4)

According to Small & Lohrasbi (2003), "The increase in the attractiveness of offering distance learning courses by educational institutions is in part attributed to declining enrollments and rising costs of traditional educational delivery" (p. 19). But why do students take distance learning courses? Distance learning offers the flexibility of accessing learning anytime, anywhere, anyplace. Rural and remote students seeking educational opportunity benefit immensely from the availability of distance learning offerings. There is an increasingly diverse population of students with widely different social, economic, cultural, and language backgrounds; and some students seeking educational opportunities contend with a wide range of physical, cognitive, and sensory disabilities. In addition, many Colleges and Universities are recruiting new target populations, such as working adults, and these students frequently enroll in online courses because of scheduling conflicts or availability issues (Taniguchi, 2003). Adult students, who need to balance many life-roles and responsibilities, find that distance learning is a time-saving and flexible mode of receiving and education. In a 2007–2008 survey that measured American students' use of distance learning, The Primary Research Group found that approximately 60% of distance learners in higher education are female (The Primary Research Group [PRG], 2007). Single and/or working mothers are able to pursue educational goals via distance learning, while still spending time with their children at home. Also, economic factors seem to be playing an ever-increasing role in the expansion of distance learning enrollments, particularly higher fuel costs (Allen and Seaman, 2008). Younger, traditional-age students who must work to pay their education expenses find distance learning beneficial, with respect to efficiently allocating their time and resources. The Instructional Technology Council (2006) specifically mentions the important aspects of students' reasons for participation in distance education:

> Students come to college for various reasons. They could be interested in changing careers or they might simply want to expand their knowledge base for work or personal reasons. They might want to expand their cultural background, learn a new language, or start a degree program that was postponed due to family or career needs. Their main reasons for choosing distance education as a delivery method is that they want to learn at their own pace, and at a time and location that is convenient to them. (Instructional Technology Council, 2006)

Another factor contributing to the popularity of distance learning among students in higher education is the expectation for distance learning offerings by a generation of students that have grown up with the dynamic wealth of resources on the Internet. The millennial generation of students (ages 18 to 25), savvy users and consumers of the Internet and all the forms of multimedia and social networking therein, are entering colleges and universities demanding not only a variety of distance learning course offerings, but a repertoire of e-services as well. The 2007–08 survey of distance learning programs in higher education (PRG, 2007) suggests that since more than 57% of students enrolled in distance programs reside within 75 miles of the host institution, distance learning may be a preferred mode of instruction, rather than an access issue.

Issues to Consider

There are many issues to consider when contemplating offering distance learning courses or programs. Several of the key issues are discussed in the following sections. It is important to remember that facilitating a distance course and teaching a traditional course require different sets of skills for the instructors, as well as different formats and structures for the development and delivery of course content.

Lack of Universal Standards

Despite the many positive aspects of distance learning, initially there were concerns, many of which continue to linger, about its appropriateness and effectiveness. The Institute of Higher Education Policy (1999) identified several areas of concern, including (1) inadequate control of extraneous variables, (2) non-random sampling of subjects, (3) questionable validity and reliability controls and measures, and (4) lack of control of reactive effects of students. Instructors and administrators expressed concern about course quality and the value of learning activities.

Historically, the research claimed no discernable difference between distance learning and traditional classes. Early research focused on (1) student outcomes, (2) student attitudes, and (3) student satisfaction. However, recent research examining the distance learning phenomena more closely has begun to reveal measureable results. A new meta-analysis released by the United States Department of Education (USDOE, 2009) indicates that "students who took all or part of their instruction online performed better, on average, than those taking the same course through face-to-face instruction. Further, those who took 'blended' courses—those that combine elements of online learning and face-to-face instruction—appeared to do best of all" (p. xiv).

Although there are many strands of ongoing research, compared to other fields under study, there is a scarcity of established research devoted to the effectiveness of distance learning. Compounding this problem is the lack of nationally accepted universal standards of quality for distance learning. The authors maintain that not all studies are equally rigorous and many studies contain bias. Some considerations of best practice recommendations are:

1. Quality course design should be a greater priority than attention to the media characteristics
2. For asynchronous courses, active learning and collaboration among students seems to result in higher achievement and attitude outcomes
3. Opportunities for communication, whether face-to-face or through course tools, appear to be beneficial for both synchronous and asynchronous learning
4. Supplemental one-way videos were found to promote better achievement and attitude for both synchronous and asynchronous learning

5. Interactivity between students appears to enhance better attitudes in asynchronous courses;
6. Provision of advance course information is beneficial for students

Attempts to develop national quality standards include the March, 2000 *Quality on the Line* report from the Institute for Higher Education, commissioned by the National Education Association (NEA) in collaboration with Blackboard, Inc. This report outlined twenty-four benchmarks (measures of quality) for distance learning courses and programs. A link to the full report can be found at www2.nea.org/he/abouthe/distance.html. More recently, in 2006 the North American Council for Online Learning (NACOL) issued *National Standards for Quality Online Teaching,* a guide designed to provide quality standards for course development and delivery.

Inasmuch as the Istitute for Higher Education/NEA/Blackboard benchmarks and the NACOL guide provide direction for the creation and delivery of Internet-based distance learning courses, the missing piece is "how to." This text focuses predominantly on the "how to" of three categories: (1) Course Development, (2) Teaching and Learning Strategies, and (3) Course Structure. Accordingly, the authors have developed six tenets of distance learning course development that set minimum standards for creating online courses and facilitating online instruction. The ability to meet these tenets results in an instructor that is fluent in the delivery of distance instruction. The six tenets are as follows:

1. Educators fluent in the delivery of distance instruction possess the knowledge, skills, and attitudes that encompass all aspects of teaching online including administrative, design, facilitation, evaluation, and technology—from pre-course planning to post-course wrap up.
2. Educators fluent in the delivery of distance instruction facilitate effective online communication that establishes a sense of community among all course participants, fosters information sharing and open dialogue, and supports active student participation.
3. Educators fluent in the delivery of distance instruction accommodate differing learning styles and intelligence types by incorporating multimedia to help students connect to and find meaning in the course content and relate their learning to the world beyond the online classroom.
4. Educators fluent in the delivery of distance instruction utilize a variety of teaching strategies to actively engage and motivate a

diverse student population to participate in the learning process, resulting in deeper understanding.

5. Educators fluent in the delivery of distance instruction understand the need to assess student performance using a variety of assessment strategies to ascertain that the essential skills and knowledge being taught is actually being learned.

6. Educators fluent in the delivery of distance instruction employ sound instructional design focused on delivering a quality learning experience that includes consideration of design principles such as content organization, layout, and use of color and graphical elements.

One final point should be made. Although distance learning provides flexibility and abundant opportunity for individuals to access higher education, there are contexts and content better-suited for traditional classroom or face-to-face instruction. Preferably, consultation occurs between instructors and program administrators to best determine the most effective delivery options.

Technology

One only has to review the history of education to note that change and reformation have been stimulated by technology and innovation. Interestingly, the history of distance education is marked by some as beginning in the early 1700s with correspondence education. Technology enhanced distance learning began with the advent of instructional films in 1910 (Reiser, 1987), leading Thomas Edison to predict in 1913 that school systems would experience dramatic changes throughout the next decade. Television and radio broadcasted instructional programs began as early as the 1930s, but it was the rapid development and expansion of computers and communications technologies in the 1980s that escalated the distance learning movement. Treat, Ying, Rajat, and Dixon (2006) explain that the 1990s saw tremendous growth in educational and home access of computers and networks. This advance in educational technology enabled the design and increased the availability of more student-centered learning experiences.

In 2005, the Internet was used by 72 percent of United States residents. In addition, approximately 54 percent of senior citizens, age 65 or older, regularly used the Internet. By 2008, Internet use had increased to 74 percent of total adults, with the fastest growing group of Internet users being seniors between the ages of 70–75. Approximately 45 percent of this age group is online, compared to 26 percent in 2005. These survey results released by the Pew Internet and American Life Project (2008) also revealed that 11 percent of online American adults reported using a service like Twitter to share updates about themselves and to see the updates of others. And 75 percent of online adults age 18–24 report having a profile on a social networking site (Pew, 2008).

The Pew project reveals that individuals using the Internet do so to take part in a wide range of activities, including a large percentage of online adults who use classified ads on websites such as Craigslist. The use of online classified ads more than doubled from 2005–2008, although email remains the most popular online activity, particularly among older Internet users. The Pew project indicates that 74 percent of Internet users age 64 and older send and receive email, while email use among teens has declined from 89 percent in 2004 to 73 percent in 2008 (Pew, 2008).

The Pew report, *The Internet Goes to College* (Pew, 2002), disclosed that 79 percent of college students believed the Internet had a positive impact on their college academic experience. Contending that the Internet is a core activity of most college students' educational experiences, the report states that (1) 73% use the Internet more than the library for research, (2) 60% think the Internet improved their relationships with classmates, and (3) 56% believe that email enhanced their relationship with professors (Pew, 2002).

In addition to the Internet, the use of digital technologies to educate learners extends the opportunity to reach larger numbers of students. Digital technologies such as video and audio have enabled educators to develop new teaching and learning strategies that help students develop the skills needed to thrive in a continuously changing world. Delivering instruction via the Internet and utilizing digital technology creates a framework for instructors and students to access knowledge and collaborate in the construction of new knowledge and understanding. In the end, the ultimate goal is not to utilize distance learning for the sake of competition and keeping up with what other institutions are doing, but to enrich the educational experiences and opportunities for all students.

As technology continues to advance, there are innumerable ways to design and deliver education at a distance. For instance, Web 1.0 technology was about reading content accessed from a website. Distance learning provided through Web 1.0 tools was static, with little opportunity for student interaction. The new Web 2.0 technologies allow learners to engage in peer-to-peer collaborative learning through blogging, videos, wikis, and webinars. A free Internet-based communications software program, Skype, allows individuals to talk to each other all over the world for free through the Internet. A webcam can be used to send video, and Skype can handle conference calls for up to nine users. Even more exciting is the ability to schedule Skypecasts, a jumbo conference call with up to 100 people participating. After downloading the free software and logging into the Skypecast, participants can listen to the conversations, indicate a desire to talk and then wait for their turn to talk, and contribute to the conversation. Imagine the possibilities for education! Students and faculty around the globe can share ideas, concerns, and discoveries. Students can create Skypecasts for an international audience as easily as they prepare an in-class presentation for their local classmates. Additionally, with Skype's video capability, instructors can demonstrate techniques and procedures.

Web 2.0 technology enabled the social networking of the chat room to evolve into the social media collaboration and connections happening in Facebook (www.facebook.com) and MySpace (www.myspace.com). Higher education is seeing potential and grasping opportunities to put these networks to work. From increasing student access to textbooks, to helping students find a roommate, to connecting students to a variety of student services, college and university departments are relating with students through the social media they are already familiar with. Hoffman (2009) shares:

> Many advocates promote the use of social networking for community building and increasing student engagement in higher education classrooms...Mazer, Murphy and Simonds (2007) indicate that teacher self-disclosure via social networking can increase motivation and improve classroom climate thus impacting student outcomes. In many of these debates, the focus is often limited to the massive and most well known of the social networks, MySpace and Facebook, particularly because media coverage has ensured that even those who have limited familiarity with social networking have heard about these Internet environments. However, social networking tools are more diverse and in fact, some may better fit specific class needs. (p. 92)

Colleges and universities are exploring ways to utilize other Web 2.0 tools, through the use of mobile technologies, in innovative and effective ways. As mentioned previously, the new generation of college students is plugged into their mobile devices, preferring the immediacy of information available through cell phone technology, such as emailing or texting classmates and professors. Massachusetts Institute of Technology (MIT) launched the MIT Mobile Web project in summer 2008 with 7000 screens. The mobile portal offered information on class schedules, grade reports, directions to classes, the best ways to get from one campus location to another, and bus schedules. In three months, the number of screens increased from 7000 to 55,000, with plans for the 2.0 version to offer access to the MIT learning management system and the ability to pay and manage debit card accounts (Raths, 2009).

Finally, virtual worlds are opening up a whole new realm of learner-centered engagement with Web 3.0 technology, based on intelligent web applications where users will create new tools and applications through open-source software and systems. A few years ago, placing a narrated PowerPoint online was advanced strategy; then video-conferencing enabled students to experience live lecture from a distance, albeit usually with limited or no interactivity. Now, with the availability of collaborative video systems, such as Elluminate, instructors and students communicate with each other online, either through a chat room or through video webcams, increasing the ability to interact synchronously and reinforce concepts in real-time.

Today, there exists a plethora of digital lecture capture and broadcast solutions that greatly enhance the ability to deliver instructional content remotely. Many products allow the creator to produce a lecture that can be placed in a learning management system and played back on a computer, but that can also be played back on a cell phone or downloaded to an iPod. There is no doubt that as technology continues to evolve, so will the face and possibilities of distance education.

Learning Management Systems

Software that facilitates the delivery of distance learning content is generally known as a learning management system (LMS). The anytime, anyplace, any pace access to instruction is a hallmark of LMS systems and is achieved through web-based communication. Most LMS systems deliver learning activities through the Internet, and typically include online tools that allow assessment, such as surveys and quizzes; communication tools, including email, discussion boards, and live chat; and content pages containing text documents and multimedia instruction via video and audio files. Well known LMS systems include Angel, Desire2Learn, Moodle, and WebCT/Blackboard.

Currently, there are over ninety different LMS systems, ranging from the most basic text-driven model to systems that offer new social learning features, such as blogs and wikis, peer rating of content, bookmarking, team calendaring, and file and media sharing, in addition to the features mentioned above. LMS solutions will continue to evolve as web technologies become more advanced. The reason is that LMS is considered a mission-critical investment, not only for academic institutions, but for private industry as well. According to Chapman (2009), over 65 percent of organizations (both academic and non-academic) utilize a learning management system, with 17,738 total LMS implementations, and 83.3 million registered e-learners.

The multitude of technologies and techniques presented in *Fluency in Distance Learning* are discussed in the context of teaching/learning strategies utilized within an LMS. The purpose of this approach is that, while some academic institutions are at the forefront of innovation, conducting classes in virtual worlds, or through open source gaming, or in even more inventive environments and pioneering techniques, the fact is that the majority of schools and colleges are just beginning to understand the potential of distance learning through their learning management systems. It has been our experience in working and consulting with a variety of institutions and school districts that the actual use and mastery of technology lags behind its availability. Therefore, through this book we endeavor to acquaint educators with the teaching and learning possibilities available within an LMS. Our goals are to (1) demystify the process of transforming face-to-face curriculum for online delivery, (2) help novice distance learning instructors adopt sound instructional practice for teaching online, and (3) encourage experienced distance learning instructors to try new strategies and explore new innovations.

Lecture Capture and Collaborative Broadcast Systems

Besides the tools available in an LMS, digital lecture capture and broadcast systems capture content in a particular form and make the output available to a user through a specific medium, such as the Internet, an iPod, or cell phone. Most of the systems include desktop sharing applications that allow students access and control of a virtual desktop. Students make presentations on the whiteboard, and other students may add comments or questions to the session by "raising their hand" (i.e., activating an icon to indicate a desire to "speak" in class). The systems vary widely in cost, features, and functions; a list of some of the systems is displayed in Table I.1.

The lecture systems use video and audio capture software to record lecture sessions, along with archiving and playback tools, so learners can view sessions asynchronously. Peripheral equipment such as webcams, video cameras, and microphones are used to deliver streaming live instruction over the Internet, and interactive whiteboards involve students in synchronous collaboration. Typically, users view a divided screen that displays the video lecture, while the other section of the screen contains the whiteboard and operational tools. The lectures can be edited for asynchronous viewing and/or broadcast on iPods, MP3 players, and cell phones. Depending on the system, title slides, annotations, text, and illustrations can be added to the video lecture.

TABLE I.1 List of Common Lecture Capture and Collaborative Broadcast Systems

System	Website
Accordent	http://www.accordent.com/solutions/education.aspx
Adobe Connect	http://www.adobe.com/products/acrobatconnectpro
Cisco Systems Digital Media Center	http://www.cisco.com/web/solutions/dms/index.html
Echo 360	http://www.echo360.com/index.asp
Elluminate	http://www.elluminate.com/
HaiVision Systems	http://www.haivision.com/applications/education/
Media POINTE	http://www.everythingavoverip.com/
Panopto Coursecast	http://www.panopto.com/
Polycom	http://www.polycom.com/
Sonic Foundry	http://www.sonicfoundry.com/
Tandberg	http://www.tandberg.com/
Tegrity	http://www.tegrity.com/
Wimba	http://www.wimba.com

Student Preparation

The meta-analysis by the United States Department of Education (US-DOE, 2009) found that students who took all or part of their instruction online performed better, on average, than those taking the same course through traditional classroom instruction. The report also relayed that students in online courses typically spent more time on task than students in face-to-face courses. However, student dropout rates are a concern held by most educators and educational institutions. Frankola (2001) reports that "dropout rates may be ten to twenty percent higher for online courses and programs, potentially due in part to the fact that distance learning may not be an effective mode of learning for some students" (p. 54). More current research indicates that the dropout rate may actually be higher than initially reported. The average attrition rate for college freshmen is approximately 20%, while estimates for online students' dropout rates appear to be around 35% (Clark, 2007).

There are a number of possible reasons why some students do not persist in distance learning courses. First, one of the most significant reasons may be found in the makeup of the distance learning student demographic: full-time workers with families. The time intensiveness of working full time, caring for children, and successfully completing college courses can be exhausting (Cochran, 2009). Second, the learning institutions may also be responsible for high dropout rates, due to their "one size fits all" manner of providing services to students. Failure by distance learning providers to engage each student on her or his own merits and according to individual needs increases dropout rates (Cochran, 2009).

Additional reasons for high dropout rates include the lack of necessary technical skills that are required to utilize common LMS tools, as described above. In addition, some students do not have access to necessary technical equipment needed to obtain course resources. Also, even though many college students have sufficient technical skills and equipment, they may never have had a previous opportunity to take a distance learning course. For these students the tasks of navigating the course, locating course materials, posting assignments, and utilizing communication tools associated with distance learning courses is challenging. Finally, many students lack the "self-management" skills needed for distance learning. Without the pressure of seeing the instructor and classmates each week, some students find it easy to procrastinate in completing required course activities and assignments. Research reveals that successful distance learning students are self-directed and able to manage their time and their own learning (Worcester Polytechnic Institute, 2007).

But, there is good news! And the good news rests with you, the Instructor. According to Palloff & Pratt (2003), research conducted on student perspectives regarding distance education suggests that (1) the level of interaction between instructor and student has a significant impact on student satisfaction and learning, (2) students prefer distance courses to be structured with expected outcomes and requirements clearly stated, and (3) students respond best when a variety of learning activities are utilized that appeal to multiple learning styles and intelligence types. Additional research (Sahin, 2007) further indicates the important role the instructor plays in student success and satisfaction with distance learning courses, relevant to the following categories: (1) instructor support, (2) student interaction and collaboration, (3) personal relevance, (4) authentic learning, (5) active learning, and (6) student autonomy.

By itself, simply putting lecture notes on a web site does not equate to effective use of distance learning resources and would not benefit a majority of students. However, stimulating a student's visual learning style via their attentiveness to a PowerPoint presentation, or engaging a shy/tentative student in an online discussion are just two examples of the impact that distance learning can have in opening up learning opportunities for all students.

Instructor Preparation and Attitudes

Deciding to implement a distance learning course should be made because an instructor, department, or institution is committed to reaching students who may not otherwise have access to education due to distance, time, or learning constraints. With regard to researching faculty perspectives regarding distance learning, Watts (2003) concluded that there is (1) frustration at being pressured to transform traditional courses to distance learning format, (2) a lack of experience in creating and managing distance learning courses, and (3) a lack of time to transform traditional classroom instruction to a distance learning mode. Additional concerns expressed by faculty include limited technical training and lack of support from administration; factors rated as important to faculty who currently teach distance learning courses include personal satisfaction, flexibility for students and instructor, and the ability to increase personal knowledge and skills (Carthan, 2007).

Getting Started

This book offers a practical, hands-on, workshop style approach to creating an effective distance learning course. Even if you are currently teaching online, we think you will find many valuable tips and strategies within the pages of the book to help you make your course more engaging and meaningful. Much of the guidance offered in the second edition of *Fluency in Distance Learning* is channeled to those who use conventional LMS systems. However, even if you deliver your distance courses via a different platform, this book contains a multitude of ideas and resources for developing fully interactive and engaging courses. Full of specific recommendations, step-by-step instructions, and templates that you can customize, the authors guide you through the process from beginning to end.

References

Allen, I. E. & Seaman, J. (2008). *Staying the course: Online education in the United States.* Sloan Consortium. Retrieved Jan., 2009, from http://www.sloan-c .org/publications/survey/pdf/staying_the_course.pdf

Carthan, E. (2007). *An analysis of faculty attitudes toward online courses at selected historically black colleges and universities.* Retrieved July 2, 2009, from http://www. sloanconsortium.org/conference/proceedings/2008/1209587688560 .ppt

Chapman, B. (2009). *LMS Knowledge Base 2009*. Brandon Hall Research, Harvard, CT.

Clark, D. (2007). *The pros and cons of elearning*. Retrieved July 2, 2009, from http://www.skagitwatershed.org/~donclark/hrd/elearning/proscons. html

Cochran, S. (2009). *Why a high rate of drop out for distance learning students?* Retrieved March 26, 2009, from: www.brighthub.com/education/online-learning/articles/33547.aspx

Frankola, V. (2001). Why online learners drop out. *Workforce, 80*(10), 52–60.

Hoffman, E. S. (2009). *Evaluating social networking tools for distance learning*. White paper presented at the TCC 2009 Proceedings. Retrieved July 2, 2006, from http://etec.hawaii.edu/proceedings/2009/hoffman.pdf

The Institute of Higher Education Policy. (1999). *What's the difference: A review of contemporary research on the effectiveness of distance learning in higher education.* Retrieved April 25, 2003, from http://www.ihep.com/Pubs/PDF/Difference.pdf

The Institute of Higher Education Policy. (2000). *Quality on the line: Benchmarks for success in internet-based distance education*. Washington, DC.

Instructional Technology Council. (2006). Retrieved May 7, 2007, from http://144.162.197.250/definition.htm

Mazer, J. P., Murphy, R. E., & Simonds, C. J. (2007). I'll see you on "Facebook": The effects of computer-mediated teacher self-disclosure on student motivation, affective learning, and classroom climate. *Communication Education, 56*, 1–17.*National Standards for Quality Online Teaching* (2006). Retrieved July 7, 2009, from http://www.inacol.org/.../nationalstandards/NACOL%20Standards%20Quality%20Online%20Teaching.pdf

Palloff, K. & Pratt, K. (2003). *The virtual student: A profile and guide to working with online learners*. San Francisco, CA: Jossey-Bass.

Pew Internet and American Life Project (2008). Retrieved July 7, 2009, from http://www.pewinternet.org/

The Internet Goes to College (2002). Pew Internet and American Life Project. Retrieved July 7, 2007, from http://www.pewinternet.org/Reports/2002/The-Internet-Goes-to-College.aspx

Prime Research Group (2008). *The Survey of Distance Learning Programs in Higher Education* (2007–08 Ed.). (2008).

Raths, D. (2009). Admin on the fly. *Campus Technology*. 25–29.

Reiser, R. A. (1987). Instructional technology: A history. In R.M. Gagne (Ed.) *Instructional technology: Foundations* (pp. 11–48). Hillsdale, NJ: Lawrence Erlbaum Associates.

Sahin, I. (2007). Predicting student satisfaction in distance education and learning environments. *Turkish Online Journal of distance Education-TOJDE*, Volume 8, Number 2, Article 9.

Small, M. & Lohrasbi, A. (2003). Student perspectives on online degrees and courses: An empirical analysis. *International Journal on E-Learning, 2*(2), 15–28.

Taniguchi, M. (2003). Introduction: Technology: Taking the distance out of learning. *Internet Metaphors Matter.* San Francisco, CA: Wiley.

Treat, A., Ying W., Rajat, C., & Dixon, M. (2006). Major developments in instructional technology: During the 20th century. *IDT Record.* Indiana University Bloomington. Retrieved June 29, 2009 from: http://www.indiana.edu/~idt/shortpapers/documents/ITduring20.html

United States Department of Education, Office of Planning, Evaluation, and Policy Development. (2009). *Evaluation of evidence-based practices in online learning: A meta-analysis and review of online learning studies.* Washington, DC: U. S. Department of Education.

United States Distance Learning Association, (2005). *Resources: Research, statistics and distance learning resources.* Retrieved June 16, 2009, from http://www.usdla.org/html/about Us/researchInfo.html

United States Distance Learning Association. (2009). DL Glossary. Retrieved February 17, 2010, from http://www.usdla.org/html/resources/dictionary.htm

Watts, M. (2003). Introduction: Technology: Taking the distance out of learning. *Technology as Catalyst.* San Francisco, CA: Wiley.

Worcester Polytechnic Institute (2007). *Characteristics of distance learning students.* Academic Technology Center. Retrieved July 2, 2009, from http://www.wpi.edu/Academics/ATC/Collaboratory/Teaching/students.html

1

KSA: Knowledge, Skills, and Attitudes of Effective Distance Learning Instructors

An effective distance learning instructor is a facilitator of learning, rather than the provider of knowledge. As stated in the introduction, creating a distance learning course or transforming a traditional class to a distance learning format is more than just uploading lecture notes or existing course materials. The process involves, above all else, careful planning and preparation. Upon completion of Chapter One, readers will be able to:

1. List the knowledge, skills, and attitudes (KSAs) necessary for effective online teaching
2. Write learning objectives that are specific and measurable
3. Utilize the Course Flowchart to map two units of instruction
4. Using the Course Planning and Delivery Guide, identify strengths and weaknesses of an existing or proposed distance learning course
5. Construct a plan for transitioning face-to-face course materials to distance learning format
6. Build a "Start Here" folder
7. Identify copyright violations

Fluency in Distance Learning, pages 1–33
Copyright © 2010 by Information Age Publishing
All rights of reproduction in any form reserved.

Knowledge, Skills, and Attitudes of Effective Online Instructors

The design, development, and maintenance of distance learning courses is often time intensive...a necessity, to ensure that learning activities are matched appropriately to desired learning outcomes. Research has identified five key categories of knowledge, skills, and attitudes (KSAs) necessary for the successful facilitation of online learning: Administrative, Design, Facilitation, Evaluation and Technical (Carroll-Barefield, et al., 2005; Shank, 2004). These categories are described in greater depth as follows:

1. *Administrative* traits include: (a) elimination of ambiguity and guessing by students about what is expected of them; (b) providing specific objectives, expectations, and policies; (c) posting course materials (syllabus, assignments, discussion topics, etc.) in plenty of time for students to access and plan; (d) communicating changes and updates; (e) engaging students in an introductory activity to take "attendance" and/or reduce anxiety; (f) providing timely feedback to student calls/emails; (g) referring issues and problems to appropriate sources and following up to assure resolution; and (h) providing information to students about institutional resources, such as tutoring services, location of computer labs, library hours, disability services, and so on.

2. Good *design* requires instructors to: (a) include activities that encourage students to attach personal meaning to content; (b) plan activities that allow students to connect content to the world outside of the course; (c) provide opportunities for active learning and application; (d) balance activities and assignments in order that students can manage time and workload; (e) include mechanisms for students to assess their learning; and (f) provide opportunity for discourse between students to overcome anonymity, share discoveries, and present multiple viewpoints.

3. *Facilitation* of online learning necessitates that instructors: (a) state expectations of frequency of communication; (b) provide examples of appropriate discussion responses; (c) describe group decision-making rules; (d) provide dynamic opportunities for online discussion, negotiation, and debate; (e) monitor discussions and moderate, as necessary, without "taking over"; (f) contribute resources or insights to spur further investigation of topics and content; (g) encourage class sharing of knowledge, questions, and expertise; (h) acknowledge student efforts and contributions; and (i) provide summary or wrap-up of discussions.

4. *Evaluation* is conducted to: (a) provide learners with unambiguous grading criteria; (b) use rubrics, checklists, and examples that help students understand expectations; (c) respond to and provide feedback to students having problems completing the assignments; (d) allow students to track assignment progress and cumulative grading; and (e) acknowledge receipt of assignments.
5. *Technical* considerations call for distance learning faculty to: (a) become proficient with the learning management system, (b) help students learn how to navigate the course and troubleshoot technical problems, and (c) report problems to the technical team for resolution.

Further research indicates specific traits that successful online teachers possess. These traits include clarity, creativity, and compassion (Pierce, 2008). At the November 6, 2008 Sloan-C Conference on Online Learning, Phillips presented to his audience that many believe an effective online instructor must "exude authority...and gain students' trust from day one or before." One suggestion for gaining trust is to send each student an individual email prior to the start of class. The email can include a brief instructor introduction, clear goals and expectations for the course, and an inquiry as to the student's personal goals for the course. The email message should be informally written, but clear in its content. Finally, the successful online instructor is an effective writer who uses humor judiciously, spends many hours online providing an abundance of feedback, is caring, flexible, organized, and creates a lot of redundancy by posting directions and reminders in many locations throughout the course (Phillips, 2008).

From the lists above, it is evident that the KSAs necessary for successful online teaching extend beyond just providing course materials in a distance learning format. Competencies in follow-through, organization, communication, and evaluation carry through from the course planning stage to post-course wrap-up. In the hectic and demanding world we live in, it is rewarding to know that, as a facilitator of distance learning, you are helping a student to access learning when it is most convenient for them to focus on their personal learning goals.

Suggested Activity

If you and/or your department are considering offering distance learning courses, suggest the KSA activity, displayed in Figure 1.1, for your next department faculty meeting. Performing this brief activity will allow you and your peer instructors to identify specific knowledge and skills required for distance learning course facilitation.

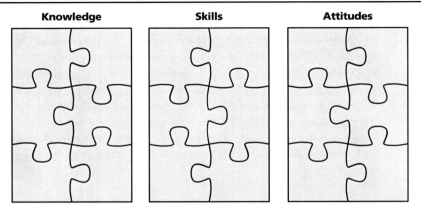

Knowledge – Skills – Attitudes (KSA)

It is important for distance learning instructors to identify the knowledge, skills, and attitudes that are necessary to facilitate effective online learning.

Form teams of four, preferably with those who are interested in, or currently teaching, distance learning courses.

1. Each team is assigned one of the following roles: (a) Advocate for Knowledge, (b) Advocate for Skills, (c) Advocate for Attitudes.
2. Each team brainstorms (for their assigned role) what Knowledge, Skills, and Attitudes are necessary for effective online instruction.
3. Each team lists their responses.
4. Then, each team prioritizes their top six responses.
5. One person from each team writes the top six choices on their KSA puzzle— one choice per puzzle piece.
6. Each team summarizes rationale/decisions to the Group for clarification.

Figure 1.1 Instructions to facilitate the Knowledge, Skills, and Attitudes (KSA) professional development activity.

Planning Your Distance Learning Course

Planning instruction through analyzing objectives, organizing learning activities, and preparing resources is a necessary skill that effective instructors practice. Being able to develop a cohesive strategy for communicating necessary information and engaging students in the learning experience is essential for all learning environments, including traditional face-to-face and distance learning. Simonson, Smaldino, Albright, and Zcavek (2009) advise that considerable effort be allocated to the early planning of distance instruction, both synchronous and asynchronous. There are many considerations that must be well thought-out and anticipated. The instructional design process is especially useful in this planning process, and many researchers suggest treating the planning process as a system of interrelated components (Simonson et al., 2009; Dick, Carey, & Carey, 2004). Initially, effective online instructors carefully consider how the facilitation of the desired learning outcomes will be achieved by conducting a thorough examination of the following: (1) course format: design and organization of the online course; (2) instructional design and delivery: learning objectives and activities; (3) resources: learner support; (4) evaluation of student learning: assessment strategies; (5) technology: selection and integration of technology resources; and (6) course revision: improvement based on evaluation and student feedback.

Regardless of the Learning Management System (LMS) or web-based environment your institution utilizes, there are some basic steps in designing a distance learning course that help insure a student-centered course that is easy to navigate. Historically, questions for consideration when planning a distance learning course have included information regarding target audience, curriculum, delivery methods, and additional resources required for student success (Boaz, 1999). The next several sub-sections frame these questions within the context of important considerations and corresponding recommendations.

Who is the Primary Student Population or Group?

Gathering information about your students is valuable when designing the course structure and scope. For example, adult students with specific goals and career needs are usually more self-directed, independent learners than younger students. Students with physical or learning challenges may require certain accommodations, such as extra time to complete assignments. Your course or program may have a specific student demographic that would allow you to pre-plan your course prior to the beginning of the term or semester. However, you can also gather information about your students once the course begins. Keep in mind that one of the benefits of obtaining this type of information is that you can use it to partner students or to place them in small groups comprised of people who have varied backgrounds and experiences. This is a workplace model that our graduates will most likely encounter at some point as they move into their chosen careers. Suggested approaches include (1) the use of the discussion tool to provide a forum to be used as a "student lounge," where students introduce themselves, post pictures, and learn about each other (Some learning management systems have built-in student web pages.), (2) a structured survey using the LMS quiz or survey tool, and (3) personal conversations using email or chat tools.

What Should the Students Learn?

Before a lesson or unit of study can be designed, specific course objectives and desired learning outcomes must be identified. Defining specific learning objectives for the distance learning course is not a different task from that performed for a traditional course. However, the objectives may or may not be the same. For instance, one objective that might be included in your distance learning course is to enhance students' ability to locate and utilize online resources, or to work effectively in groups, whereas this may not be a reasonable or necessary objective for a traditional face-to-face class.

Writing Good Learning Objectives

It is practiced skill and sound planning that enables instructors to communicate internal knowledge about a particular process and explain complex concepts in such a way that learners will grasp the important ideas and demonstrate competencies. Good teaching also engages students in problem-solving, as well as training them how to see beyond the immediate and to take initiative in analyzing issues for deeper exploration and alternative solutions. These challenges are accomplished more readily when instructors have a plan. The instructional plan should be based on goals, objectives, and expected learning outcomes that are mapped to state curriculum frameworks and standards. Gray and Herr (1998) advise that instructional design is the component of curriculum development focused on organizing an instructional delivery plan. Attention is paid to designing and selecting teaching methods, learning activities, and assessment strategies that support the intended learning outcomes. In addition to the desired learning outcomes, a variety of variables are considered when designing curriculum, such as time, learner needs and characteristics, technology and equipment, learning environment, learner skill, prior knowledge of concepts, assessment, and evaluation.

Learning results in a change of behavior, thus, learning objectives specify what learners will know or be able to do. Learning objectives are usually expressed as knowledge, skills, or attitudes. A learning activity is what students do to learn the knowledge, skills, or attitudes necessary to demonstrate mastery of the learning objectives. Objectives are detailed statements that outline specifically what students will be able to do at the conclusion of a unit, course, or program, as well as the conditions and criteria that indicate the acceptable level of performance. Learning outcomes specify what the achieved results of student learning should be as the result of the instruction, that is, how the learning that took place will be evidenced. It is recommended that learning outcomes reflect state or industry standards. The learning outcomes for a course drive the selection of teaching methods, learning activities, and assessment strategies to support the learner's acquisition of desired knowledge, skills, and attitudes. When devising learning outcomes, an instructor may find the following questions helpful:

1. At what level of conceptual awareness does the learner need to be?
2. Is contextual understanding necessary? Or can concepts be generalized across contexts?
3. What, if any, unlearning needs to take place?
4. What are the most necessary things learners need to be able to do or know?
5. What skills or strategies will the learners need?
6. How will learners demonstrate mastery?
7. What assessments are appropriate to measure learning?
8. What barriers, if any, will learners face?
9. What workforce rationale exists?
10. How well does the learning prepare students for continuing education and training?

Since learning outcomes and objectives describe what learners should be able to do or know, they should be written in terms that are observable and measurable. In other words, how can the change in behavior (i.e., learning) be evaluated? Ambiguous learning outcomes result in vague expectations for learners. For example, consider the following outcome: *Learners will understand the value of cultural diversity in the workplace.* How can this outcome be measured? Fuzzy statements of learning can be sharpened by changing the verb and the expected action. Observe the difference in the previous outcome by replacing a few words: *Learners will demonstrate understanding of the value of cultural diversity in the workplace by summarizing their feelings and observations in a weekly blog journal.* The revised outcome offers learners a more precise statement of the expected task. The use of action verbs (*demonstrate, summarizing*) describes observable behavior that can be measured.

A list of suggested action verbs are contained in Table 1.1. The words in Table 1.1 are probably familiar to you as belonging to Bloom's taxonomy. The taxonomy, which we will cover in greater depth in Chapter Two, refers to intellectual processes involved in developing intellectual understanding, such as knowledge and comprehension, to facilitate skills for application, analysis, synthesis, and evaluation of concepts and ideas.

TABLE 1.1 Action Verbs (from Bloom's Taxonomy) Useful in Constructing Learning Objectives

	Domains of Knowledge				
Knowledge	Comprehension	Application	Analysis	Synthesis	Evaluation
Arrange	Classify	Apply	Analyze	Arrange	Appraise
Define	Describe	Choose	Appraise	Assemble	Argue
Duplicate	Discuss	Demonstrate	Calculate	Collect	Assess
Label	Explain	Dramatize	Categorize	Compose	Attach
List	Express	Employ	Compare	Construct	Choose
Name	Identify	Illustrate	Contrast	Create	Compare
Order	Indicate	Interpret	Criticize	Design	Defend
Recognize	Locate	Operate	Differentiate	Develop	Estimate
Recall	Recognize	Practice	Discriminate	Formulate	Judge
Repeat	Report	Schedule	Distinguish	Manage	Predict
Reproduce	Restate	Sketch	Examine	Organize	Rate
State	Review	Solve	Experiment	Plan	Identify cores
	Select	Use	Question	Prepare	Select
	Translate	Write	Test	Propose	Support
				Set Up	Value
					Evaluate

Learning statements for outcomes and objectives should (1) align with state curriculum frameworks; (2) include specific knowledge, skills, and attitudes learners must demonstrate; (3) identify conditions or criteria under which learners must demonstrate learning; (4) contain action verbs; and (5) be measurable. Consider the difference between the two statements:

Generic: *Learners will understand how to use software.*

Specific: *Learners will be able to utilize spreadsheet software to categorize data.*

Connecting the learning to the learning outcomes and learning objectives is vital. Verbs such as *know, become aware of, appreciate, learn, understand,* and *become familiar with* are unclear and may be interpreted in various ways, depending on the action they specify. These verbs suggest behavior that is difficult or impossible to observe or measure. Avoid including these types of verbs in learning outcome statements.

The action verbs should clearly define behavioral objectives useful for interpreting student behavior as a demonstration of learned concepts. In other words, including a definitive action verb in the learning outcome and objectives assists the instructor in classifying the learning behavior of students and understanding if what a student is doing demonstrates the desired behavior. Students demonstrate specific behaviors when they participate in learning activities defined by the instructor. The examples offered in Table 1.2 distinguish, and provide an overview of the connection, between the learning outcome, the learning objective, and the learning activity.

How Will Courses be Delivered?

Once the learning objectives are identified, you can begin to decide what types of learning activities are required, and the tools and resources

---

TABLE 1.2 Examples of Learning Outcomes, Learning Objectives, and Learning Activities

Item	Example
Learning Outcome	The student will demonstrate understanding of the operation of the equipment.
Learning Objective	The student will explain why a piece of equipment is working improperly.
Learning Activity	Given examples of a variety of scenarios, the student will categorize possible problems and develop a troubleshooting guide.

necessary, for students to achieve the specific learning objectives. Bernard, et al (2004) found, in analyzing data on effective distance learning, that opportunities for communication appear to be beneficial for students in distance learning courses, and interactivity between students seems to foster better attitudes. Consider these brief recommendations as you begin to plan your course.

1. Activities that integrate a variety of disciplines usually receive a positive response from students, since they appreciate activities that reach beyond the scope of the unit or course and incorporate tangible, real-world associations.

2. Utilize teamwork and collaborative activities, such as research and report projects, role play, peer assessment of work, and discussion groups. Most of today's Learning Management Systems provide a variety of collaborative tools, including discussion boards, email, interactive whiteboard, and student presentation pages where PowerPoint and other multimedia files can be uploaded. Web-based instruction may take advantage of a variety of Web 2.0 tools, such as wikis, blogs, and social networks, and many Learning Management Systems contain these or similar tools, as well. Utilizing collaborative activities requires that students be present online and be active learners, rather than passive observers. You will find many of the activities described in later chapters valuable for achieving your learning objectives, while keeping students actively engaged with learning material as a community of learners.

3. As mentioned above, communication tools such as email and the discussion board provide opportunities for ongoing dialogue in the exchange of ideas and information. By participating in ongoing discussion and/or email communication, students develop the ability to formulate thoughtful and concise responses. It is important for you, the instructor, to establish a non-judgmental and supportive environment where students are comfortable sharing their ideas and thoughts. In addition, encourage your students to reflect interactively with each other about the course content. Later in the course, we will help you establish rubrics and guidelines to structure an open, responsive, and respectful environment.

4. The inclusion of distance learning as a prime method for delivering instruction indicates a need to shift from a behaviorist passive approach of learning to a constructivist orientation that encourages active, reflective, and social learning (Lewis et al., 2005). Provide investigative problem-solving activities and case studies where students apply their new knowledge and present their findings via

multimedia files, communication tools, and peer review. Detailed instructions on how to facilitate a variety of activities, as well as links to additional online resources, are included in subsequent chapters.

5. Strive to create authentic learning opportunities for students in which they may apply their understanding of concepts to real-world situations. With the availability of web and collaboration tools, the possibilities are limited only by the imagination. Students can join a list or blog, where they contribute questions and ideas, post their resumes online, analyze and evaluate products and services, collaborate synchronously with peers to create a work of art or piece of music, or conduct an online interview with a subject matter expert in real time.

6. Utilize a variety of assessment strategies, including individual and group projects, discussion participation, e-portfolios, e-journals, reflective papers, web site development, pre-tests, post-tests, quizzes, and tests. Use benchmarks to measure growth in knowledge, comprehension, and application. Be specific about minimum participation requirements, and communicate your expectations up front. Let students know what each learning activity is worth in points, via a rubric, as well as the point system used for assigning grades. In our chapter on assessment, we will help you select which assessment strategy is the best fit for your objectives.

What Resources are Needed for Student Success?

In addition to instructional content, the resources needed so that students can achieve the stated learning objectives must be articulated. Be sure that students are aware prior to, or at the very beginning of the course, what equipment (computer hardware and software) is required. Provide information or links to download necessary programs, plug-ins, or templates. If CDs, videos, or textbooks are a required part of your course, be aware of distance barriers some students might face. As part of your course syllabus, provide students with specific tips for success, or use FAQs to help answer students' questions and concerns.

Remember that distance learning may be a new experience for many of your students. It is recommended that you add a link to your course homepage that includes this information. In addition, email students prior to the first day of classes to provide them with specific course information. Consider regularly scheduled "virtual" office hours that are conducted asynchronously or synchronously. Answer student questions and concerns via the email or chat tool.

The Tasks

Once the target population and learning outcomes are identified, objectives and learning activities are developed to match each outcome. Tasks necessary for the transformation of traditional course materials and development of online activities often include: (1) converting documents into .html and .pdf formats; (2) converting lecture materials, such as adding narration to PowerPoint and developing video lectures; (3) creating a template for each course, which, depending upon the Learning Management System utilized by your institution, will require the identification of appropriate course tools (Calendar, Discussion, Content Modules, etc.); (4) uploading course materials (files) to the online course file manager; (5) organizing the course materials into manageable units and chunking unit content into manageable activities; (6) planning and deciding communication strategies and formats; (7) planning and deciding assessment strategies; (8) managing student access to each course, which might include activities such as taking online "attendance"; and (9) at the end of the course, administering and compiling surveys and course evaluations. Note that later in this chapter, you will be introduced to the *Distance Learning Course Planning and Delivery Guide*. Another excellent resource for course planning is the Lesson Planner from the North Central Regional Technology in Education Consortium (2001), available online at: http://www.ncrtec.org/tl/lp/. Both are designed to assist you in designing and developing a distance learning course.

Distance Learning Course Planning and Delivery Guide

We are certain you and your faculty colleagues identified, from the KSA activity depicted in Figure 1.1, two of the predominant skills required to deliver an effective distance learning course: *planning* and *organization*. While developing your course, 75 percent of your time should be spent in planning and organizing, with 25 percent of your time actually spent uploading course content into your Learning Management System. As promised, the authors have provided a tool to help start the planning and organizing process. Adapted from resources developed by the Kentucky Virtual University (2001), the Distance Learning Course Planning and Delivery Guide revealed in Figure 1.2 is a tool used to guide the planning process. The complete guide, provided in Appendix A, lists major features of best practices for distance learning courses, and is designed to be used as a checklist while developing your course. The planning guide provides structure during the course

Course Welcome Page (Home Page)			
	Created	Reviewed	Revised
1. Course Title			
2. Course Number and Section			
3. Instructor Contact Information			
4. "Getting Started" instructions – what to do first (include a "Start Here" page or folder.)			
4a. Course Introduction			
4b. Instructor Introduction			
4c. Media Player Downloads			
Orientation (video)			

Figure1.2   The Distance Learning Course Planning and Delivery Guide.

development process by addressing the major components of every distance learning course including: (1) Course Home Page (Welcome page); (2) Course Syllabus; (3) Course Calendar; (4) Course Content; (5) Teaching and Learning Strategies; (6) Communication; (7) Assignments, Projects, Quizzes, Tests; (8) Assessment; and (9) Course Evaluation and Feedback.

As you work your way through the planning guide, you will find yourself identifying the instructional goals and analyzing them in terms of what you want the students to learn, how they will learn, what tools will facilitate their learning, and how they will demonstrate their progress. In addition, the planning guide provides an organized structure for continuous improvement throughout the process by providing Creation, Review, and Revision sections for each category topic.

Start Here

Upon logging in at the course level, students will need to be directed to their first task. In the course home page section of the Delivery Guide, you will note a section called "Getting Started." This can be a page or a folder linked directly from the course home page that includes all of the materials and information students will need to begin the course. It is recommended that you make this section of the home page stand out so that student's attention is immediately drawn to it. To accomplish this, you can make the page link a different color and/or font style. Or, you can use a special graphic to denote the "Start Here" link.

Once you have created your "Start Here" folder, you will need to decide upon the folder contents. There are many options. But, the goal is to avoid overwhelming the students. Keep the contents simple, while making sure to provide as much information as is needed. Suggestions for inclusion in the "Start Here" folder include:

1. A welcome message (can be printed text in the header of the page)
2. A course introduction video (or audio podcast, or narrated PowerPoint presentation, etc.)
3. A "Meet Your Instructor" video, audio podcast, or print bio
4. Tutorials for the most commonly used features of the learning management system
5. Links to media player downloads so that students can access your multimedia course content
6. Instructions for navigating the course site
7. Introductory activity (e.g., *Meet Your Course Mates Discussion Forum* where students post brief bios of themselves, Scavenger Hunt to find important materials within the course, etc.)
8. Instructions for what to do next

Course Introduction

It is recommended that you include a course introduction in your "Start Here" folder. The introduction can be a video, an audio podcast, a narrated PowerPoint presentation, or another form of multimedia. It is recommended that you use a multimedia program to create the orientation, as opposed to having them read a printed document. Multimedia will immediately capture the students' interests and will encourage them to continue reviewing the remaining contents of the "Start Here" folder. We will explore various multimedia programs in Chapter Three, many of which are suitable for your course introduction.

The course introduction should minimally include an overview of course topics and course objectives, instructions for navigating the course site, and other important information that students must know in order to be successful in your course. It is not a problem if some of this information is also included in the course syllabus. Duplicating information in several places throughout the course is a recommended strategy to help make sure that all students see it.

Instructor Introduction

Also included in the "Start Here" folder is an instructor introduction. The introduction can be a video, an audio file, a narrated PowerPoint presentation, or printed format curriculum vitae. Again, multimedia is recommended, but any of these will be sufficient. The purpose of the instructor introduction is to provide students with the opportunity to learn about your credentials, your interests, and gain a bit of insight into your personality. It is possible that your students will never meet you in person. Therefore, an introduction is important chance to begin to build a connection, and bonds of trust and rapport with your students.

Organizing a Distance Learning Course

Organizing an entire distance learning course can be a daunting task, especially for those new to the online delivery format. As mentioned before, utilizing a *systems* instructional design approach can help make the activity more manageable. The previously discussed Distance Learning Course Planning and Delivery Guide is one tool you can use to effectively manage course development.

What the eLearning design will look like depends on several factors, such as learner population, learning environment, and learning objectives. The most common academic distance learning design of learning events is sequenced in a linear progression (Figure 1.3), but some instructors might view and approach learning in a less prescribed arrangement of learning

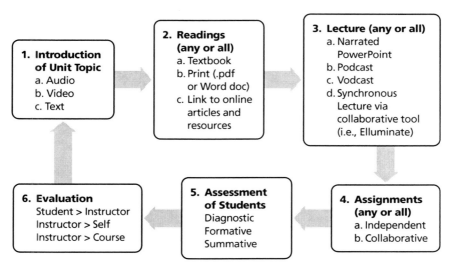

Figure 1.3   Linear model of distance learning course unit design.

experiences, using a more open entry model (Figure 1.5), which allows the student greater control over choice of assignments and learning methods. Corresponding examples of how each model might appear on a course homepage are provided in Figures 1.4 and 1.6.

Note that the linear design is created in such a way that a learner completes units/modules in a specified sequence. This is the most popular form of distance learning course organization. Also that the circular design may be created in such a way that a learner could enter any module of his choosing, and move onto the next module of choice upon completion, without having to complete modules in a specific sequence. This is less popular than the linear model. We will share more information about the visual layout and design of an online course in Chapter Six.

Planning and Organizing a Unit of Instruction

It may help to segment the course into discreet units of instruction and begin to identify learning objectives, required readings, unit activities, assignments, and evaluation methods for each unit. The purpose of this section is to provide you with guidelines in selecting the Learning Management tools, teaching and learning strategies, and multimedia software programs you can use to deliver your course content. It is recommended that each unit of instruction contain a minimum of one of each of the items included in this section. You will note that we have adopted a linear approach to designing an online course, and the Unit Content Guide is an excellent tool for organizing thoughts, decisions, and the collection/creation of materials for your course in a sequential. The Companion Website includes this Guide as a digital form that can be used during unit development. The remaining chapters in this book will assist you in selecting and developing

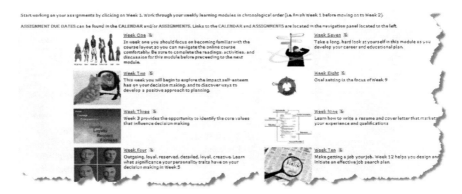

Figure 1.4   Example of course home page for linear model.

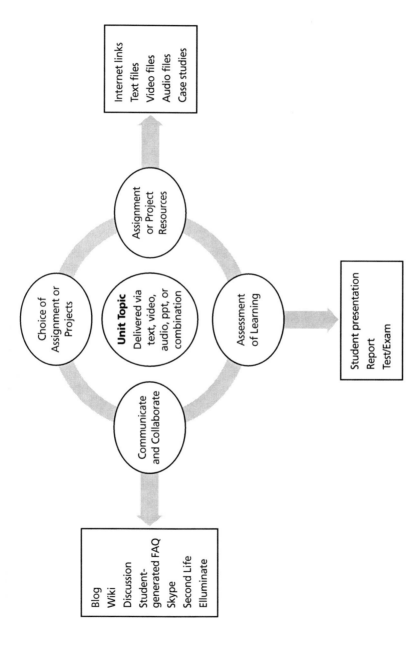

Figure 1.5 Open Entry model of distance learning course design.

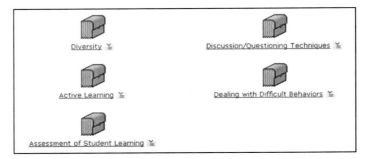

Figure 1.6   Example of course home page for Open Entry model.

each of items included in the Guide. Following is a brief description of each of the items.

Unit Overview and Objectives

The Unit Overview and Objectives should provide students with a general overview of the topics to be covered within the unit, including specific, measureable learning objectives. Use the Unit Overview to link the current unit to the previous unit, as well as to reinforce "why" this unit is important. The Unit Overview and Objectives can be presented within the course in a variety of formats, such as a text document, narrated PowerPoint, or audio file.

Required Readings

First, identify how information and instructions will be communicated about reading material. Each required reading should have a direct link to subsequent unit content. Include information from readings as part of the overall unit assessment. Instructions for Required Readings can be presented within the course in a variety of formats. Your options include a text document; graphic with audio, such as a picture of the textbook with an audio file explaining reading assignment; graphic with text explanation of reading assignment; or text instructions with accompanying hyperlink to an online reading.

Unit Activities

Unit Activities are usually developmental in nature. They may or may not be graded, but link directly to unit assignments and assessments. It is critical that the instructor provide frequent and rich feedback to unit activities. Unit Activities can be presented within the course in a variety of formats. Good choices for unit activities include (1) digitized lecture with narrated PowerPoint, video inserted in PowerPoint, or audio file with a print transcript; (2) demonstrations via an instructor-created video, print document with graphics of required process enhanced with text instructions, or existing demonstrations found on the internet; (3) video recorded or audio recorded interview with guest speakers or presenters, live synchronous chat with guest experts, an asynchronous discussion board topic facilitated by a content expert, podcasts downloadable from the Internet, conference presentations or white papers available on the Internet; (4) Internet-based activities such as interactive websites, blogs, direct link to website(s) that contain videos, activities, and so forth, or PowerPoint with hyperlinks to sites; (5) interactive class activities that utilize at least one interactive communication strategy (discussed in Chapter Four), projects with group and individual components, such as, WebQuests, case studies, and research projects.

Communication Strategies

Communication strategies and activities should be selected to reinforce unit objectives. Develop specific communication standards and policies to be included in the course syllabus. Effective communication is a critical component for student success and satisfaction. Communication strategies should be selected to lessen the sense of isolation and support student learning, as follows: (1) identify a strategy to provide ongoing feedback and motivation to students, (2) identify a strategy or strategies to utilize the synchronous chat tool, (3) identify a strategy or strategies to utilize the asynchronous discussion forum, (4) utilize a course calendar, and (5) utilize the course syllabus template.

Assignments

It is recommended that a variety of Assignment types be used to impact multiple learning styles and intelligence types. Assignments can be presented within the course in a variety of formats. Assignment formats and types can include readings with written reflection, hands-on activities (demonstration of skill, creating of finished product), group/team assignments, blogs, discussion forums, chat sessions, and student presentations. Specific instructions for course assignments should be provided in written format and/or audio or video format. It is also good practice to provide examples of both exemplary and unacceptable work.

Assessment Strategies

Assessment is an integral part of the teaching and learning process. Identify the ways in which you will verify student learning and the tools/software you will use to create unit assessments. Assessment activities should directly correlate to unit objectives. Assessments can be presented within the course in a variety of formats including (1) class discussion/chat participation, which may utilize a discussion/chat rubric that specifies evaluation criteria (include discussion/chat guidelines and rubric as part of course syllabus); (2) quizzes/tests/exams created with the LMS assessment tool or delivered within an on-site testing center; (3) lab demonstrations that are completed during on-site lab time; and (4) student presentations, such as a student-created video demonstrations. In addition to the traditional assessment strategies, alternative forms of assessment strategies, such as peer- and self-assessment, may be used. An important element of assessment is instructor feedback. Instructors can utilize course email for private, individualized feedback and evaluation, course discussion for general feedback, and course chat for private, group, or general class feedback. Finally, it is prudent to develop rubrics that establish guidelines and criteria for successful assignment completion.

Important Principles of Lesson Planning

As you begin to use the Unit Content Guide to develop your course, it is important to remember that the learning outcomes underpin the overall process of designing the course and the individual lesson plan(s) by providing guidance for writing learning objectives, as well as for selecting appropriate teaching strategies, learning activities, and assessment strategies to support learner attainment of desired course learning outcomes. Each course unit or module will contain a set of expected learning objectives that are aligned with the course learning outcomes. The teaching strategies and learning activities selected for the unit must be directly aligned with the assessment method for the unit and, ultimately, the course. Thus, the learning outcomes must be considered when selecting the assessment tool. Likewise, identification of the learning outcomes and assessment method should be part of the selection process for teaching and learning activities.

Instructors must deliberate what teaching method is appropriate for group size, learners' past experiences, special characteristics of the group, and special needs. Rarely will the classroom contain a homogeneous population of students with skills at the same level. Teaching strategies and lessons need to recognize and accommodate the variety of skill levels across the group. An astute instructor designs learning experiences that build on existing knowledge and experience, and also creates opportunities to assimilate new information.

Consider the principles of adult learning in creating the unit lesson plans. Learning is most effective when learning activities are relevant, based on real needs, and situated within authentic contexts. For instance, in the workplace, problems are usually solved in teams or by committee; adults learn well when able to learn from each other. Therefore, when possible, include peer learning by designing or selecting team activities or, at least, providing informal opportunities for students to share information. For example, group discussion is valuable for communicating challenges, observations, and discoveries in conceptual understanding and application.

Assessment types may include instructor, peer, and self. Students need opportunities for self-reflection in order to make connections between previous learning, new knowledge, and application. Provide an opportunity for students to reflect on their own learning, identifying strengths as well as areas for improvement. Learning contracts offer a venue for this type of self-assessment.

Finally, in addition to learning outcomes, learner characteristics and a variety of practical issues must be considered when devising lesson plans. Practical issues include giving careful thought to whether the teaching methods and learning activities are feasible, given the online environment, the time available (both for preparation of course materials and for online facilitation, as well as the time required for students to successfully complete the activity or assignment), and the materials and equipment required. Weber and Berthoin (2003) believe that "[t]ime pressure can both accelerate and slow down learning processes... [and] is experienced as motivating or threatening... [I]f the sense of threat becomes too excessive, however, learning can be slowed or made impossible altogether" (p. 355). Some research suggests that situational circumstances, such as time and practice, influence successful learning for adults. Weber and Berthoin (2003) contend that learning processes that require practice are much slower than those that do not require practice. Variables such as practice and time influence the type and scope of learning activities. An astute instructor will analyze time considerations when designing curriculum that must meet specific deadlines, and accommodate time needed for practice and review opportunities.

Unit Flowchart

Taking the time to flowchart each unit of instruction will help you organize curriculum and avoid student confusion. The Companion Website contains an Online Course Planning Flowchart (Figure 1.7) document that can be printed and used for developing units of instruction. The flowchart

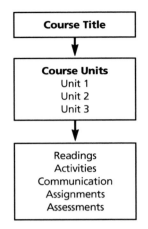

Flowchart of Unit Construction

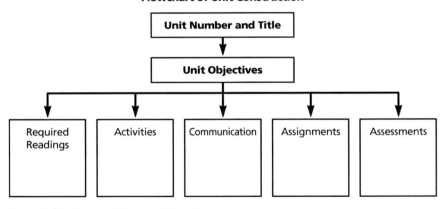

Figure 1.7 Course Planning Flowchart.

is another tool that will help you manage the selection of activities and necessary course materials and resources, such as those listed below:

1. Required Readings: textbook chapters, online articles, journals and periodicals, and lecture notes
2. Activities (includes how or in what format you will deliver content): digitized lecture, video demonstration, PowerPoint presentations (narrated or text-added), guest speakers (via live chat or hosted discussion), and Internet activities
3. Communication (includes student activities and instructor feedback): cooperative communication activities that promote active learning, frequency of feedback, and frequency of contact

4. Assignments (graded assignments): written reports/reflections, creation of finished product, skill demonstration, presentation (individual or team), participation

5. Assessments: class discussions, chat session, quizzes and tests, evaluation of finished product, evaluation of skill demonstration, and rubrics

Copyright and Fair Use

The power of the Internet will offer many avenues to help you create custom course materials and locate ready-made resources. Therefore, knowledge of and careful attention to how these resources can be used is important. Copyright law protects the works of others, while the Fair Use Policy provides a means for instructors to utilize materials for educational purposes.

Copyright law provides authors and artists the right to deny others from copying and/or using their work without appropriate permission. There are seven categories protected by copyright law: (1) literary works; (2) musical works; (3) dramatic works; (4) pantomimed and choreographed works; (5) pictorial, graphic, and sculptural works; (6) motion pictures and audio-visual works; and (7) sound recordings. The exact expression of content is protected, but not the use of facts or ideas. For example, content from a website, book, or play devoted to Benjamin Franklin would be protected, but the events and details of his life would not be.

Another important condition of copyright is the tangible expression of ideas. The work must be established in an actual medium. In addition to the venues of expression mentioned above, Web content, along with original contributions to a blog, wiki, twitter, social network site pages, or other forums for expression, is also covered under copyright provisions. Some contents of a distance learning course, such as instructor lectures, discussion forums, and other instructional materials, may meet the criteria for copyright protection.

A common mistake made by educators is to copy and save graphics from the Web. Utilizing even a small portion of another's work may be risky. Considering the vast amount of inexpensive commercial clip art available, copying an image off a webpage is not worth the chance of a copyright infringement charge. Similarly, copying video or music files is also a violation of the law. The superior tactic is to provide the Web address or a hyperlink to the desired file.

Once a work reaches a certain age, the copyright expires, and the work passes into the public domain and may be used freely. Currently, works published prior to 1923 are in the public domain. Works created on or after January 1, 1978 are protected for the lifetime of the author, plus an additional 70 years. Copyright for corporate authorships is set at 95 years from the date of publication. Also excluded from copyright protection and included in the public domain are most U.S. government documents and publications.

Fair Use Policy sets restraints to copyright protection, by allowing that limited use of a copyrighted work for certain purposes is not an infringement. Such uses include: criticism, comment, parody, news reporting, teaching (including multiple copies for classroom use), scholarship, or research. However, exploiting a copy of a written work to generate income and/or for commercial purposes is not considered fair, particularly if the owner's income is impinged. A short excerpt of a speech, article, book, poem, or report would be considered fair use if the commercial value of the work were not devalued. One must also cite (i.e., give credit to) the original artists and authors; failure to do so is considered an infringement. Although many persons find the vague definition of Fair Use troubling for interpretation, four standards guide the copyright exemption:

1. Purpose of use: spontaneous, temporary use of copyrighted works for specific educational purposes
2. Nature of the work: short excerpts, such as paragraphs, are acceptable; copying and using an entire work or several chapters would be questionable
3. Proportion/extent of the material used: short excerpts that do not represent the major essence of the work are acceptable
4. Effect on marketability: copying and use of the work should not adversely impact its marketability or revenue

Everyone, but perhaps educators, in particular, have a moral obligation to model appropriate ethical behavior in respecting the rights of the artist/author. Copying software and duplicating publications may save money for the instructor or institution, but it is also taking rightfully earned income away from the works' creators. Faculty should also communicate copyright policy to students, encouraging honorable actions, and discouraging plagiarism and academic dishonesty.

End of Chapter Activities

The end of chapter activities provide opportunities for you to acquire new knowledge, gain skill, and apply principles and concepts. These activities are located on the Companion Website, and are divided into three subsections: Knowledge Building, Skill Building, and Practical Application.

Appendix A

Course Planning and Delivery Guide

Course Welcome Page (Home Page)	Developed	Reviewed	Revised
The course welcome page or home page should include the items listed below.			
1. Course Title			
2. Course Number and Section			
3. Instructor Contact Information			
4. "Getting Started" instructions—what to do first (include a "Start Here" page or folder)			
4a. Course Introduction			
4b. Instructor Introduction			
4c. Media Player Downloads			
4d. Course Orientation (video)			
5. Help desk information (for technical support)			
6. Links to major course items (Calendar, Content, Syllabus, Communication tools, etc.)			
7. Course meeting dates (if applicable)			

Course Syllabus			
The course syllabus should include the items listed below.	Developed	Reviewed	Revised
1. Complies with Institutional requirements			
2. Course objectives are clearly stated in measureable terms			
3. Includes a course description.			
4. Includes a rationale for the course and its relationship to previous courses in the program area (if applicable)			
5. Includes textbook information including where/how to order; includes information regarding other required course materials			
6. Includes grading criteria, scoring components, and grading scale			
7. All required on-campus meeting dates and times are listed (if applicable)			
8. All required synchronous "chat" session dates and times are listed (if applicable)			
9. All technology requirements are described including hardware components, software, and minimal technical competency			
10. Alternate plans are identified, in the event of technical difficulties that prohibit course access for an extended period of time			
11. Required media players are listed (to view multimedia course content) and links to download sites are provided			
12. Includes instructor contact information, physical office hours, and virtual office hours			

	Developed	Reviewed	Revised
13. Frequency and timing of participation expectations are stated and described			
14. Frequency and timing of instructor feedback is stated and described			

Course Calendar

The course calendar should include the items listed below.	Developed	Reviewed	Revised
1. A schedule of specific course activities is included			
2. All course meeting dates are included (if applicable)			
3. Course start/end dates, withdrawal dates, important institution dates, etc. are included			
4. Assignment due dates, quiz dates, test dates are included			

Course Content

Course content should meet the minimum established guidelines listed below.	Developed	Reviewed	Revised
1. Each section or module contains an introduction and background information that connects it to the previous module			
2. Specific objectives and learning outcomes are stated at the beginning of each module and are written in measureable terms			
3. Each module includes required readings (from textbook, Internet, or other sources)			
4. Content is accurate, relevant, and current (content is reviewed every semester and updated as needed)			

	Developed	Reviewed	Revised
5. Content is logically sequenced (within each module, as well as having each module build upon the previous)			
6. Multimedia content is appropriately "chunked" as a means to reduce media file size (recommendations are included in Chapter Three)			
7. Content is free of cultural, racial, religious, gender, and age bias			
8. Various media formats are used, including audio, video, print text, etc. to provide for multiple learning styles and intelligence types			
9. A glossary of key terms is included with each module			
10. The length of each module is appropriate to the priority of the objective(s)			
11. Copyright issues are addressed; appropriate permissions have been received and/or proper citations provided			
12. All web links are checked and working prior to the start of the course			
Teaching/Learning Strategies			
Each course should include evidence of the teaching and learning strategies listed below.	**Developed**	**Reviewed**	**Revised**
1. A variety of learning activities are included that address various learning styles and intelligence types			
2. Learning activities vary in level of difficulty and all levels of the Cognitive Domain of Bloom's Taxonomy of Learning are represented in the course			

	Developed	Reviewed	Revised
3. Learning activities facilitate active engagement in the learning process (students are required to interact with each other; all levels of the Cognitive Domain of Bloom's Taxonomy of Learning are represented in the course)			
4. Learning activities provide opportunities for weekly interaction between students and instructor			
5. Students are sometimes given a choice of learning activities			
6. Instructions for each activity are clear			
7. Samples of exemplary assignments, discussion postings, etc. are provided; samples of unacceptable assignments and discussion posts are provided			
8. Students are given opportunities to work in teams			
Communication			
Minimum communication standards must be developed and should include the items below.			
1. Email is available to enable private communication between student and instructor, as well as between student and student			
2. Discussion groups/forums are used frequently to encourage interaction between student and instructor, as well as between student and student			
3. Discussion Forum questions are presented in question bundle format (see Chapter 2)			
4. Students are required to respond to a specific number of classmates' posts; a rubric is provided to help guide the responses			

	Developed	Reviewed	Revised
5. Strategies are in place to provide prompt instructor feedback to discussion board postings (provide feedback within 24 hours of post)			
6. Discussion rubrics and guidelines are provided for discussion board postings (establish ground rules for appropriate public communication; establish specific evaluation criteria)			
7. Chat rooms are available for team interaction and for synchronous communication			
8. For team assignments and activities, each team is provided with a team discussion forum for asynchronous communication and file sharing			
9. Opportunities are available for students to lead discussion forums and chat sessions (instructor-monitored)			
Assignments, Projects, Quizzes, Tests			
Assignments, projects, quizzes, and tests should meet the standards listed below.	Developed	Reviewed	Revised
1. A variety of assignments are offered that directly correspond to module/course objectives			
2. The number of assignments is appropriate for the estimated time of module completion			
3. Assignments consider various learning styles and intelligence types; assignments vary in difficulty level by utilizing the Cognitive Domain of Bloom's Taxonomy of Learning			

	Developed	Reviewed	Revised
4. Assignment instructions are clear; assignment due dates are provided			
5. Assignment submission instructions are provided and include a description of acceptable file/software formats			
6. Short-term and long-term course project(s) are included			
7. At least one course project provides students with the opportunity to work in teams			
8. Assignments are included for the purpose of providing formative feedback			
9. Assignments are included for the purpose of providing summative feedback and evaluation			
10. Formative self-tests are included			
11. Test items provide clear instructions and submission requirements			
12. A format and timeline for quiz/test results and for assignment feedback is provided			
Evaluation and Feedback			
Evaluation and Feedback strategies should minimally include all of the items listed below.	**Developed**	**Reviewed**	**Revised**
1. Scoring rubrics are provided for all assignments and projects			
2. Multiple forms of assessment are included in the course, including both formative and summative assessments			
3. Strategies are in place to provide consistent and prompt evaluation and feedback (evaluate assignments within 24 hours of submission)			

	Developed	Reviewed	Revised
4. Strategies are in place to provide descriptive feedback as a means to enable students to improve their learning (ungraded formative feedback and graded summative feedback)			
5. There are opportunities for students to evaluate their own learning (self-assessment rubric)			
6. There are opportunities for student peer evaluation (using a peer evaluation rubric)			
7. Evaluation methods are consistent with course objectives and learning outcomes (each module includes evaluation and assessment activities that directly measure the attainment of the specified module learning objectives)			
8. An evaluation process exists to assess student satisfaction with the course and services			
9. An evaluation instrument exists for students to assess the instructor's performance			

References

Bernard, R. M., Abrami, P. C., Lou, Y., Borokhovski, E., Wade, A., Wozney, L., et al. (2004). How does distance education compare with classroom instruction? A Meta analysis of the empirical literature. *Review of Educational Research.* Retrieved May 7, 2007 from http://www.unb.ca/naweb/proceedings/2002/Po2Bernard.htm

Bicknell-Holmes, T. & Hoffman, P. S. (2001, June). Elicit, engage, experience, explore: Discovery learning in library instruction. *Reference Services Review.* 28:4 (2000) 313–322. Simmons College Library.

Boaz, M. (1999). *Teaching at a distance: A handbook for instructors.* Phoenix, AZ: The League for Innovation in the Community College and Archipeligo Publications.

Carroll-Barefield, C., Smith, S., Prince, L., & Campbell, C. A. (2005). Transitioning from brick and mortar to online: A faculty perspective. *Online Journal of Distance Learning Administration,* 8(1), State University of West Georgia, Distance Education Center. Retrieved June 8, 2007 from http://www.westga.edu/~distance/ojdla/spring81/carroll81.htm

Dick, W., Carey, L., and Carey, J. O. (2004). *The systematic design of instruction* (6th ed.). New York: Longman.

Gray, K. & Herr, E. (1998). *Workforce education: The basics.* Needham, MA: Allyn and Bacon.

KYVU Course Development Resource. (2001). Kentucky Virtual University. Retrieved May 7, 2007 from http://www.kyvu.org/partners/quality_audit_1-23-01_screen.pdf

Lewis, B., MacEntee, V., DeLaCruz, S., Englander, C., Jeffery, T., Takach, E., et al. (2005). *Learning management systems comparison.* Proceedings of the 2005 Informing Science and IT Education Joint Conference, Flagstaff, Arizona.

North Central Regional Technology in Education Consortium Lesson Planner. (2001). Retrieved August 1, 2007, from http://www.ncrtec.org/tl/lp/

Phillips, B. (2008, November 6). In a presentation at the 14th annual Sloan-C International Conference on Online Learning.

Pierce, D. (2008). These traits make online teachers successful. *eSchool News.* Retrieved May 28, 2009, from http://www.eschoolnews.com/news/top-news/?i=55930

Shank, P. (2004). Competencies for online instructors. *Learning Peaks.* Retrieved May 7, 2006 from http://www.learningpeaks.com/instrcomp.pdf

Simonson, M., Smaldino, S., Albright, M. & Zvacek, S. (2009). *Teaching and Learning at a distance: Foundations of distance education* (4th ed.). Boston, MA: Pearson.

Weber, C., & Berthoin Antal, A. (2003). The role of time in organizational learning. In M. Dierkes, A. Berthoin Antal, J. Child & I. Nonaka (Eds.). *Handbook of organizational learning and knowledge* (pp. 351–368). New York: Oxford University Press, Inc.

2

Active Learning in Online Courses

By now you can see that teaching, learning, and technology in distance learning work together as a system to accomplish an effective transfer of knowledge. The way you utilize technology to enhance your teaching and learning activities has a direct impact on student learning and retention. We now turn our focus to active learning strategies appropriate for distance learning courses. Upon completion of Chapter 2, readers will be able to:

1. Describe the levels of Bloom's taxonomy, as they relate to designing learning activities that satisfy desired learning objectives
2. Explain the benefits of differentiated instruction for distance learning teaching
3. Utilizing the *How Hot Are You?* Activity, self-assess knowledge of, and comfort with, a variety of teaching strategies
4. Structure questions in a Question Bundle format
5. Utilize the assignment template to develop an assignment that provides instructions appropriate for online learning
6. Use the Course Planning and Delivery Guide to identify strengths and weaknesses

Introduction to Active Learning Strategies

Not all students learn in the same way. In this age of accountability educators are challenged to reach every student. Students do not come to us as blank slates. Some administrators and instructors are often skeptical that course activities and assignments in distance learning classes can equal, or even approximate, the quality of face-to-face instruction. Questions and concerns expressed by the American Federation of Teachers (2000) include:

1. Will deep understanding of complex concepts occur in the absence of face-to-face instructor-led classroom learning?
2. Are particular types of subjects inappropriate for delivery via distance learning?
3. Do higher dropout rates occur because of the isolatory nature of distance learning, that is, lack of face-to-face instruction and/or limited social interaction?
4. Are there limitations on equipment, or technical or learning resources that adversely impact student learning in distance education courses? (p. 5)

It is apparent that face-to-face and distance learning environments are very different. Conway (2003) explains that the disagreement revolves around a belief that students cannot receive the same quality of education online as they can in a face-to-face learning environment. However, what is really being disputed here is not whether the educational experience for the student is *equal* in these different environments, but whether the educational experience for the student is *equivalent* in each environment. She contends that utilizing a variety of technologies and teaching strategies is important in facilitating desired learning outcomes for students.

One of an instructor's first considerations when developing a distance learning course is to understand the needs of the learner. Motivating students to access information, complete assignments, and apply learning is always challenging. The unique characteristics of the distance learner often involve additional insight from instructors to reach their students. Students new to distance learning may experience confusion in determining what the expectations are of the course. Obstacles for these students include lack of (1) support from a peer group, (2) access to learning resources, (3) access to or familiarity with appropriate technology resources, and (4) confidence in their ability to successfully complete the course. Instructors often report that students new to distance learning initially engage in surface learning, memorizing facts, rather than becoming immersed in deep learning—an understanding and application of course concepts.

In order to help students reach beyond the surface, many of the same types of class activities and assignments that are currently used in traditional face-to-face courses *can* be utilized in the distance learning environment. Active learning practices have a more significant impact on student performance than any other variable, including student background and prior achievement (Darling-Hammond et al., 2008). Learning is deeper when students are embroiled in activities that require application of theory and concept to real-world contexts. The old adage, "I hear and I forget, I see and I remember, I do and I understand," is a truism. Inquiry-based learning is not about finding the right answer, but more about developing curiosity and investigative skill. Its sister, project-based learning, incorporates inquiry skills to present a realistic product or simile to an intended group. Thomas (2000) identified five key components for project learning:

1. Centrality of project to curriculum
2. Driving question(s) that guide students to engage with central concept(s)
3. Investigation and inquiry for knowledge building
4. Student-driven processes
5. Authentic problem that is of interest to real people in the real world

In conclusion, utilizing a variety of active learning strategies that include student-to-student interaction is critical for all types of courses, but is especially important for distance learning courses (Lamb & Smith, 2000). However, given the isolatory nature of distance learning courses, using active learning may seem like a daunting task. But, keep in mind that current learning management system (LMS) tools allow students unlimited opportunities to interact with course content and course materials, as well as to interact with each other. As such, distance learning courses are an excellent mode for implementing active learning strategies. This chapter explores the role of active learning in designing assignments and activities for the distance learning course. In addition, step-by-step instructions are offered for implementing specific active learning strategies.

Learning Styles and Intelligence Types

The typical classroom mirrors the diversity of the institution, the community, and the world beyond, and the distance learning classroom is no exception. This multiplicity of cultures, ages, and abilities means instructors must motivate a heterogeneous population of students with different preferences, experiences, and abilities, and who respond to information differently. Studies (e.g., Montgomery, 1995) reveal that although a majority of students are active, visual learners, the prevalent method of instruction is a passive lecture style. Research on learning (Dunn & Dunn, 1978; Riding & Ratner, 1997; Rasmussen, 1998) reveals that students learn in different ways and that learning can be enhanced when students are taught concepts in ways that match their individual learning styles. Typical learning styles include visual, auditory, and kinesthetic.

Gardner's (1985, 1993) theory of multiple intelligences suggests that each individual has a unique pattern of strengths and weaknesses, which he deemed "intelligence types." Gardner has theorized, and academia has widely accepted, that a variety of distinct intelligence types exist, including:

1. Logical/Mathematical: well-developed reasoning capabilities, scientific thinking, and investigation; easily reads diagrams and maps
2. Verbal/Linguistic: good with words and languages; enjoys reading, writing, and story telling
3. Interpersonal: extroverted; sensitive to others; enjoys working in groups
4. Intrapersonal: introspective; self-reflective; enjoys working individually
5. Musical/Rhythmic: sensitive to sounds, tones, rhythms, and music; can easily learn to sing and play musical instruments; discerns patterns
6. Bodily–Kinesthetic: learns best by doing something physically; may enjoy acting or performing; often excels in sports
7. Visual–Spatial: can visualize and mentally manipulate objects; easily solves puzzles
8. Naturalistic: sensitive to nature and her or his place within it; able to grow things and interact well with animals
9. Existential: can reflect on philosophical questions about life, death, and reality
10. Spiritual: a propensity for intuition and cognition, as it relates to spirituality

Reading textbooks and answering static, low-cognition type questions will not meet the needs of all learners. One of the goals of this book is to assist instructors with developing a variety of learning activities that address multiple learning styles and intelligence types. Typically known as *differen-*

tiated instruction, varying one's teaching strategies allows each student to be ultimately successful in completing course components, internalizing course content, and transferring her or his new knowledge and skills to the workplace and beyond.

So what does differentiated instruction look like? It is an environment rich in differentiation, and is respectful of student differences. This atmosphere would offer many opportunities for collaboration, and provide the means for students to explore, discover, and access pertinent learning materials and resources appropriate for their projects and overall learning objective(s). Differentiated instruction is supportive of a project-based online environment that sets the tone for individualistic and collaborative studying and learning that allows students some choice as to the end product they will construct that evidences learning.

Bloom's Cognitive Domain (Taxonomy of Learning)

In 1956, Benjamin Bloom led a group of educational psychologists who developed a classification of levels of intellectual behavior important in learning. This became a taxonomy including three overlapping domains: the cognitive, psychomotor, and affective. Cognitive learning is demonstrated by knowledge recall and the intellectual skills: comprehending information, organizing ideas, analyzing and synthesizing data, applying knowledge, choosing among alternatives in problem solving, and evaluating ideas or actions. Bloom identified six levels within the cognitive domain, from the simple recall or recognition of facts as the lowest level (knowledge level), through increasingly more complex and abstract mental levels (comprehension, application, analysis, synthesis), to the highest order (evaluation level). This domain on the acquisition and use of knowledge has become the gold standard to use when developing educational objectives and learning activities, and must be considered when creating distance learning courses.

Quick Strategies to Actively Engage Students

This section includes a list of quick strategies that online instructors can use to actively engage students while meeting the needs of students with multiple learning styles and intelligence types. Many of the strategies can be structured to engage students at all levels of Bloom's cognitive domain. Each strategy includes specific examples of ways to structure the activity using current LMS tools. We will revisit these strategies in Chapter 5 from the perspective of assessment of student learning.

Background Knowledge Probe

The background knowledge probe consists of short surveys or questions to use at the beginning of the course, beginning of a new unit, or prior to introducing a new concept. The objective is to determine pre-existing knowledge (both accurate and inaccurate), as well as to determine cognitive level (depth) of pre-existing knowledge. This strategy reinforces the Verbal and Intrapersonal learner. This strategy may be facilitated via:

1. Discussion forum: Post a "write what you know" question to the LMS discussion forum, wiki, or Blog and ask students to respond.
2. LMS quiz tool: Create a 5–10 question survey using the LMS quiz tool. (Structure questions using various levels of Bloom's cognitive domain.)

Focused Listening

Focused listening draws students' attention to a single term or concept from the unit. It allows the instructor to see if students understand important concepts. The primary objective of focused listening is to determine what learners recall as the most important points of the lesson. This strategy reinforces the Auditory, Verbal, Interpersonal, and Intrapersonal learner. This strategy may be facilitated via:

1. Chat
   a. Synchronous chat session; ask students to clarify most important concept from unit using a single sentence
   b. As a class, determine the top three most important concepts from the unit.
2. Discussion forum
   a. Ask students to clarify most important concept from unit using a single sentence
   b. Ask students to review a minimum of 3–5 of their course-mates' posts
   c. Following review, students post a final list of the top three most important concepts from the unit
3. Twitter
   a. Ask students to clarify most important concept from unit in a Tweet (140 characters)
   b. Utilizing a wiki, the class builds a study guide of important unit concepts

Empty Outlines

With empty outlines, the instructor provides students with an empty or partially completed outline of a digital lecture, presentation, or text reading. The primary objective of empty outlines is to provide students with an organized way to capture notes and focus attention on important concepts. This strategy reinforces the Visual, Intrapersonal, Verbal, and Logical learner. Empty outlines may be facilitated via:

1. Discussion forum
   a. Document posted online to students for their completion
   b. Re-submission via attaching to a discussion forum
2. Assignment tool
   a. Document posted online to students for their completion
   b. Re-submission by uploading in the assignments section

Memory Matrix

The memory matrix is a rectangle divided into rows and columns to organize information and to provide a visual illustration of relationships. The primary objective of the memory matrix activity is to assess recall of course content and skill at organizing and categorization. This activity supports the Visual, Logical, Intrapersonal, Spatial, and Interpersonal learner, and can be structured as a team activity. Memory matrix may be facilitated via:

1. Discussion forum: attach a file to the forum
2. Wiki
3. Assignment attachment

Minute Paper

With the minute paper, instructors ask students to respond to a specific question in one or two sentences. The primary objective of the minute paper is to reinforce advanced levels of Bloom's cognitive domain. This activity supports the Visual, Auditory, Verbal, Intrapersonal, and Interpersonal learner. Minute paper may be facilitated via students posting responses using:

1. Chat
2. Twitter
3. Email
4. In addition, students can create an Audio File response and upload it to the assignments section.

Muddiest Point

With muddiest point, the instructor asks students to respond to the question: "What is your muddiest point in...?" The primary objective of muddiest point is to reveal what students find least clear or most confusing about a particular lesson, activity, or text reading. This activity reinforces the Visual, Auditory, Verbal, Intrapersonal, and Interpersonal learner. It can be facilitated in the same manner as the minute paper.

One-Sentence Summary

Using the one-sentence summary, students answer investigative questions, such as: "Who does what to whom, when, where, how, and why?" Student responses must be written in one sentence. The primary objective of one-sentence summary is to promote synthesis of information, as well as critical thinking. This activity supports the Auditory, Verbal, and Intrapersonal learner. One-sentence summary can be facilitated via students posting responses to:

1. Chat
2. Twitter
3. Email
4. Discussion
5. In addition, students can create an audio file or a paper response and upload it to the assignments section.

Word Journal

With word journal, the instructor asks students to summarize a short text in a single word, and then to write a paragraph on why that word was chosen. The primary objective of word journal is to encourage students to read carefully, as well as to improve skills at explaining and defending with brevity. This activity supports the Verbal, Intrapersonal, and Interpersonal learner. Word journal may be facilitated via students posting responses to:

1. Blog
2. Wiki
3. Discussion forum
4. Assignment (paper submission)
5. In addition, you may have students conduct a peer review for feedback.

Approximate Analogies

With approximate analogies, the instructor presents a term or concept and asks students to complete the second half of the analogy. The primary objective of approximate analogies is to determine students' understanding of relationships between concepts. This activity supports the Logical, Verbal, and Intrapersonal learner. One suggestion is to have students search YouTube for for videos of an appropriate analogy. Approximate analogies may be facilitated via students posting a response to:

1. Discussion forum
2. Assignment (paper submission)

Concept Map

With concept mapping, the instructor provides drawings or diagrams (visuals) of mental connections that should be made between a major concept and other learned concepts. The primary objective of concept mapping is to provide an observable graphic record of students' conceptual schema and associations made in relation to a given focal concept. This activity reinforces the Visual, Kinesthetic, Logical, Verbal, Intrapersonal, and Spatial learner. Concept mapping can be facilitated via students accessing, completing, and re-submitting the concept map document to the:

1. Discussion forum
2. Assignment tool
3. Wiki: Students can each contribute one idea to the concept map wiki.

Invented Dialogues

With invented dialogues, instructors ask students to synthesize knowledge of issues, persons, or events into a structured and illustrated conversation. The primary objective of invented dialogues is to reveal the ability of students to capture the essence of personalities and expression styles, theories, controversies, and opinions. This activity supports the Verbal, Interpersonal, Musical, and Kinesthetic learner. Invented dialogues may be facilitated by:

1. Students creating dialogue with media of their choice: Power-Point, audio file, video file, picture show, or webpage
2. Students posting responses in one of the following: blog, wiki, discussion forum, or social network

Annotated Portfolios

Using the annotated portfolio strategy, students compile selected examples of their work and provide written commentary on each artifact. The primary objective of annotated portfolios is to assess synthesis, critical thinking, communication skill, and progressive achievement. This activity reinforces the Visual, Verbal, Logical, and Intrapersonal learner. Annotated portfolios may be facilitated through the following:

1. Students utilizing a variety of media to demonstrate skills
2. Students submitting portfolio via social network site, assignment (paper submission), e-portfolio, website, or LMS student presentation page
3. Students creating a documentary-type video that presents their accomplishments and demonstrates understanding: post video on YouTube

Problem Recognition Tasks

Using problem recognition tasks, instructors provide examples of common problems, direct students to determine the specific type of problem for each example given, and direct students to flowchart the steps to solve the problem. The primary object of problem recognition tasks is to assess recognition of problem types (which is critical for problem solving) and critical thinking for problem solving. This activity reinforces the Visual, Logical, Verbal, Interpersonal, and Kinesthetic learner. Problem recognition tasks may be facilitated via students posting responses to:

1. Discussion forum
2. Wiki
3. Blog
4. Or, students create a video presenting the problem solving steps; post video to YouTube

What's the Principle?

The *What's the Principle* strategy allows instructors to provide examples of problems and ask students to state the primary principle that best applies to each problem. The primary objective of *What's the Principle* is to determine students' abilities to connect specific problems with specific solution principles. This activity supports the Interpersonal, Visual, Logical, and Verbal learner. *What's the Principle* may be facilitated via:

1. Students posting responses to assignment (paper submission), discussion forum, wiki, blog, or social network site

2. Students locate a video on YouTube that approximates the stated problem (or antithesis); provide link to video in an appropriate forum (blog, wiki, discussion, etc.) and discusses the principle(s) within the problem

Audio and Video-taped Protocols

With audio or video protocols, students record themselves working through the problem-solving process. The primary objective is to evaluate the ability of students to employ problem-solving techniques and to promote critical thinking. This activity reinforces the Visual, Auditory, Kinesthetic, Logical, Verbal, Interpersonal, and Musical learner. Audio and video protocols may be facilitated by:

1. Student-produced narrated PowerPoint or Windows Movie Maker File
2. Upload file to student presentation page, wiki, social networking site, or YouTube

Application Cards

With application cards, students describe real-world workplace applications for the important principle, theory, or process that they just learned. The primary objective of application cards is to depict whether or not the student clearly understands the concept and applications. This activity reinforces the Visual, Auditory, and Verbal learner. Application cards may be facilitated by asking students to:

1. create responses in a media type of their choice (i.e. PowerPoint, audio file, video, etc.)
2. post responses to discussion forum, wiki, blog, social network site, YouTube, or LMS student presentation page

Students Create Test Questions

For this activity, students develop test questions from course materials such as textbook, online discussions, group chat sessions, instructor feedback, etcetera. The primary objective is to reveal what students remember and what they consider to be most important. This activity reinforces the Logical, Verbal, and Intrapersonal learner. Student test questions may be facilitated with students posting responses to:

1. Email
2. Blog

3. Wiki
4. Discussion forum

Prospectus for a Paper or Project

Students prepare a prospectus, which can be a brief first-draft or plan for a research paper or course project. The primary objective of the prospectus activity is to help students to organize their thinking, outline the steps needed to complete the task, and focus on the product to be created. This activity reinforces the Visual, Logical, Verbal, Intrapersonal, and Interpersonal learner. Prospectus may be facilitated via students posting a response to:

1. Blog
2. Wiki
3. Discussion forum
4. Assignment (paper submission)

Questioning Strategies in Online Courses: The *QB*

The previous section focused on easy-to-implement active learning strategies, as they relate to the delivery of content and assignments in distance learning courses. However, in many instances the instructor may desire quick, individual responses from students and, thus, will create questions for each student to answer via email, discussion, or chat. Well-developed questions can spark students' interests and serve to motivate them to pursue additional information. In addition, asking questions allows the instructor to evaluate student preparation and learning, as well as assess the achievement of course objectives.

There is an abundance of research with regard to questioning techniques in traditional face-to-face classes. Placement and timing of questions, oral versus written questions, the amount of wait-time allowed after asking a question, and cognitive level of questions are topics that have been well-researched. However, these topics are not the focus of this section, since placement, timing, and wait-time do not necessarily apply to asynchronous forms of communication in online courses delivered via an LMS. The focus here is how to group or "bundle" activity/assignment questions so that students are required to recall facts and/or specific knowledge, interpret the facts/knowledge, use the knowledge to solve problems, and evaluate/make choices based on the knowledge. (You may recognize this as the cognitive domain of Bloom's Taxonomy of Learning, discussed in a previous section of this chapter.)

By using *question bundles* (QBs) instructors avoid asking yes/no questions. This is critically important, since the ultimate purpose is to generate discussion that allows students to internalize the content. In addition, avoid asking questions that require a purely factual answer, unless that question is the first part of a QB.

Before we explore QBs, it is important to be aware that, in general, online questioning can often be more effective than in-class questioning, especially if asynchronous forms of communication, such as the discussion board and/or the assignments tool, are used. Asynchronous communication allows learners more time to process the questions and to develop responses, thus encouraging critical thinking. However, since it is difficult and often time-consuming for instructors to post single questions to the discussion board and ask students to respond, then post follow-up questions, and, again, ask students to respond; we recommend that you post QBs.

What Exactly Is a Question Bundle? (QB)

It is often beneficial in guiding students to think about a concept or topic in an organized way by creating question bundles, or QBs. The supportive nature of QBs helps students to sort out the elements of the query or problem, limits ambiguity, and allows for critical analysis of specific issues in explicit or implicit contexts. It is helpful to think of QBs as a package of parts that, when assembled, comprise an intact artifact. To create QBs appropriate for distance learning delivery, instructors must first identify a list of questions that would normally be asked in the traditional, face-to-face class. Remember to consider Bloom's Taxonomy when crafting questions: knowledge, comprehension, application, analysis, synthesis, and evaluation. You may wish to revisit the action verbs located in Table 1.1 from Chapter 1. Once the initial list of questions is created, create two or three follow-up questions (increasing in cognitive level requirements) for each of the initial questions.

To illustrate, if you begin by asking a question that requires the answer to be a fact or simple recall of information, reflect on what question you would use as a follow-up to determine that your students comprehend the knowledge, can apply the knowledge, and can make choices based on the knowledge. Combining the initial question and follow-up questions creates a QB.

The first question in a QB is often a knowledge level question requiring simple recall or recognition of facts. The content of this question should be such that it leads nicely into follow-up questions that increase in cognitive level. Sentence prompts for knowledge level questions include: arrange, define, duplicate, label, list, name, order, recognize, recall, repeat, reproduce, and state.

In comprehension type questions, students are typically asked to classify, describe, discuss, explain, express, identify, indicate, locate, recognize, report, restate, review, select, or translate. These types of questions would be appropriate for the second question in the bundle. Or, in some cases, comprehension questions can be the first question in the bundle.

Next, questions that challenge students to think about the topic or concept in a more in-depth manner, such as applying their knowledge of the topic to a specific context or setting and/or anticipating outcomes would be appropriate for the third question in the bundle. These types of questions may challenge students to apply, choose, demonstrate, dramatize, employ, illustrate, interpret, operate, practice, schedule, sketch, solve, use, or write (application), as well as analyze, appraise, calculate, categorize, compare, contrast, criticize, differentiate, discriminate, distinguish, examine, experiment, question, or test (analysis).

Finally, request that students synthesize and evaluate their learning experience. Stimulate their synthesis of information by asking them to arrange, assemble, collect, compose, construct, create, design, develop, formulate, manage, organize, plan, prepare, propose, set up, or write. Usual requests for evaluation type responses are for students to appraise, argue, assess, attach, choose, compare, defend, estimate, judge, predict, rate, identify cores, select, support, value, and evaluate. These question types are appropriate for the final, culminating question in the bundle.

A number of sample question bundles are contained in Table 2.1. The question topics vary, but we recommend that you use these samples as a guide when developing questions for your distance learning instruction.

Additional Course Activities for Distance Delivery

There are a multitude of active learning strategies that can be implemented to create effective learning activities and assignments for distance learning courses. The previous section focused on quick activities and assignments, as well as online questioning strategies, using QBs. However, many of the major or long-term assignments given to students in face-to-face courses can be utilized in the distance learning environment. The asynchronous characteristics of distance learning, combined with web delivery, allows for dynamic types of learning activities and assignments. The list of activities displayed in Table 2.2 is classified from the simple uploading of documents, to multifaceted activities involving group work, to the new Web 2.0 social networking tools.

TABLE 2.1   Sample Question Bundles

Topic	Question Bundle
Social Change	From our literature readings, identify three major social changes that occurred from 1865–1910 (knowledge-based question). Post your response to the Discussion Board. Read two or three of your classmates' responses, then compare the changes you identified with the changes that your classmates identified. Discuss the merits of the changes your classmates identified that you did not by replying to your classmates' posts (comprehension question). After you reply to your classmates, write a one-page abstract indicating how current literature reflects one of the changes you or a classmate identified (analysis, synthesis, and evaluation).
School Segregation	After reading your text and viewing the required video, identify five significant events/court cases that led to school desegregation (knowledge-based question). Based on your opinion, prioritize the events from most significant to least significant (analysis and evaluation).
Career Preparation	This unit focused specifically on issues related to the world of work. What types of experiences does your text recommend as preparation for the world of work? In what ways can you demonstrate and provide documentation of your life and workplace skills? List five strategies for getting a job. Identify five work place behaviors that will help you keep a job. Compose a one- to two-paragraph outline of your educational and career plan; include specific strategies that you will employ to support your plan. Finally, what is your opinion of the direction the labor market will take in the future (10 to 25 years from now)? Share how you plan to prepare for it.
Nursing	Explain how theories are used in nursing. Identify a situation where a theory from another field, such as Psychology (Maslow's Hierarchy, Piaget's growth and development, etc.), may be useful in guiding a nurse's actions and decisions when working with patients. Discuss the advantages and disadvantages of using a theory to guide practice. Compare and contrast the three categories of theories.
Early Childhood/ Childcare	According to your text, which learning strategies are effective for teaching young children? Explain the intended effect of these strategies. Discuss the changes or innovations that you feel have impacted the teaching/learning environment, and why. What resources and/or references do you believe will be instrumental in helping you develop your own philosophy of teaching/childcare?

TABLE 2.2 Active Learning Strategies

Active Learning Strategy	Learner Preferences	Learning Domains
Documents/Assignment Files		
Fill-in-the blank handouts presented and turned in via a Word document	Visual Intrapersonal Linguistic/Verbal Logical	Knowledge
Reflective Discussion/ Reflective Journal Writings	Linguistic/Verbal Intrapersonal	Understanding, Application, Analysis, Synthesis, Evaluation
Written report on a research topic	Linguistic/Verbal Logical Intrapersonal	Knowledge, Understanding, Application, Analysis, Synthesis, Evaluation
Problem-Based Learning		
Group Work/Collaborative Learning	Auditory Interpersonal	Application, Analysis, Synthesis, Evaluation
Case Study	Linguistic	Application, Analysis, Synthesis, Evaluation
Investigative Inquiry	Logical	Analysis, Synthesis, Evaluation
Service Learning	Kinesthetic Interpersonal	Application, Analysis, Synthesis, Evaluation
Web-Based Projects		
WebQuest	Visual	Knowledge, Understanding, Application, Analysis, Synthesis, Evaluation
Virtual Fieldtrip	Visual Kinesthetic	Knowledge, Understanding
Simulation	Visual Kinesthetic	Knowledge, Understanding, Application, Analysis
Interactive Internet Resources	Visual Kinesthetic	Knowledge, Understanding, Application, Analysis, Synthesis, Evaluation
Web 2.0 Tools		
Blog	Linguistic/Verbal Kinesthetic	Knowledge, Understanding, Analysis, Synthesis, Evaluation
Wiki	Linguistic/Verbal Kinesthetic	Knowledge, Understanding, Analysis, Synthesis, Evaluation

Active Learning Strategy	Learner Preferences	Learning Domains
Twitter	Linguistic/Verbal Interpersonal Kinesthetic	Knowledge, Understanding, Analysis, Evaluation
Social Networking	Linguistic/Verbal Interpersonal Kinesthetic	Knowledge, Understanding, Application, Analysis, Synthesis, Evaluation
Multimedia		
Podcast	Auditory Kinesthetic	Knowledge, Understanding
Video	Visual Kinesthetic Musical/Rhythmic	Knowledge, Understanding, Application, Analysis
Gaming	Visual Kinesthetic	Knowledge, Understanding, Application, Analysis, Synthesis, Evaluation
Virtual Worlds and Avatars	Visual Kinesthetic	Knowledge, Understanding, Application, Analysis, Synthesis, Evaluation

Documents/Assignment Files

The focus of this section is the linguistic/verbal learner who enjoys working independently. However, depending on how the assignments are structured, collaboration can be built in, such as asking students to respond to their classmates' reflective journals posted to a discussion forum. Also, visual learners and those with strong analysis and synthesis skills are well accommodated by the strategies included in this section.

Fill-in-the Blank Handouts

In the early days of teaching online, students accessed lectures and supplemental readings and handouts that their instructors had uploaded as Word documents and PDF files. And, although online technology has advanced to enable streaming audio and video, this technique is still prevalent. Other instructors prefer to create web pages using Web authoring programs such as FrontPage or Dreamweaver. The purposes of handouts include:

1. Form to be saved, completed, and submitted as an assignment
2. Organizers that help prepare students for upcoming content
3. Introduction of, and instructions for, learning activity

4. Rubric
5. Supplemental information (additional readings, charts, graphs, data, illustrations)
6. Summary of key points for a unit of study
7. Study guide for quiz or test
8. Anecdotal information about topic (community resources, events related to topic, volunteer activities, instructor's personal views and observations)

When creating a handout, it is important to keep the focus on a single topic. If multiple topics are incorporated into one document, they should be separated into logical categories with headings that alert the readers about the nature of the content. The visual appearance and functionality of the document should also be ascertained. When critiquing a document handout, certain considerations should be made, including (1) visual appeal and professional appearance; (2) organization, including numbered and bulleted lists; (3) the amount of white space to balance and highlight information; (4) appropriate use of color and graphics, so as not to detract the learner from important information; and (5) adequate space for students to take notes and answer questions.

Reflective Discussion/Reflective Journal Writing

In reflective discussion and journal writing, students have the opportunity to contemplate what they have learned, share their observations and discoveries through interactive discussion or personal journal writing, and extend their knowledge and comprehension of information. The reflective dialogue allows students to clarify their thoughts and feelings, rediscover concepts, and recreate events in context and sequence. Personal interpretations assist students in understanding phenomena from different perspectives and demonstrate that diversity of opinion is valued. By giving students control of their engagement with curriculum and prompting reflection, online learning can be enhanced (USDOE, 2009). A meta-analysis of research conducted by the USDOE (2009) determined that "manipulations that trigger learner activity or learner reflection and self-monitoring of understanding are effective when students pursue online learning as individuals" (p. xvi). Muirhead (2001) identifies seven significant advantages to journal writing:

1. Provides an aid to memory
2. Provides a basis for creating new perspectives; creates a framework to explore relationships between ideas

3. Enhances critical thinking skills by learning to analyze the under-lying assumptions of our actions and those of others
4. Provides psychological/emotional advantages by enabling indi-viduals to work through difficult work or personal situations
5. Offers opportunities to increase empathy for others by enhancing understanding of our society and the world
6. Provides a practical way to understand books and articles
7. Provides support for self-directed learning activities by establish-ing individual learning goals to complete the journal assignments

To facilitate reflective responses, whether in a group discussion or private contribution, pose a question or questions to provoke thought and structure the direction of rumination. Reflective questions begin with "Who," "What," "When," "Where," "Why," and "How," rather than questions that can be an-swered with a simple "Yes" or "No." The question, "Did you enjoy the vol-unteer experience?" does little to illicit thoughtful discussion, as compared to, "What was the volunteer experience like?" where the student must think more deeply about their reaction to the incident. Open-ended questions stimulate variety and encourage students to make inferences and interpre-tations. Allow students to post their initial reactions to the question. Then, ask the same question, but posed in a different context, and ask students to respond. As part of their response, ask students to identify how the context of the question changed their opinions. For instance, an initial question might ask, "What conclusions did you draw from your reading/research?" The follow-up question, altered slightly to challenge their application of concepts to a new context, might query, "If the gender of the central figure in your reading/research changed, would this change your perspective, and why?" The QB strategy is effective for this type of activity.

Written Report on Research Topic

The written report—formal or informal research paper—is a staple of learning strategies. Considerable thought about the goals and objectives for the paper, format expectations, and evaluation criteria initializes the creation of the assignment. The written paper assignment is valuable when it requires students to frame their own question(s) about the topic and/or construct a thesis statement. Requiring students to locate, analyze, and draw conclusions from researched information makes the research paper mean-ingful, as it moves the student to operate at higher cognitive levels, rather than merely restating facts and opinion. A list of questions to help guide the goals and objectives for a meaningful written paper assignment is provided in Table 2.3. Options for receiving the written paper from students include

---

TABLE 2.3   Guiding Questions That Help Develop a Written Assignment Activity

Scope:
- What topics are appropriate for the paper?
- Will all students research the same topic or different topics?
- Will topics be assigned to or selected by the students?

Deadlines:
- When is the due date for the assignment?
- Will a draft be required? If so, when?

Format:
- What types of references and sources will be accepted?
- Will the instructor provide any source materials?
- How many sources are required?
- What format is required (e.g., APA, MLA, etc.)?
- How many pages should the paper be?
- What font styles and font sizes are acceptable?
- How should the paper be spaced (single-spaced, double-spaced, etc.)?

---

requiring students to submit the assignment through the LMS assignment tool, email the paper to the instructor, or post the draft or final paper to a discussion board or wiki.

Another interesting strategy to stretch student imagination and perspective is the multi-genre paper, which uses different genres within the body of the paper to reflect a facet or subtopic of the main focus. The writer of a multi-genre piece may use a diary entry, interview dialogue, story-telling, cartoon, advertisement, personal letter or correspondence, birth/death announcement, advice column, recipe, motto, horoscope, poem, instruction manual excerpt, yellow pages advertisement, classified advertisement, resume, or any other artifact that adds credence to the topic. In short, anything that would add value and insight in describing and understanding the subject is considered a worthy addition to the multi-genre paper.

Problem-Based Learning

The exploration by students of a problem within structured guidelines is commonly referred to as problem-based learning. Students typically work collaboratively to define, conduct, and analyze a challenging question or issue, often anchored in real-world circumstances. The focus of this section is the analytical learner who enjoys working with others. However, again, depending on how the assignments are structured, collaboration among students is not necessary.

Group Work (Collaborative Learning)

Research indicates that collaborative/cooperative learning promotes deep understanding of concepts and applications. In fact, one of the guiding principles for effective learning advocated by Chickering and Gamson (1987) is the opportunity for cooperative learning. Therefore, effective distance learning courses must include interactive assignments and activities that are carefully structured.

Many faculty cringe when told that collaborative group work should be incorporated into their course, even though it has been known for decades that collaboration and sharing discoveries and ideas amplifies new learning (Reynard, 2008). Part of the problem stems from the muddling of cooperative and collaborative work. Cooperative group work does not necessarily require that students be actively involved in the exploration, decision making, or creation of a learning product. Collaboration necessitates that all members of the group be committed and engaged in the sharing of new ideas for construction of new learning. In addition to the strategies mentioned in this section, Web 2.0 social networking tools can adroitly accomplish the aim to have learners see beyond themselves as valuable contributors to a community of fellow learners with common goals and challenges.

Since learning requires students to reconstruct knowledge or create new information, it is desirable that learning occur in real-world contexts that are significant and relevant to learners' experiences. In the real world, people interact to consult, observe, instruct, learn, share, and negotiate to accomplish a task objective. Classroom learning, whether face-to-face or via distance learning, should incorporate opportunities for students to engage in similar behavior. However, as previously mentioned, some students may be reluctant to take part in group activities for a variety of reasons. They might have participated in prior group work that was poorly organized and resulted in a negative outcome. Other students may not have been included in a collaborative learning activity, and thus do not know what is expected of them. Thorough planning in structuring collaborative active learning assignments will result in a positive experience for you and your students. Please note that careful consideration should be given to how the groups will be configured and organized; simply placing students into groups and expecting them to move forward on the assignment with little direction rarely works well. Utilizing early course activities such as class introductions can help to break the isolation of distance learning and lay the foundation for collaborative work.

Tips for Incorporating Group Work

The first consideration for group work is how the activity will contribute to the learning goals and objectives for the concept(s) to be learned. Communicate to students how and why the group activity will further their understanding of course work and strengthen their abilities in other areas, such as teamwork skills, that are valued in the workplace. Share with students that research indicates that learning is enhanced when there are opportunities for student collaboration. In addition, allow group members a short period of time to bond and build their teamwork skills.

Second, plan how to communicate the group assignment to the students in a way that it is easily understood. The dynamics of group work can create frustration and misunderstanding if the assignment instructions are not straightforward and specific. Provide step-by-step directions; outlines and checklists are effective organizer tools. Give students an indication of the time to be spent on different tasks, as some students have difficulty in managing their time effectively. This also helps to alleviate conflicts that may form between students familiar with distance learning and group work, novice students, those who normally work fast, and/or who tend to procrastinate. Groups are more effective when there are specific directions for tasks and time limits to complete them. For instance, instead of directing students to "Work in groups and discuss the implications of theories of X, Y, and Z" or "Critique the first draft," provide detailed instructions that help guide the groups to produce a tangible product or result with a timeline that includes benchmarks along the way. This means requiring that groups generate concrete work corresponding to a structured schedule. For example, call for groups to produce a certain number of drafts, reports, questions, explanations, reasons, clarifications, solutions, and/or presentations by a certain date. Provide a worksheet with specific benchmarks that guides groups through the process. Ask groups to provide weekly progress reports.

Next, consider involving students in pre-project activities. Many instructors find that pre-project activities build student confidence in the group process, as well as communication and teamwork skills. The following two activities may be adapted to most group projects:

1. Drafting: students read and critique each other's drafts

   How it works: students post drafts in presentation area, discussion board, or in email so that coursemates have access; critique responses can be private or public

   Instructor responsibility: provide guiding questions and timeline for responses

Benefits: supports revision, peer learning, and helps instructors manage time

2. Setting the bar: students establish rubric or grading criteria for project

   How it works: students examine several examples of anonymous work from previous classes, and in groups establish a rank order for quality of work, even providing a written summary that justifies their conclusion; following the group submissions, the instructor reveals their rankings, inviting discussion about any discrepancies

   Instructor responsibility: provide samples of work, and possibly a rubric

   Benefits: helps students internalize criteria by which their work will be evaluated

Fourth, clearly identify expectations for student participation and performance. Many distance learning instructors find rubrics to be particularly effective in clarifying how grades or points will be earned for collaborative activities. Chapter 5 will provide additional information on using rubrics for assessment.

Finally, be sure to provide ample opportunities for collaboration among team members by setting up a team discussion board, chat room, presentation area, and email. Without the use of available communication tools, the primary learning value of group work would be lost.

Constructing Groups

There are five general characteristics of effective collaborative learning that must be considered when deciding upon a grouping strategy. The five characteristics are:

1. Students work together on a common project, activity, or assignment that could not be effectively completed by an individual.
2. Groups should be small, with a maximum of four to five group members; this is the ideal size because it provides diverse perspectives but is still manageable, in the sense of forming a consensus.
3. Students must cooperate and use socially acceptable behavior to complete the assigned task. You may want to consider assigning group roles, or requiring students to volunteer for a role within their team. Examples of group roles include leader, recorder, technology expert, researcher, presenter, nurturer, and devil's advocate.
4. Students are positively interdependent, in the sense that they need the contribution of each team member in order to complete the assigned task.

5. Students are individually accountable and responsible for their shares of the workload.

There are myriad ways that groups can be assigned in a distance learning course. Examples of grouping strategies include:

1. Instructor Assigned Teams: The instructor creates teams and uses the Email tool to notify students of the names of their team members.
2. Discussion Board Activity: Determine how many teams are necessary for the desired project and create a discussion board topic that contains a thread for each team (Team 1, Team 2, etc.). Use the Announcements tool or the Email tool to notify students that they are to access the discussion board and assign themselves to a team by posting a message to the appropriate team thread.
3. Online Assessment: Create an online assessment (using the Assessment tool included with your LMS) that ascertains students' current knowledge regarding the specified topic. Ask the students to complete the assessment. Order the students by score, in order of highest to lowest. If four teams are required, assign numbers to the students based on their assessment score. The student with the highest score is a 1; the student with the second highest score is a 2, etcetera. The student with the fifth highest score is a 1; the person with the sixth highest score is a 2, etcetera, until all students are assigned to a team. This grouping method insures that each team has a wide array of topic knowledge levels represented.

Additional Issues with Collaborative Learning. Once the group work has begun, continue to monitor progress for both the group and individual group members. Course communication tools are valuable for monitoring student progress and answering questions. Staying in close contact with students allows the instructor to ascertain the level of student learning and motivates students to stay committed to their achievement. Since students must be held accountable for their own contributions to the group assignment, keeping an eye on student progress motivates the "hitchhikers" and restrains the "workhorses," so that all students assume their shares of responsibility for the group work and take ownership of their individual academic achievements.

As mentioned above, one of the key elements of effective collaborative learning is positive interdependence among team members. At the same time, it is important to strike a balance between independence and interdependence. Just as employees in the workplace engage in cooperation for the mutual benefit of the organization, group members should realize that they share a common goal, and contribute to each other's learning. Positive interdependence can be achieved by having students (1) reach a consensus on a decision, (2) produce team-generated resolutions, (3) construct a report or presentation with components developed by individual team members, (4) spend time in each of the group's roles (leader, recorder, researcher, nurturer, etc.), and (5) review and evaluate group and individual participation.

Grading of group work should have no connotation of competition between group members. As mentioned previously, the preferred grading scheme for group projects is criterion-referenced and comprised of scores for individual productivity, as well as a group score based on the quality of the finished product. Moreover, some instructors choose to include a score for overall group performance, cohesiveness, cooperation with each other, and overall group effectiveness.

Problems may arise. Address them immediately. Continuous monitoring of group and individual progress goes a long way toward resolving misdirection and other issues before they escalate. During collaborative activities, poll the class via an email or discussion board with questions such as, "How is the activity progressing?" "What questions do you have concerning this task?" After completion of a task, ask students to respond to informal questions or a task survey with inquires of: (1) Were all group members active in the completion of the task? (2) What recommendations would you make for better group effort? (3) List three contributions you made to the group effort, (4) What was the most important thing(s) you learned from this activity? and (5) What information from this activity do you still need to have clarified?

It is recommended that the instructor intercede in group conflicts only when absolutely necessary. Encourage group members to negotiate and resolve their disagreements through good communication strategies, such as active listening and reflecting back. Teams can use a designated team discussion forum or chat room for communication.

The Companion Website contains sample group projects and assignments that are appropriate for distance learning courses, along with step-by-step instructions for facilitating each project. In addition, the website contains a template for creating customized team activities. Review the samples carefully. Then, access the template and print a copy. You will use the template to complete one of the End of Chapter Activities.

Case Study

A case study includes a specific situation or scenario. The situation or scenario may be fact or fiction. However, in both instances, the students are provided with detailed background information. After reviewing the background, students are given a specific problem to solve. Students explore solutions to the problem by asking "what if" questions. Exploring a variety of "what if" questions eventually leads students to solve the problem and/or form a conclusion. Yin (1994) cautions that when using case studies as a teaching/learning strategy, it is necessary to provide specific information to the students, including:

1. An overview of the case study project, which should include background information, objectives, issues, topics being investigated, and the purpose of the case study
2. Research procedures: involves the collection of information, including access to websites and additional resources
3. Case study questions, which should include specific "what if" questions that the student must keep in mind while conducting research
4. A guide for the case study final report that includes information regarding report format, length, etcetera (p. 64)

The use of case studies in distance learning requires ongoing communication between the instructor and students, as well as between the students. The use of synchronous and asynchronous communication tools, which will be discussed in Chapter 4, is highly recommended. Case studies are usually group activities. However, simple case studies can be used for individual student assignments, as well.

An example of a case study is contained in Table 2.4, about Francie Berger, the "Lego Lady." Begin to think of ways in which you could use this or similar cases in your distance learning course(s). At the end of each case study segment is a list of questions. What additional questions would be relevant to each segment that would add relevancy to your course?

TABLE 2.4   Case Study Example

The Lego Lady

Part One. *Read to the bottom of this page then stop.*

What do you want to be when you grow up? Francie Berger could have answered this question when she was three and received her first set of Lego bricks: Build things with Legos! At age eight, she decided to be an architect, since that was an occupation where she could design and build. Although she had an extensive collection of Legos, this budding architect needed more; so she wrote to Lego Systems, Inc. to order a couple million more. They declined her request. While attending Virginia Tech, Francie finalized her occupational

choice, deciding to pursue a career at Lego after hearing a lecture on designing toys. She began routinely writing and calling Lego to inquire about job possibilities. When she made a visit to the company's U.S. headquarters in Enfield, Connecticut, they were well aware of who Francie Berger was. They declined her offer to come to work for them. Not to be discouraged, Francie used her passion for building and Legos to design a working farm, using only Legos, for her architectural thesis—and as a job application for Lego. She was hired for a three-week trial probationary period. Francie became a master builder for Lego, and through the decades has created some of the most fascinating and well-loved Lego designs.
STOP

Reflection and investigation:
1. Why do you believe Lego hired Francie?
2. What qualities that employers usually value did she demonstrate prior to being hired by Lego?
3. How did Francie pursue her idea of getting a job at Lego?
4. Why do you suppose her persistence paid off?

Part Two. *Read to the bottom of this page then stop.*
All work and no play? Francie spent her work day in Lego Heaven—a roomful of the colorful plastic bricks. Her job was to design the wonderfully elaborate displays that evoke oohs and ahs from customers in stores like F.A.O. Schwartz or at the Toy Trade Fair in New York. When asked what the downsides of her job were, Francie commented, "There are none. There really is nothing better than this."
Some of her creations include a six-foot roller coaster, parts of an animal amusement park, a thirteen-foot-tall and twenty-seven-and-a-half-foot-wide replica of the U.S. Capitol, and Francie's favorite, a six-foot-tall surfing hippo. The models are constructed entirely of Lego bricks, the same kinds that are sold in stores. A team of model-designers and model-builders under master builder Francie's supervision construct the models, some of which use more than a half-million bricks.
Clickity-clickity. Clackity-clickity. The sound of Legos being snapped together to build fanciful creations like spaceships, cowboys riding horses, dancing sultans with yellow pointed slippers and voluminous blue pantaloons. The master builders are the elite force at Lego, working in an environment that is part fantasy and part corporate privileged. There are only about 10 master builders in the U.S., and only slightly more at the corporate headquarters in Denmark. They all have degrees in engineering, architecture, or science, as well as practical experience in wood crafting, pottery, art, or a related craft.
STOP

Reflection and investigation:
1. What processes do the model builders follow when executing a project?
2. How is this similar to procedures for construction projects? Manufacturing? Landscaping? Culinary? Writing a report?
3. How is this process important in completing a project?
4. What other steps not mentioned do you suppose are part of a project process?

(continued)

TABLE 2.4   Case Study Example (continued)

Part Three. *Read to the bottom of this page then stop.*
Born in 1960, Francie Berger, in her mid-forties, worked in an office filled with
bins of colorful Lego blocks of all sizes. There are about thirteen thousand
different elements in the Lego system, and Francie can have as many of
them as she wants, say…a couple million? Lego blocks have been a part of
her life for as long as she can remember. Years ago, when she was getting
married, her wedding invitation was decorated with a photograph of a three-
foot-tall red Lego hippopotamus bride and groom. The actual wedding cake
was topped with a Lego model of a bride and groom. At Christmas, Francie
used Lego bricks to build seasonal decorations beneath the Christmas tree
and throughout the house. In addition to creating models in her office, she
travels to different cities and participates in exhibit events and demonstrations
building models while people watch. Sometimes people are so intrigued they
ask Francie how they can get hired to create models at Lego. Every year, Berger
receives dozens of letters from children, art students, engineers, architects,
and others, all wanting to know the same thing: "What do I have to do to get a
job like yours at Lego?" When Francie replies, she explains that when she was
hired, her job didn't exactly exist. With her passion and talent, she just kind of
made it happen: a career playing with Lego bricks that are sold in 140 countries
and played with by over 300 million people. With a little imagination, and an
endless supply of bricks…anything is possible!
STOP

Reflection and investigation:
   1. What impresses you about Francie, the woman who was determined to spend
      her life "doing the thing she likes best?"
   2. Life Coaches, Employment Counselors, and Psychologists advise people
      to follow their passions. Francie followed this advice. How might you
      incorporate your passions and strengths into your work?
   3. Since the article was written (around the mid 1990's) what types of models do
      you think Francie has developed since then?
   4. What do you suppose the future holds for Francie?

It is recommended that instructors create original case studies that reflect course content and meet the course objectives, as well as the needs of
students. However, there are a multitude of case studies available on the
Internet. Examples and information about case study learning is presented
in Table 2.5. Consider adapting a previously-created case study by modifying the investigative questions to meet your course needs.

Investigative Inquiry
   Many distance learning assignments involve students responding to
pre-established questions. A strategy appropriate for the distance learning

TABLE 2.5 Case Study Resources

National Center for Case Study Teaching in Science
   http://ublib.buffalo.edu/libraries/projects/cases/case.html
Template for creating case studies
   http://www.bgfl.org/bgfl/18.cfm?s=18&m=469&p=262,index
Teaching materials using case studies
   http://www.materials.ac.uk/guides/casestudies.asp
Harvard business case studies
   http://hbsp.harvard.edu/product/cases
Technology case studies from MIT
   http://web.mit.edu/d-lab/resources/nciia_files/cases.pdf

course involves the use of "investigative" questions. When using investigative questions, you must provide students with a specific problem to solve. Then ask students to respond to the following questions:

1. What do you know now? (What information is provided?)
2. What additional information do you need to know? (What information is missing?)
3. Where can you find the additional information needed?
4. Can you now solve the problem?

Investigative inquiry encourages students to explore and elucidate their findings, based on their discoveries. Student learning is strengthened by their own active investigation. As emphasized in the information regarding the cognitive domain of Bloom's Taxonomy of Learning, in the process of investigative inquiry, students acquire skills in locating, analyzing, interpreting, synthesizing, and applying information. An example of an investigative learning activity is displayed in Table 2.6. Please note that additional examples can be found on the Companion Website.

Service Learning Projects

Service learning is a strategy intended to promote academic enhancement, personal growth, and civic engagement. Service learning integrates academics with serving the community in ways that benefit both. Students engage in meaningful service at a site within the community; the encounter presents the opportunity for real-world experiences that support course curriculum. Guided by the instructor, students reflect on the experience, articulate their learning, and make connections to learning goals. Service

---

TABLE 2.6 Sample Investigative Inquiry

Students investigate a mass beaching of whales off the coast of Australia and identify the oceanic conditions that may cause such an event. Students will work individually to investigate the event and will be allowed to utilize Internet resources to determine a possible cause or causes. Students are asked to describe their findings using the course discussion board, blog, or wiki. Once each student has posted his/her response, they are to review the responses of three coursemates and respond to one.

The instructor will want to ask some guiding questions to prompt the direction of inquiry. Examples of questions are provided below. Note that questions follow the Bloom's taxonomy model.

1. How many whales were beached in this incident?
2. Discuss three major oceanic conditions that contributed to the beaching.
3. In your opinion, which of the conditions is the most important factor?
4. How does knowledge of this factor play an important role in our own hemisphere?

---

learning is based on the idea that students learn best by constructing knowledge that is rooted in personal experience.

Service learning programs and projects help students understand the complexities of the world in which they live by participating in activities that help them make a tangible connection to that world, and perhaps make a difference in people's lives. True service learning, as an educational endeavor, seeks to not only have students work in food pantries and homeless shelters, but to also ask and reflect upon significant issues, such as, (1) Why is there hunger in our society? (2) Why is there homelessness in our society? and (3) How can I make a positive contribution to the lives of the hungry and the homeless? An excellent resource from Florida International University contains a plethora of ideas for service learning projects. The resource, *101 Ideas for Combining Service and Learning*, is accessible at http://servicelearning.org/resources/lesson_plans/index.php?popup_id=211.

If you choose to incorporate a service learning project into a distance learning course, it is important to make sure that continuous opportunities for students to interact and communicate with each other are included. Consider using course communication tools, such as synchronous chat, asynchronous discussions, and email, to allow students to reflect on their experiences.

Web-Based Projects

One of the key elements of web-based projects is the introduction of Internet resources as an element of the activity. These types of projects usually require students to collaborate to conduct research, compile and analyze data, and formulate responses based on the results. Web-based projects lend themselves well to all learning styles (visual, auditory, kinesthetic), and support those with logical, verbal, and interpersonal intelligence types.

Student Presentations

A number of the current LMS systems include a Student Presentation tool that allows students to share electronic files. Students simply upload their file (PowerPoint presentation, document, .html file, etc.) to the presentation page. Then, all students can access and review each presentation, as well as provide feedback via the discussion board, structured chat session, etcetera. Collaborative systems, such as Elluminate and DyKnow, offer even more sophisticated many-to-many presentation options.

Following is a brief list of strategies for using student presentations in your distance learning course. Note that the Companion Website contains a template for creating presentation activities.

1. Students can be asked to prepare information for a scheduled synchronous session. A handful of students can be identified for each session so that by the end of the course, each student will have had the opportunity to present.
2. Students can upload their presentation file (PowerPoint, document, multimedia file, etc.) to the discussion board; students can email their presentation file to all of the other students in the course.
3. Individual students can give oral presentations to the class by uploading previously recorded audio files and/or webcasts.

WebQuests

"A WebQuest is an inquiry-oriented activity in which some or all of the information that learners interact with comes from resources on the Internet, optionally supplemented with videoconferencing" (Dodge, 1997). WebQuests are student-centered learning activities that present a question or problem centered around a topic or concept, and challenges students to use Internet resources to obtain information on the topic. Most WebQuests include direct links to web sites that students can use to research the problem(s) or question(s).

There are two types of WebQuests: short-term and long-term. The primary objective of a short-term WebQuest is for students to acquire knowledge, and it includes substantial amounts of information, primarily factual in nature. A short-term WebQuest can be completed within one week, and is usually included as one assignment within a specific module or unit of instruction.

The primary objective of a long-term WebQuest is for students to extend their current knowledge of a topic, analyze the new information, and demonstrate understanding via application of the new information to a specific situation. In addition, with a long-term WebQuest, students should be given the opportunity to discuss the information and its application by using online discussion and/or chat forums to interact with and respond to the ideas of other course participants. A long-term WebQuest will typically be completed within several weeks, and sometimes spans several modules or units of instruction.

Regardless of whether a short-term WebQuest or a long-term WebQuest is chosen, every WebQuest contains specific components, including an introduction, a task, a process, a list of resources, and an evaluation. Following is a detailed description of the typical components of a WebQuest. An example of a WebQuest is offered in Appendix C.

Introduction

The purpose of this section is to provide an overview and purpose for the WebQuest, as well as to prepare and hook the students by describing their quest. Present the main topic in three or four sentences. The introduction should provide the context that the students need to complete the WebQuest task.

The Task

In this section, the task is clearly described. The task is what leads the students to process and transform the information they gather. It is important to provide a specific and detailed description so that students are clear regarding expectations for their completed work. The task can be any type of active learning strategy, including but not limited to (1) a problem, (2) a position to be formulated and defended, (3) a creative work, and (4) a case study.

The Process

Here, the steps are listed that the students should go through to accomplish the task. Again, it is important to provide clear, specific, step-by-step instructions. Consider preparing worksheets or forms for students to fill in as they use the different resources. Or provide ways for the students to organize the information they will be gathering by instructing them to make a flowchart, summary table, concept map, graph, and/or checklist.

Resources

This section includes links to the web sites that students will use to accomplish the task. (Resources are not confined to web sites—print resources can be used as well.) Provide a list of web sites or annotate each web site, telling the students what kind of information to look for in each site. It is not necessary to provide web sites that include all of the information that the students will need to complete the task. It may be necessary for students to search the Internet for additional information.

Evaluation

The purpose of this section is to describe for students exactly how their performance and/or final product will be evaluated. Consider linking to a separate rubric document from here, or briefly summarize the evaluation criteria. (The use of rubrics will be discussed in detail in Chapter 5.) Specify whether there will be individual grades, a common grade for group work, or some combination. Following are the steps for creating a WebQuest.

1. Select a problem to be solved, a position to be defended, a question to be answered, etcetera.
2. Select the appropriate tool to construct your WebQuest, such as Microsoft Word or PowerPoint. Or consider using one of the multimedia programs discussed in Chapter 3. Visual Communicator, Captivate, and Camtasia are excellent programs for creating WebQuests.
3. Based upon the component descriptions listed above, organize the WebQuest in sequential order, as follows:
   a. Introduction: Present the main topic of the WebQuest in three to four sentences. Stimulate student interest in the topic.
   b. The Task: Clearly describe what the learning outcomes will be, what questions should be answered, and/or problems to be solved.
   c. Process: Provide step-by-step directions, such as role play, group interaction, method of reporting findings, etcetera.
   d. Resources: List resources on the Internet that students can use to accomplish the task.
   e. Evaluation: Share with students how their work will be evaluated and graded; provide a rubric as a guideline.
   f. *Note*: Create a wrap-up activity or a "Conclusion" to the WebQuest. Consider using one of the collaborative communication activities found in Chapter 4 to provide a summary activity for the unit.

TABLE 2.7   Ready-Made WebQuests

WebQuests for a variety of topics
http://www.spa3.k12.sc.us/WebQuests.html

Gallery of Artifacts (high school)
http://www.teachtheteachers.org/projects/PWalker2/index.htm

Career WebQuest (high school)
http://www.macomb.k12.mi.us/wq/WebQ97/CAREER.HTM

A variety of award-winning WebQuests
http://www.iwebquest.com/?CFID=11981842&CFTOKEN=41952012

WebQuests for Health Professions' Students
http://technology-escapades.net/?q=node/2

A variety of WebQuests for Post-Secondary
http://midsolutions.org/samples/index.htm

WebQuest for people of all ages to learn about the Dakota Conflict of 1862
http://www.nativeweb.org/resources.php?name=Dakota&type=1&nation=154

You are encouraged to create original WebQuests that are customized to specific course learning objectives. However, there are literally thousands of ready-made WebQuests available on the Internet. WebQuests can be found for virtually any topic, teaching discipline, and age level. A few of the available websites that include ready-made WebQuests are listed in Table 2.7. Note that links for many more WebQuests can be found on the Companion Website.

Virtual Fieldtrips

Would students benefit from visiting a location that is too far, too dangerous, or just plain unrealistic? If the answer is yes, then consider using virtual fieldtrips as a structured course activity. Virtual fieldtrips are available on the Internet, including those appropriate for any age level and across many disciplines. Trips can be as simple as a photo tour of an art museum, to an interactive marine laboratory exploration, replete with a live webcam and video segments. Many virtual fieldtrip sites allow students to ask questions of experts, such as resident scientists, librarians, or historians, through email or phone. Virtual fieldtrips allow students to journey to places they may not otherwise ever be able to visit, and to make connections with course curriculum and the real world.

Many exceptional virtual fieldtrips can be found on the Yellowstone website at http://www.windowsintowonderland.org/. Since 2001, Yellowstone has been offering award-winning virtual fieldtrips as a window to exciting adventures that investigate the resources and treasures of the world's first national park. Two outstanding trips are *The Firehole River* and *On the Scene of the Yellowstone Hotspot,* both found in Table 2.8.

Links to interactive virtual fieldtrips available on the Internet are provided in Table 2.9. In addition, the Companion Website contains additional virtual fieldtrip websites appropriate for distance learning courses, a template for building custom trips, and sample virtual fieldtrips created using

---

TABLE 2.8   Virtual Fieldtrips

The Firehole River
The Firehole River fieldtrip takes you on a journey through three major geyser basins as the Firehole River in Yellowstone National Park flows through some of the most remarkable country on earth.
   http://www.windowsintowonderland.org/hotwater/index.html

On the Scene of the Yellowstone Hotspot
Become part of an investigative team reporting the story on Yellowstone National Park Geysers, earthquakes, and shifting shorelines in On the Scene of the Yellowstone Hotspot fieldtrip.
   http://www.windowsintowonderland.org/hotspots/index.shtml

TABLE 2.9   Virtual Fieldtrip Resources

Williamsburg, Virginia
   http://www.history.org/history/
Dive and discover the excitement of ocean exploration
   http://www.divediscover.whoi.edu/
Miami Hurricane Center
   http://www.miamisci.org/hurricane/
Franklin Institute Science Museum
   http://www.fi.edu/learn/learners.html
Vietnam
   http://www.vietvet.org/visit.htm
Chicago Museum of Science and Industry: Old Ben mine
   http://www.msichicago.org/exhibit/coal_mine/index.html
Chicago Museum of Science and Industry: Genetic engineering in a chick hatchery
   http://www.msichicago.org/exhibit/chick/index.html
American Museum of Natural History Fossil Halls
   http://www.amnh.org/exhibitions/permanent/fossilhalls/
Worldwide Museum of Natural History
   http://www.wmnh.com/
Metropolitan Museum of Modern Art
   http://www.metmuseum.org/
Berkeley seismological laboratory
   http://seismo.berkeley.edu/seismo/

multimedia software. Remember, the multimedia software programs previously discussed are excellent tools for creating virtual fieldtrips.

Tips for Using Virtual Fieldtrips.   Following are several tips for using virtual fieldtrips in your distance learning course. Proper preparation for both you and your students will help ensure a beneficial learning experience.

1. Explicitly state the learning goals for the activity to focus student purpose in moving forward. Students must understand the reasons why they are being asked to take this journey.
2. It is important to choose a trip that has a strong correlation to the course curriculum, and to preview the trip prior to giving students instructions to engage in connecting activities.
3. Help students to prepare for the fieldtrip by assigning them a specific related topic for research. (Asking students to gather information connected to the upcoming trip prepares them to engage more fully in the experience by activating prior knowledge, stimulating curiosity, and building anticipation.)
4. Provide step-by-step instructions on how to access the virtual fieldtrip, what to expect once students begin the fieldtrip, and how to complete connecting activities. It is wise to provide a checklist for students to follow.
5. Rubrics can be invaluable in structuring the expectations for fieldtrip participation and contributions to fieldtrip assignments.
6. Conduct at least one follow-up session after the fieldtrip activity to review learning goals and to sum up the main points of knowledge confirmation and discovery. Consider conducting a chat session or providing a discussion board topic. Other potential activities are included in Table 2.10.

Virtual fieldtrips enrich the learning experience by helping students to make connections not only with other environments, but also with other learners. The experience enables students to appreciate their own and other cultures and viewpoints. The Companion Website provides a substantial list of virtual fieldtrip resources and websites organized by categories.

Simulation

A simulation is similar to a case study, except that only real-world situations are explored. When using a simulation in a distance learning course, instructors must provide the specific scenario to be explored and the question/problem to be solved. Simulations can be group or individual activities. However, if groups are used, it is recommended that each group mem-

---

TABLE 2.10 Follow-Up Activities for Virtual Fieldtrips

Scrapbook

Tasks:

1. Have students collect text, images, video, and website addresses.
2. Working in groups or independently, students organize media into an e-portfolio that expresses their interpretation of the fieldtrip experience.
3. Students share their e-portfolio in an online presentation.

Cultural Exchange with Another Class

Tasks:

1. Instructor or students contact another class (preferably in a different geographic region) to create an exchange of information and perspectives.
2. Students share photos and narratives, and utilize online communication tools to discuss varied experiences, perceptions, concerns, and reactions to the concepts presented through the fieldtrip.
3. Students learn from their global peers by imparting information about the relationship between the fieldtrip experience to their communities, lives, traditions, challenges, resolutions, etc.

WebQuest

Tasks:

1. Instructor or students (independently or in groups) create a WebQuest that focuses on a particular aspect of the fieldtrip.
2. The WebQuest(s) are posted online and students are responsible for participating in one or more of the posted WebQuests.

Scavenger Hunt

Tasks:

1. Instructor or students (independently or in groups) create a checklist as a culminating activity.
2. Students search for information via the clues provided in the scavenger hunt checklist.

Note: This activity can also be utilized as pre-fieldtrip preparation

ber be assigned a specific role within the group, especially given the fact that the profile of the typical distance learning student indicates that many prefer to work independently. This inclination, combined with possible prior experience in team projects that have been managed poorly, contribute to students' reluctance to participate in group work. However, with careful planning and organization, collaborative endeavors such as simulations can be rewarding learning activities for both you and your students.

Once each individual or group generates a solution to the specified problem, they can share their solutions with the other course participants via the use of online communication tools (discussion, structured chat ses-

TABLE 2.11   Simulation Resources

Physics lab
  http://www.myphysicslab.com/
Virtual labs and physics simulations
  http://www.hazelwood.k12.mo.us/~grichert/sciweb/applets.html
Simulations on the Internet
  http://www.kented.org.uk/ngfl/software/simulations/index.htm
Free trial and virtual tour
  http://www.educationalsimulations.com/
Biology simulations
  http://serendip.brynmawr.edu/sci_edu/biosites.html
Medical simulations
  http://www.medicalsimulations.com/

sion) or by posting a multimedia presentation to a public folder. Links to examples of and information about simulations in learning are contained in Table 2.11. Also, the Companion Website contains sample simulations appropriate for distance learning courses.

Interactive Internet Resources

Interactive websites can be used to supplement course curriculum. It is recommended that instructors use these types of sites as a means for students to practice and review important aspects of the course curriculum. These sites are a fun and engaging way to introduce students to new information, reinforce content, or expand current understanding. With Google Earth 5 Beta, users can visit space one minute, and dive leagues beneath the seas in the next. A free download, Google Earth 5 beta utilizes materials from the National Science Foundation to explore the world's oceans. Users can also explore areas of the Martian surface. The Beta program includes Google Earth features, such as zoom, panoramic view, digital media, and corresponding Wikipedia entries.

Most LMS systems allow direct Web links to be added to course pages. Consider creating an "Additional Resources" folder within the course and including links to these supplemental sites. Or, add the links directly to course content pages and include them as part of required course activities and assignments.

Following are just a few of the interactive educational sites that are available. And, while there are an abundance of sites related to math and science curriculum, interactive websites can be found on most any subject. A variety of excellent examples of interactive websites are included in Table 2.12.

TABLE 2.12   Interactive Websites

The Virtual Body
   http://www.medtropolis.com/VBody.asp

The Healthy Body Calculator
   http://www.dietitian.com/ibw/ibw.html

Interactive Mathematics Tutorials
   http://www.analyzemath.com/

Science Animations
   http://nhscience.lonestar.edu/biol/animatio.htm

3-D Human Anatomy
   http://www.visiblebody.com/

Cells Alive: Interactive Plant Cells and Animal Cells
   http://www.cellsalive.com/cells/cell_model.htm

Digital History of the United States
   http://www.digitalhistory.uh.edu/timeline/timelineO.cfm

S.O.S. Math: list of interactive sites and tutorials
   http://www.sosmath.com/wwwsites.html

Web 2.0 Tools

Web 2.0 is the new buzz phrase. But what exactly is it? Web 2.0 refers to what is commonly known as the second generation of web tools. It is predominantly characterized as facilitating collaboration by transitioning from static webpages to dynamic "community" pages that allow for shareable content. Examples of Web 2.0 technologies include blogs, wikis, Twitter, and social networking. While the focus of Web 2.0 is on these new collaborative tools, the phrase also signals a change in behavior, in respect to how people use the Internet.

Blog

A form of interactive reflective expression that has become increasingly popular is blogging. Blogs are commentaries published on the Internet in reverse chronological order, and are an asynchronous form of Internet discussion. Blogs offer a forum for people to share their opinions or provide commentary on other's opinions. Blogs are typically a collection of thoughts on diverse topics, and may contain a variety of media, such as text, graphics, video, audio, and Web links. Educators are beginning to consider blogging a tool for community reflection and inquiry. Cameron and Anderson (2006) note:

> Blogs have many pedagogical and technological aspects that make them suitable tools for this type of lifelong learning. Lifelong learners could blog

to record thoughts and experiences over time, to build and maintain connection with peers, to compile resources and to create a body of knowledge representative of personal growth and achievement.

In addition to the reflective value, blogs are used by educators for a variety of reasons. Instructors utilize blogs to share class information, assignments, and links to related readings and resources. As a course progresses and interests evolve, an instructor may include relevant data, new discoveries, interesting literature, and information specific to certain students. Another inventive use of blogs in education is their ability to organize class seminars through collaborative dialogue and posts of reading and research summaries. Other possible uses for blogs include journal writing, story starters, and daily oral language activities. Blogs can be used as a tool to improve literacy skills by having students read and peer edit other students' blogs. Examples of these kinds of activities facilitated via a blog are included in Table 2.13.

There are numerous free guides and sites to help set up blogs. Or you may choose to use existing blogs. Utilize Google to search for a specific blog if the blog title is known. If the blog title is unknown, but you want to search for blogs on a specific topic, use a blog search engine. Links to blog search engines and custom blog sites are included in Table 2.14.

TABLE 2.13   Specific Blog Activities

Activity Title	Purpose	Blog Strategies
Reflective Journal Writing	Allows students to document experiences, thoughts, questions, ideas, and conclusions about a specific topic as a means to internalize the subject matter and relate it to personal experiences	Ask students to add one comment or detail to three of their classmates' blogs Ask students to read classmates' blogs until they find a shared experience
Story Starters	Creative writing prompts that can be used for writing practice or for free writing; instructors provide the first two or three sentences of a story and allow students to finish the story in one or more paragraphs	Ask students to select the three best stories among their classmates' posts and to justify their choices Instructor starts a blog with the first two or three sentences; each student adds one sentence to the story until every student has posted an entry

Activity Title	Purpose	Blog Strategies
Daily Oral Language	To build student success in using proper grammar, punctuation, and spelling; students find the errors and re-write sentences correctly; each day the errors focus on a different skill such as spelling, capitalization, or punctuation	Place student into teams. Assign each team a topic such as grammar, spelling, punctuation, etcetera. Post three erroneous sentences to the blog (errors focus on one of the topics) and ask the team who has that topic to post corrections; the remaining students must review the team's posts to make sure they are correct and to make corrections if needed
Peer Editing	Instructors break class into small groups of students who share their written drafts with each other and offer feedback; feedback is usually based on criteria established in a rubric provided by the instructor	Each student posts his or her draft (of a research paper, report, presentation, etc.) to the blog; teams review the posts of their team members and offer constructive feedback based on a pre-established rubric

TABLE 2.14   List of Blog Search Engines and Custom Blog Sites

Blog search engines:

A blog about blogs, with links to blog resources
   http://www.blogsearchengine.com/

Searches weblogs by keyword
   http://technorati.com/

Searches for information from syndicated feeds
   http://www.blogdigger.com/index.html

A blog portal
   http://blogstreet.com/

Librarian list of blogs
   http://pubsub.com

Sites to create custom blogs:

Xanga
   http://www.xanga.com

Live Journal
   http://www.livejournal.com

Blogger
   http://www.blogger.com

Blogspot
   http://www.blogspot.com

Wiki

What is a wiki? According to Leuf and Cunningham (2001) a wiki is "the simplest online database that could ever work (p. 42)." In general terms, a wiki is a composition system that allows users to create and edit web page content using any Web browser. For educational purposes, a wiki can serve as a discussion medium, a repository of ideas and contributions, and a tool for facilitating cooperative learning and collaboration. What makes a wiki unusual, as compared to other group communication formats, is that a wiki allows the organization of contributions to be edited, in addition to the content itself. Content on a wiki web page can be edited by those visiting the web page.

Many instructors use wikis as collaborative writing tools. How do you add a wiki to your course? A wiki matrix, http://www.wikimatrix.org/wizard.php, can help you make the decision of which Wiki to use. The wizard asks you a few questions about your course needs, then will present you with a list of matching wikis that are compared in a side-by-side table. Wikis are generally easier to revise than discussion board content, lending itself to a dynamic shared learning experience. Especially useful for writing classes, the use of wikis encourages students to create drafts and make frequent revisions of their writing. Wikis provide a medium that is useful for student collaboration by enabling feedback between students. The public nature of wikis often encourages students to take particular care with their writing, since they are aware that they may have an audience reading their work.

Constructivist and social learning theories tell us that students attach and build meaning into what they read, observe, and experience, and incorporate this knowledge into their structures of knowing in ways that it can be evoked in relevant circumstances. The Wiki tool is useful in helping students with this developmental task. Wikis are valuable assessment tools that reveal students' knowledge development and their progression through Bloom's taxonomy: knowledge, comprehension, application, analysis, synthesis, and evaluation of useful information. The primary goal of a wiki is not merely communication, but the collaboration by participants to building understanding and application of shared information (Reynard, 2009). Examples of educational uses of wikis are included in Table 2.15.

Collaborating in a wiki to produce an assignment or product requires a variety of skills. Students must establish a goal or agenda; identify tasks; negotiate to assign and accept individual responsibility for the various tasks; define guidelines for managing the tasks; assign individual roles, as they relate to the group goal; assimilate individual ideas to generate a collective idea; communicate prior knowledge and new discoveries; brainstorm; analyze information; edit and annotate; offer feedback; revise; and create

TABLE 2.15   Educational Activities Involving Wikis

Activity	Wiki Strategy
Media Project	Students contribute ideas and post media files to a wiki with the goal of producing a video storyboard and, ultimately, a collaborative video.
Report	Working in teams, students tackle components of a research question, case study, posting their findings to the wiki; through further collaboration via the wiki, students refine their writings and make decisions on what the final report should look like and the information it will contain.
Marketing Plan	As a group or whole-class project, students participate in the contribution, review, and editing of needs assessment survey, analysis of results, and formulation of plan based on analysis; students participate to input information that contributes to the understanding and application of the shared information in producing a marketing plan.
Solving a math problem or puzzle	Students can try out various theories and solutions in the wiki where trial and error remains visible and traceable. "Often remembering the process of thought is useful for students so that they can then use the same process in different classes. Often it is precisely the learning process that is not valued and, therefore, soon forgotten by students" (Reynolds, 2009, p. 4).

(make individual contributions to the wiki). Although wikis are an integrated writing and editing tool, simply telling students to collaborate in the wiki is likely to not engender superlative results. The wiki may offer the environment for teamwork, but the instructor must provide general and specific learning goals and expectations for individual/team participation and progress.

Twitter

Twitter is an online communication system that allows individuals to connect in real time via frequent and quick exchanges. Initially begun to respond to one question, *What are you doing?* Twitter is now used by organizations to exchange minute-to-minute information about public sentiment, disaster response, retail services, and most recently, as a method of political communication. Conventional use of Twitter requires signing up for Twitter service, allowing users to deliver and/or restrict access to text-based messages, commonly known as *tweets*. Tweets are a maximum of 140 characters and can be thought of as micro-blogs or micro-text messages.

Educational use of Twitter is quickly gaining in popularity. While many educators require students to sign up for specific Twitter messages, such as those from CNN or other news or content-related entities, it is possible to use the Twitter strategy without utilizing outside sources. Instructors can use the discussion forum, the assignment tool, the chat forum, or other learning management system tools to post a specific question to students. Students are asked to respond in "Twitter" format, meaning that they must answer the question in a maximum of 140 characters. (Note that a *character* is a letter, punctuation mark, or blank space.)

The primary advantage of using the Twitter strategy is that students are required to succinctly respond to questions. Instructors can quickly determine if students understand the main point of a text reading, a digital lecture, or a course activity. Students might initially struggle with this activity. In the activity instructions, it is important that the purpose of the strategy be explained, as well as the benefits. Also, provide students with a tip for completing the activity assignment. For example, in the instructions, tell students to answer the question in one paragraph, and then begin to eliminate and change information until they have answered the question in 140 characters or less.

Through Twitter, students can acquire a sense of a person's personality outside the context of the classroom. That type of insight dynamically influences the synergy of the classroom. Educators report that of all the new social tools embraced for classroom use, Twitter has been the favorite. As referenced by Briggs (2008), one professor imparts:

> We're always trying to teach students, especially in their writing, that context determines meaning. And because Twitter has very refined rules about what you can do—posts of only 140 characters, for example—it's developed its own sort of discursive grammar set. That can serve as an example of how rules can be productive for communication and also can limit communication. (p. 13)

Suggestions for educational uses of Twitter or the Twitter strategy are outlined in Table 2.16. These activities include having students analyze a particular course topic or phenomenon, tweet their findings and/or opinions, and then respond to the tweets of others.

Social Networking

The popularity of social networking has captured the attention and time of so many individuals across the world that it has earned its own nomenclature: Web 2.0. Although there has not been any real new technical

TABLE 2.16   Suggested Twitter Activities

Activity	Description
Reading Response	Students use tweets to send out questions and/or observations to group
Analyzing Ideas	Students analyze tweets to assess opinion, examine consensus, determine patterns of thought, and find outlying ideas
One Minute "Paper"	A new twist on an old CAT; students state their perception/understanding of the main ideas of a concept, lecture, reading, etcetera
Muddiest Point	Another twist on a CAT strategy; students succinctly state what they are confused about or need more information
Global Perspective	Compare events and perspectives with peers across the world
Sounding Board	Students post topic drafts, tentative ideas, hypothesis and receive immediate feedback
Cutting Edge	Students can follow industry and media leaders to stay up to date on news, current affairs, and latest trends and developments

version of the World Wide Web created, the Web environment has fundamentally changed, in that developers and users have redefined how the Web is used. Web 1.0 involved users in reading text online. Web 2.0 engages users in reading, participating, commenting, contributing, and networking with each other.

The introduction of any new technology as an educational method generates great debate in academia. And so it is with social networking, which sparked an online debate about its value for instruction. The outcome revealed that 63% believed social networking would engender positive transformation of educational approaches to teaching and learning (Economist Debates, 2008). And while social networking has its advocates and detractors, Hoffman (2009) offers perhaps the best guidance in the evaluation of social networking technology, stating that it is "only a tool that is successful when carefully evaluated to meet learner needs and course goals" (p. 93).

Social networking refers to several of the Web 2.0 collaborative online environments. Boyd and Ellison (2007) list four conditions of social networks, including (1) they are web-based structured environments that enable individuals to contribute information in a public forum; (2) they contain a list of users that share an affiliation with the network; and (3) they allow users to view and track the contributions made to the network by other users. A number of networks include the ability to add media files, create and edit content, and link to external content. Structures such as wikis, blogs, YouTube, eBay, Amazon, and many of the social networks contain tools that rival or surpass those in some LMS systems, and are standardized to accommodate various browsers. An additional feature of some social networks is to allow users to develop a "private" structure within the network, whereby they can invite only certain "friends" or "fans" to view and contribute.

Two excellent sources of information regarding the features and potential educational uses of social networks is Eduspaces at http://eduspaces.net and Classroom 2.0 at http://www.classroom20.com. As with most instances of teaching with technology, social networking has advantages and disadvantages, with particular implications for distance learning. The particular positive uses include the collaborative learning opportunities, where students are personally engaged in effective contribution, analysis, and feedback. Research indicates the students appreciate the collaborative and interactive functions, and felt they had a positive impact on their course experience (Hoffman, 2009). On the cautionary side, students may lose focus on academic goals, and become distracted and immersed in personal concerns unrelated to the course topic. The following sections provide more detailed information about the most common types of Web 2.0 social network tools.

MySpace and Facebook. Two of the best known and most popular social networking sites are MySpace and Facebook. Many students use these networking sites on a regular basis. They are comfortable with the format, the terminology, and the structure of this form of interaction and communication. So how can an educator use MySpace or Facebook to create profiles about historical or literary figures, develop case studies, or market a product?

How fun would it be to have students develop a social network site for Jane Austin's Elizabeth Bennett? Who would she "friend"? Pictures, songs, and videos added to the site can contribute further depth to what was once a one-dimensional textbook figure. This type of activity requires students to critically analyze the person/character and draw present-day conclusions about the person based on historical information.

Having students create social network sites based on fictional or historical figures is one way to use these tools. But, can networking sites be created based on a concept or idea? What might those sites look like? What skills would this type of activity reinforce in your students? Also, remember that you, too, can create these sites and have specific activities that students must complete when they access the sites.

TABLE 2.17   Partial List of Social Networking Sites Derived From Wikipedia

Social Network	Web site	Focus	Users
BlackPlanet	www.blackplanet.com	African-Americans	20,000,000
deviantART	www.deviantart.com	Art community	9,040,962
Disaboom	www.disaboom.com	People with disabilities	
Facebook	www.facebook.com	General	250,000,000
Flixster	www.flixster.com	Movies	63,000,000
Friendster	www.friendster.com	General; popular in Southeast Asia	90,000,000
Habbo	www.habbo.com	General for teens worldwide	117,000,000
Iw5	www.hi5.com	General; popular in India, Portugal, Mongolia, Central Africa, and Latin America	80,000,000
Last.fm	www.last.fm	Music	30,000,000
Livemocha	www.Livemocha.com	Online language learning—world's largest community of native languagespeakers	3,000,000
MyHeritage	www.myheritage.com	Family-oriented	30,000,000
MySpace	www.myspace.com	General	260,000,000
Netlog	www.netlog.com	General; popular in Europe	42,000,000
Orkut	www.orkut.com	General; popular in India and Brazil	67,000,000
Tagged	www.Tagged.com	General	70,000,000
Twitter	www.twitter.com	General; micro-blogging	25,000,000

A partial list of social network sites derived from Wikipedia (it is interesting to note that Wikipedia is, itself, a Web 2.0 source) is available in Table 2.17. Below are some basic steps for getting started using social networking sites as an educational tool. These steps are based on the idea that you are creating a social networking site around a specific person or concept:

1. Decide on a network (e.g., Facebook, MySpace, etc.).
2. Set up a profile.
3. Ask students to "friend" you (add you to their network).
4. From the site, students can access videos, audio files, graphics, and animations that reinforce the course and/or site topic.

5. Create a blog within the site and post a specific question or series of questions that students must respond to via the blog.

or

1. Create a "group" within the site.
2. Use the group message function to send out announcements such as assignment deadlines, changes in schedule, etcetera.
3. Encourage students to use the site communication tools (wall posts or discussion board) to communicate.
4. Integrate into the profile a blog feed relevant to the course topic(s); the feed will appear in the students' news stream.

Web Conferencing

Web conferencing combines video and audio tools with Internet technology to communicate and collaborate synchronously at a distance. Web conferencing can be used to deliver instruction, conduct class discussions, conduct a demonstration, or host a guest speaker. Depending on the software and video/audio technology utilized, students may see the instructor on their computer monitor and speak directly to him or her using a headset or telephone connection.

An assortment of Web conferencing options exist that enable instructors and learners to connect with classes all over the globe to learn about each other's country, culture, reaction to current world affairs, or perceptions about historical events. Each option has its advantages and disadvantages. A list and description of suggested Web conferencing activities is contained in Table 2.18. Additional information on Web conferencing is supplied in Chapter 4.

Multimedia

Technology continues to raise the bar in keeping students engaged in the learning process and in designing learning activities that enhance learning outcomes. Many distance learning instructors rely on multimedia as a way to deliver content and assess student understanding of key concepts. Many of us remember when multimedia meant using a slide show or film strip to help reinforce our course content. Today, multimedia is simply defined as multiple forms of media integrated to form a cohesive and logical flow of information. The various forms of media can include text, images, video, audio, animations, graphs, and interactive communication formats, as described in Web 2.0 tools.

TABLE 2.18   Web Conferencing Activities

Active Learning Strategy	Activity
Student Presentations	Student provides overview of student created video. Student provides narrative of PowerPoint presentation.
Case Study	Groups share findings and recommendations, facilitate discussion
Guest Speaker	Speaker presents on a topic, instructor facilitates a Q&A session
Debate	Teams or individuals debate pros and cons of specific topics
Lecture	Instructor presents lecture and provides opportunity for students to answer questions
Test and/or Exam Review	Instructor provides review of test/exam material with Q&A session
Virtual Office Hours	Instructor is available at specific times for consultation

Chapter 3 provides an in-depth exploration of numerous strategies for incorporating multimedia into your distance learning course. Various applications are explored and a detailed analysis is provided that allows you to determine which application best meets your needs. For now, however, we will focus on the basic descriptions of the finished products that multimedia applications allow you to create, active learning strategies for utilizing the products, and available Web resources.

Podcasts

Podcasts distribute multimedia files over the Internet for playback on a computer or a mobile device, such as the iPod. The fundamental nature of podcasting lends itself beautifully to distance learning, offering learners the flexibility of accessing content when it is most convenient for them. The iPod quickly revolutionized the storage and playing of music and video files, and gained popularity in the classroom. As a portable learning tool, it allows anywhere/anytime access to lectures, audio books, music files, pictures and graphics, speeches, podcasts, and video. At Georgia College and State University (GC&SU), professors and students know that the iPod isn't just for storing and playing music. Students in several classes use their iPods to listen to digital audio content, ranging from English literature to foreign history. A list of suggested activities for using podcasts is displayed in Table 2.19.

TABLE 2.19   Podcast Activities

Activity Type	Description
Sound files: animal sounds, heartbeats, voices	Students must identify and match sounds appropriately
Picture slide show with narration	Mini-lecture, Supplemental material for text readings
Recorded vocabulary list	Supplemental glossary terms; Foreign language study guide; Quiz review
Recorded interview by instructor with guest speaker	Enlightened cultural perception, historical context, insight into interviewee experience and motivation
Narratives or statements by multiple contributors	Case study, Storytelling (multiple perspectives)
Multimedia presentations	Presentations by students

Video

So you're not Spielberg! Fortunately, you have access to YouTube, TeacherTube, Hulu, and a gaggle of other websites hosting videos. The variety of videos online encompasses everything from documentaries, biographies, demonstrations, animations, short clips of theatrical releases, music videos, commercials, and TV shows, to news clips, current events, amateur contributions, lectures, and more. In addition, sites such as YouTube and TeacherTube provide space for those interested in uploading and sharing videos online. Videos that are produced to be shown on cell phones and iPods are called *vodcasts*. Like podcasts, there are many vodcasts available on the Internet that have been created by educational institutions, government, business and industry, and news feeds.

Gaming

The twenty-first century workforce requires analytical skills, teamwork, and problem-solving. Findings from a yearlong study by the Federation of Scientists suggest that computer games teach these same skills, and, minus the violence, are powerful learning tools. Other research shows that individuals who are adept at computer games are also proficient managers, because they can make quick and innovative decisions in rapidly changing circumstances (Osborn, 2008). And since 97 percent of kids play games, students are in the game! Some interesting facts about gaming that might surprise you have revealed themselves: (1) the average age of a game player is 33; (2) 25 percent of gamers are 50 years of age or older; and (3) 38 per-

TABLE 2.20 Educational Games for College Students

Online Game genres include everything from puzzles to time management challenges
  http://www.gamehouse.com/online-games
Links to online economics games where players compete to dominate market and achieve best financial results
  http://www.shambles.net/pages/learning/games/economics/
The Bean Counter: Accounting Games and Interactive Tutorials
  http://www.dwmbeancounter.com/moodle/
Games from Wisconsin Technical College
  http://www.wisc-online.com/

cent of game players are female. A list of web sites of educational games for college students is provided in Table 2.20. In addition to games available on the Internet, there are a variety of video games that can be employed as educational tools. Two notable games are the CSI video game from Xbox, in which the player is a crime scene investigator trainee, and the Trauma Center game made by Nintendo, in which players take care of patients in various situations and crises.

Avatars and Virtual Worlds

The world of Avatars allows students to create digital alter egos or doubles in a safe environment. Instructors encourage students to reflect on why they made certain choices for their avatar's appearance, such as body type, eye and hair color, skin tone, and clothing. Students can explore their own identity, perceptions, prejudices, stereotypes, fears, and biases. They can also experiment with different looks and physical attributes. An instructor might ask students a series of reflective questions, including:

1. Why did you choose to make your avatar look this way?
2. What influenced your choices (e.g., media, family, friends, etc.)?
3. How are you and your avatar different?
4. How are you and your avatar alike?

These types of lessons are meaningful for a variety of course topics, such as psychology, sociology, biology, health, marketing, management, and philosophy. History or literature faculty might find it amusing to have students "make-over" a person or character; for instance, what would Mozart look like today? Art instructors can reinforce specific design concepts, shapes, and structures by asking students to create digital avatars that meet specified requirements. In addition, instructors of all disciplines can allow students to make class presentations via their avatars.

Virtual worlds can be used to create 3-dimensional learning environments that simulate various workplaces. For example, instructors in the healthcare field can create a 3-dimensional emergency room, operating room, or exam room and ask students to perform specified healthcare functions via their avatars. Instructors in business fields can simulate office environments and reinforce concepts in professional dress and communication. Those in the hospitality disciplines can create virtual restaurants and hotels to allow students to demonstrate customer service skills. Virtual learning environments can also be created to provide students access to 3-dimensional objects, such as sculptures and art pieces (for art classes), body parts, organs, molecules, and cellular divisions (for science and biology classes), automo-

---

TABLE 2.21   Virtual Worlds

Active Worlds Educational Universe
   http://www.activeworlds.com/edu/awedu.asp
Media Grid: Immersive Education
   http://immersiveeducation.org/
Quest Atlantis
   http://atlantis.crlt.indiana.edu/
Greenbush EduSim
   http://edusim3d.com/
Web3dStudent.org
   http://www.web3dstudents.org/
Whyville
   http://www.whyville.net/smmk/nice
Caspian Learning: Leaders in Immersive Learning Simulations
   http://www.caspianlearning.co.uk/technology.html
Zora: a virtual world focused on child development and education
   http://ase.tufts.edu/devtech/projects.html
Woogi World
   http://www.woogiworld.com/
ScienceSim
   http://sciencesim.com/wiki/doku.php
The Forbidden City: Beyond Space and Time
   http://www.beyondspaceandtime.org/FCBSTWeb/web/index.html
Enter Zon: Learn Mandarin Chinese
   http://enterzon.com/
WiloStar3D: Accredited Homeschooling and 3-D Virtual Worlds for Education
   http://www.wilostar3d.com/

---

tive parts and accessories (for automotive programs), and a host of other items for instructors who need to depict objects in 3-D. A list of websites for education-focused virtual worlds is included in Table 2.21.

Assignments, Instructions, and Expectations

Regardless of which type(s) of assignments and activities an instructor chooses to use in a distance learning course, active learning is crucial. Active student involvement in the learning process, frequent interaction with both the instructor and other course participants, and varied assignment/ activity types are all critical to meet the needs of all learners. In addition, active learning strategies provide support for varied learning styles and intelligence types, and also promote critical thinking via the integration of Bloom's Taxonomy. To conclude our discussion on active learning, let's turn our attention to specific issues regarding online assignments, instructions, and performance expectations.

Assignments

The presentation of course concepts or lessons imparts the content and establishes the foundation of information for the student to access and build on with subsequent learning activities and lessons. Assignments guide the student to a deeper understanding by engaging them in learning activities that allow practice of new skills and knowledge, and demonstration of comprehension and perception. Assignments engage students to recall concepts, analyze situations, and apply learning in different contexts.

Student learning is enhanced when content is related to examples that are relevant to the real world. Much of distance learning is self-directed, and the most effective assignments are problem-centered and relevant to student needs/experiences, as well as course objectives. Given the diversity of skills and abilities of the students, it is prudent to offer more than one opportunity, ranging from simple to complex, for students to apply their learning. The active learning strategies previously discussed are all examples of types of assignments that can be utilized in a distance learning course. It is advised that these multiple opportunities be presented in a variety of formats. Differences between in-class and online presentation of assignments is outlined in Table 2.22.

Instructions

Since, in distance learning courses, instructors do not have the opportunity to provide assignment information in real time, it is important that each online assignment include specific, step-by-step instructions, as well

TABLE 2.22   Differences between In-Class and Online Assignments

Procedure	In-Class	Online
Assignments	Documents provided with printed instructions; student presentations; required readings	Can be delivered via podcast, narrated PowerPoint presentation, printed document, video, wiki, social network
Handouts	Printed paper; worksheets, Chapter-based documents	HTML, Rich-text, PDF (provide in an un-editable format)
Instructions	Print format or verbal, often minimal with less detail	Detailed, Eliminate ambiguity, Straight-forward, print format or via video or audio with graphic elements (Note that to be ADA compliant, any instructions presented in multimedia format must have a print version available.)
Expectations	In-class examples, demonstration, Textbook, outlined in course syllabus	Sample documents online, samples of previous students' work; Web site resources, reference textbook and/or companion Web site, rubrics
Submission	Hand in via printed paper, Class discussion, in-class presentation	Upload to course site, Post to a communication forum, Email to instructor, post to external source such as blog or wiki

as all of the materials and information the students will need to complete the assignment. Adequate planning time is essential for distance learning faculty to develop clear and comprehensive assignment instructions. It is recommended that instructors new to distance learning ask their faculty colleagues to preview several assignments to make sure instructions are clear and expectations are realistic. However, even when ample planning time and peer review are used, be prepared for some students feeling that assignment instructions are unclear. Make yourself available to students on a regular basis, via synchronous chat, or create an FAQ discussion forum for students to post questions. Each time you facilitate an assignment and receive questions provides you with an opportunity to refine the assignment instructions for future use. Examples of good instructions and poor instructions for the same online assignment are provided in Table 2.23.

TABLE 2.23 Sample Instructions

Poor Instructions

1. Complete the Skills Assessments.
2. Go to the following website: Complete the skills survey/assessment.
   http://www.d.umn.edu/student/loon/car/self/career_transfer_survey.html
3. Complete the Skills Chart Identify Your Skills Through Your Experiences
4. List positive experiences from your past that you are proud of. Include things from your childhood that you feel exceptionally pleased and energized about. It could be a picture you drew, an athletic competition you did well in, or an event you helped coordinate. The standard to use in choosing items for this list is your own pride in feeling "I did that myself!" or "I did that really well!"
5. Access the Skills Chart to identify the skills you feel you used in your seven positive experiences and the results of the Skills Assessment. Turn in your assignment.

Good Instructions

Skills Assessments:

1. Access the following website: Complete the skills survey/assessment.
   http://www.d.umn.edu/student/loon/car/self/career_transfer_survey.html
2. Print your results and save for the activity below.

Skills Chart: Identify Your Skills Through Your Experiences

3. List positive experiences from your past that make you feel proud. Include things from your childhood that you feel exceptionally pleased and energized about. It could be a picture you drew, an athletic competition you did well in, or an event you helped coordinate. The standard to use in choosing items for this list is your own pride in feeling "I did that myself!" or "I did that really well!"

   Some examples are:
   - A team you coached or played on had a winning season
   - A new and innovative procedure you came up with
   - Designed project with friends and won an award
   - Earned money through working extra job(s) to buy a car or take a special trip
   - Helped a friend or family member solve an important personal problem
   - Helped a boss or coworker solve an important business problem
   - Raised money for a charity
   - Put yourself through school
   - Learned an athletic or academic skill at an early age
   - Taught yourself a technical or academic skill

4. Now select seven of the experiences you feel most proud of. Write a short story (one or two paragraphs) about each of these experiences. Try to describe in detail what you did in each of the experiences. What did you accomplish? What did you enjoy? What was easy about it? What was hard? Now is not the time to be modest...BRAG ON YOURSELF!!!! How much

(continued)

TABLE 2.23 Sample Instructions (continued)

money did you make? What accolades did you receive? What people did you meet in the process? What was thrilling?

5. In writing your stories, it may be helpful to pretend you are explaining them to a small child. When we speak to children, we use clear language and a lot of detail. Describe your experiences using words from all of your senses: what you saw, heard, felt, smelled, and tasted. How did you feel at the time, and how do you feel now, as you recall and remember them?

6. Access the Skills Chart to identify the skills you feel you used in your seven positive experiences and the results of the Skills Assessment you printed.

7. Title your assignment (Your Name) Skills Chart and upload to SUBMIT ASSIGNMENTS. This assignment is worth 30 points

---

Expectations

Students want to know what to expect in your class and how to do well. Yet, many of our students come to us with under-developed study skills and poor work habits that can diminish their performance. Add to that the self-paced, self-directed nature of distance learning, and many students initially flounder. Research reveals that there is a direct correlation between high instructor expectations and high student achievement. As such, it is imperative to clearly define your expectations for students' performance and to specifically identify how academic performance will be measured, in order to set the stage for maximum student effort and success.

The syllabus is an important communication tool to provide students with information on policies, procedures, resources, grading, and performance expectations. Furthermore, allowing students to view "good" and "poor" examples of assignments should be included. These examples provide students with a reasonable idea of what your expectations are for the completed assignment. Also, rubrics are useful in designating how students earn points and what are the criteria required for success. Rubrics will be discussed in greater detail in Chapter 5.

End of Chapter Activities

The end of chapter activities provide opportunities for you to acquire new knowledge, gain skill, and apply principles and concepts. These activities are located on the Companion Website, and are divided into three subsections: Knowledge Building, Skill Building, and Practical Application.

Appendix B

Sample WebQuest

Time Traveler

Introduction. You had been hanging out at home, listening to your iPod, playing a video game, and texting friends before going to purchase groceries for the empty fridge. The day at school had not gone well, as you forgot to turn in an English assignment, and having found the math quiz quite challenging, you were wary of what grade would result. In addition, tickets for the next concert event just went on sale, but short on cash and maxed out on your credit card, chances were that you would be a no-show at the concert. Speaking of no-shows, you also pondered what your boss would say tomorrow about the two previous days when you had called in sick; the old geezer was always fussing about something!

As you locked the front door and headed to the car, the sky turned darker and a mist started to infiltrate the street. It grew shadowy and gloomy, almost eerie in the way the mist swirled with a threatening attitude, the air seeming one moment light, and heavy and sinister the next. Pulling out onto the street, you turned left toward Colonial Street, and it was at that precise moment that the ominous fog, thick and greenish-black, enveloped the car. There was no visibility beyond the windshield wipers swishing slowly from side to side; nothing but the sickening, smoky, lime-colored clouds encircling the car. The car seemed to assume a life of its own, despite your attempts to brake to a stop, moving slowly at first and then spinning faster and faster upwards and forwards, and finally at blinding speed backwards. The last thing you remember before blacking out was a white lacy hat landing on the windshield.

Awakening to the sounds of a distant hammering on metal, your eyes fly open to a bizarre scene. "Am I dreaming?" you wonder. A group of young boys and girls in strange dress walk through a small field. The girls wear long dresses of brown, gray, or dark blue fabric covered by an apron-like garment, and each wears a white lacy cap that droops down over their ears. Long tunic-like shirts of various solid dull colors paired with brown or gray pants costume the boys. Not all the kids are wearing shoes, and perhaps most astounding, some of the older boys have a rifle hanging by a strap from their shoulders—and they don't look to be over ten or twelve years old! "Where am I?" you think. "Is this some sort of colonial theme park??" Gradually, you become aware that there is no car, and those strange fashions the children are wearing . . . well, the same style now adorns your body!

You have been inexplicably transported to the year 1760. What will you need to do to start a new life in this time period? Should you go shopping? Who makes the things you will need and want to buy? How were they made? Oh ... and how and where will you get the money to go shopping with? What will your job be? What are you qualified to do in this era?

After a time, you do make a selection of an occupation and begin to adapt to life in the 1790s. One day, while walking down to the river to take your weekly bath, you see a mist building. It swirls around you with long, dark, blackish-green fingers snaking around your ankles. The mist increases to the thick black fog you remember from several years ago; the eerie murky filament between past, present, and future.

Cars that fly like jets and buildings five times higher than the Empire State building loom before your eyes as you slowly awaken. You wonder if you have been transported to a Star Wars or Star Trek movie lot. Mysteriously, you have time travelled again, this time to the year 2050. The same questions you had to answer in 1790, you must answer now in 2050. What will you need to do to start a new life in this time period? Should you go shopping? Who makes the things you will need and want to buy? How are they made? Oh ... and how and where will you earn money to go shopping with? What will your job be? What are you qualified to do in this era?

The Task. There is nothing wrong with your computer. Do not attempt to adjust the screen or browser. We are controlling the transmission of information. We will control the action. We will control the websites. We can sharpen your perspective to crystal clarity. For the next several minutes, sit quietly and read carefully, while we control all that you see and hear. You are about to participate in a great adventure. You will experience the awe and mystery of the TIME TRAVELER.

Your task is to decide which occupation you will work at during the time you are transported to the 1790s. When you are transported to the future, you will also choose an occupation to support yourself with during your stay there. Finally, you will select an occupation to perform upon your return to the present.

The Process.

1. You will familiarize yourself with six of the common occupations during the 1760s period of time. Select one of the occupations that you see yourself performing and complete the COLONNIAL section of the ORGANIZER TABLE (see RESOURCES) with information specific to that occupation.

2. Next, familiarize yourself with six of the common occupations expected for the future. Select one of the occupations that you see yourself performing and complete the FUTURE section of the ORGANIZER TABLE (see RESOURCES) with information specific to that occupation.

3. Finally, select one of the occupations that you see yourself performing now or shortly in the current era and complete the PRESENT section of the ORGANIZER TABLE (see RESOURCES) with information specific to that occupation.

4. Complete the Organizer Table and Reflections (see RESOURCES), save to computer, then submit to Week 7 Assignments.

The Resources.

Colonial Period: 1760s

http://www.history.org/almanack/life/trades/tradehdr.cfm

http://www.dcboces.org/sufsd/nassau/hhv2/colonial.html

http://encarta.msn.com/encyclopedia_1741502192/colonial
_america.html

The Future

http://www.forbes.com/2006/05/20/jobs-future-work_cx_
hc_06work_0523jobs.html

http://www.youtube.com/watch?v=2KDs3ebVSdI

http://www.youtube.com/watch?v=sKYY_8iqaB0

http://www.wfs.org/tomorrow/index.htm

http://www.et-trends.com/future50/future50.html

http://www.technologyreview.com/special/emerging/

http://www.pcmag.com/article2/0,2817,1130591,00.asp

http://www.futurehorizons.net/

The Conclusion. Reflect on the following: What did you find appealing about the occupations you selected for your stay in the past and in the future? How might this be connected to the occupation you are considering and/or preparing for in the present? Jobs change due to inventions and people's wants. How will today's jobs change in the future? What new jobs and products will you find in the future?

TABLE 2.24 Organizer Table and Reflection

Questions for consideration	Occupation of the Past (Colonial)	Occupation of the Future	Occupation of the Present
What are the main duties of the occupation?			
What knowledge and training is required for this occupation?			
What skills are necessary to perform this occupation?			
How important is the job to the economy of that period?			
What impact does gender have on the opportunity to work in this occupation?			
What did you already know about this occupation?			
Was there anything you learned about the occupation that surprised you?			
What commonalities exist between jobs of the past, present, and future?			
In your opinion, why do jobs change or become extinct?			
How did jobs in the past evolve to become the jobs of the present?			
How will the jobs of the present change for the future?			
What factors of evolvement and change persist with jobs over time?			
Create your own question and answer here:			

Use the Organizer Table and Reflection document included in the resources section; save to your computer, complete, save as "your name_webquest," then submit to Week 7 ASSIGNMENTS.

The Evaluation. Your Organizer Table and Reflection assignment will be evaluated based on the rubric below.

TABLE 2.25 Rubric for Organizer Table and Reflection

Category	Points				Score
	0–2	**3–5**	**6–8**	**9–10**	
Required Elements	Several required elements on the Organizer Table and Reflection were missing	All but 1 of the required elements are included on the Table and Reflection	All required elements are included on the Table and Reflection	The Table and Reflection includes all required elements as well as additional information.	
Task Questions	Did not answer all questions	Answered all questions	Answered all questions in complete sentences	Answered all questions creatively; in complete sentences	
Knowledge Gained	Student appears to have insufficient knowledge about the concepts discussed in the Table and Reflection	Student can accurately answer half of questions related to facts in the Table and Reflection	Student can accurately answer most questions related to research in the Table and Reflection	Student can accurately answer all questions related to research in the Table and Reflection	

Total Score

References

American Federation of Teachers, (2000). *Distance education: Guidelines for good practice report.* Item No. 36-0693. Washington, DC.

Boyd, D. M., & Ellison, N. B. (2007). Social network sites: Definition, history, and scholarship. *Journal of Computer-Mediated Communication, 13*(1), Article 11. Retrieved June 19, 2007 from http://jcmc.indiana.edu/vol13/issue1/boyd.ellison.html

Briggs, L. (2008, December). Teaching twitter. *Campus Technology.* P. 12–13.

Cameron, D. and Anderson, T. (2006). *Comparing weblogs to threaded discussion tools in online educational contexts.* Retrieved January 12, 2006, from http://www.itdl.org/Journal/Nov_06/article01.htm

Chickering, A.W., and Gamson, Z.F. (1987). Seven principles of good practice in undergraduate education. *Faculty Inventory.* Racine, WI: The Johnson Foundation, Inc. Retrieved June 19, 2007 from http://learningcommons.evergreen.edu/pdf/fall1987.pdf

Conway, E. D. (2003, January). *Teaching strategies for distance education: Implementing the seven principles for good practice in online education.* White paper presented at the 5th Annual Science, Engineering & Technology Education Conference.

Darling-Hammond, L., Barron, B., Pearson, P. D., Schoenfield, A. H., Stage, E. K., Zimmerman, et al. (2008). *Powerful learning: What we know about teaching for understanding.* San Francisco, CA: Jossey Bass.

Dodge, B. (1997). *Some thoughts about WebQuests.* Retrieved June 9, 2007, from http://edweb.sdsu.edu/courses/edtec596/about_webquests.html

Dunn, R., & Dunn, K. (1978). *Teaching Students through their individual learning styles: A practical approach.* Upper Saddle River, NJ: Prentice Hall, Reston Publishing.

Economist Debates: Social networking (2008). Economist.com. Retrieved December 5, 2008, from http://www.economist.com/debate/overview/123

Gardner, H. (1993). *Frames of Mind: The theory of multiple intelligences.* Tenth Anniversary Edition with new introduction. New York, NY: Basic Books. (original work published 1985)

Hoffman, E. (2009). Evaluating social networking tools for distance learning. White paper presented at the TCC 2009 Proceedings. Retrieved July 2, 2009, from http://etec.hawaii.edu/proceedings/2009/hoffman.pdf

Lamb, A.C. & Smith, W. L. (2000). Ten facts of life for distance learning courses. TechTrends, 44(1), 12–15.

Leuf, B. & Cunningham, W. (2001). *The Wiki way: Quick collaboration on the Web.* Upper Saddle River, NJ: Addison Wesley.

Muirhead, B. (2001). Learning leadership journal: Handout. Doctor of Management Class, DOC 791. University of Phoenix Online, Phoenix, Arizona.

Montgomery, S. M. (1995). *Addressing diverse learning styles through the use of multimedia.* Presented at the ASEE/IEEE Frontiers in Education Conference.

Osborn, H. (2008). Broccoli Brain. *Edutopia,* 4(5). North Hollywood, CA: George Lucas Foundation.

Reynard, R. (2008, December). Web 2.0 meets conventional education. *Campus Technology.*

Reynolds, R. (2009). *Why wikis?* Retrieved June 22, 2009, from http://campus technology.com/Articles/2009/02/04/Why-Wikis.aspx?p=1

Rasmussen, K. L. (1998). Hypermedia and learning styles: Can performance be influenced? *Journal of Multimedia and Hypermedia, 7*(4). 291–308.

Riding, R. & Rayner, S. (1997). *Cognitive Styles and learning strategies.* United Kingdom: David Fulton Publishers.

Thomas, J. (2000). *A review of project-based learning.* Retrieved July 9, 2009, from: http://www.bobpearlman.org/BestPractices/PBL_Research.pdf

United States Department of Education, Office of Planning, Evaluation, and Policy Development. (2009). *Evaluation of evidence-based practices in online learning: A meta-analysis and review of online learning studies.* Washington, DC: U. S. Department of Education.

Yin, R. (1994). *Case study research: Design and methods* (2nd ed.). Thousand Oaks, CA: Sage Publishing.

3

Multimedia in Online Teaching: Creating Dynamic Content

It is important to recognize that filling up a distance learning course with a variety of rich *media elements* does not automatically make the course interactive or effective. In fact, over-using flashy multimedia can distract students from learning important course concepts and skills. This chapter focuses on multimedia and the benefits and strategies for implementing multimedia into distance learning courses. Upon completion of Chapter 3, readers will be able to:

1. Create a unit introduction utilizing one or more multimedia tools
2. Digitize a lecture by creating a podcast
3. Conduct an online search for and select at least two online resources to support learning content
3. Revise current lesson plans to incorporate the newly created podcast and online resources
4. Use the Course Planning and Delivery Guide to identify strengths and weaknesses.

Multimedia in Online Teaching: Creating Dynamic Content

We have heard of the Baby Boomers, Generation X, and the Millenials. But a new cohort term for describing age and experience is the Digital

Fluency in Distance Learning, pages 99–125
Copyright © 2010 by Information Age Publishing
All rights of reproduction in any form reserved.

Generation. Today's students are no strangers to digital technology. They live in a media-rich, networked world of immediate information and access. But their experience is not just about cool tools; they engage in self-directed learning that is creative and connected. The Digital Generation plays games, builds profiles on social networks, generates web sites, makes movies and shares them online, creates music, buys and sells online, voices opinions on blogs, asks for help in wikis, and researches answers to questions through the Internet. Even students who profess an ignorance of technology do not realize the extent to which their daily lives involve Web-based services, digital media, and technical mechanisms.

Even though the Digital Generation is technologically sophisticated and uses multimedia for a variety of educational and entertainment purposes, it is not the responsibility of the distance learning instructor to entertain the students. The instructor's role is to engage, challenge, and retain them as learners in support of their academic goals. Multimedia components can help students in distance learning courses to master the course content knowledge and skills. However, multimedia has a downside. Inexperienced students can become distracted by the delivery platform, causing them to lose focus on the content (Littlefield, 2009). Therefore, the decision to use multimedia in distance learning instruction should be made in order to help students connect to and find meaning in the content, and to relate their learning to the world beyond the online classroom.

Differentiated Instruction via Technology

In support of instructors' efforts to transmit knowledge in diverse ways, institutional budgets are strained to provide up-do-date physical resources: TVs, VCRs, DVDs, CDs, and so on. Technology in distance learning can provide relief for the financial and physical demands of purchasing and housing technology tools, and provide an outlet for instructors to transmit knowledge in a variety of modes. It is important to note that, just as students possess their own dominant preferences for learning, instructors have their favored methods of teaching and expression. This is where technology can play an increasingly valuable role. Online use of multimedia allows instructors to focus student attention on core principles by providing lessons in printable text, photographs, illustrations, animations, videos, audio and/or sound recordings, website links that support content, and interactive study guides and quizzes. Students can play all of the multimedia files by downloading the media players that are available for free on the Internet. These players include Windows Media Player, QuickTime Player, and Real Player. Web links to the free downloads are listed in Table 3.1.

TABLE 3.1   Media Player Downloads

Windows Media Player
   www.microsoft.com/windows/windowsmedia/player/download/download.aspx
Quick Time Player
   www.apple.com/quicktime/download/win.html
Real Player
   www.real.com/player

Using Audio in Distance Learning Courses

Audio has been an element in distance learning courses for many years. Audio is effective, as it is more personal than text. Today's technology makes audio recording simple and cost-effective (Siemens, 2003). There are a number of issues to consider when contemplating using audio in distance learning courses. Pros and cons for using audio, as well as ways that audio can be used, are offered in Table 3.2 (Siemens, 2003). Consider these as you explore the use of audio.

Several faculty members at the University of North Florida's (UNF) Education program initially began teaching courses on the Internet in 1997. These courses were primarily textual with supporting graphics. Eventually they discovered that adding audio for specific functions improved the quality of the courses. Following are examples of appropriate uses of audio in distance learning courses and ways that audio can enhance student learning.

TABLE 3.2   Pros and Cons of Audio

Positives	Negatives	Uses
Promotes 2-way communication	Students can lose focus; easy to tune out	Explanations
Enriches a text-only course	Limits the pace	Presentations
Useful for detailed explanations and proper pronunciations	Need a "professional" voice for recording	Analysis of information
Benefits auditory learners	Can be poor quality	Synthesis of information
Time effective (audio files can be created faster than typed documents)	Instructors may not have access to proper equipment and software	

Using Audio as a Greeting

It is common knowledge that a sense of remoteness is associated with distance learning instruction. One way to counteract this isolation is to offer a friendly greeting. Consider a greeting that introduces you as the instructor. Realizing that people find comfort in associating a voice with text or graphics, it is recommended that you include a photo of yourself along with the audio greeting. Even major news shows usually include a picture of the reporter along with their audio report (Bratina, Bratina, & Bratina, 2001). Other types of greetings appropriate for audio files are the use of audio as a welcome and overview to the course, or as an introduction to each lesson or major unit of study.

Using Audio for Housekeeping Tasks

Most instructors utilize a few minutes of their face-to-face class doing "housekeeping" or administrative type tasks, such as communicating policy, procedure, expectations, and tips for success in the course. Consider recording this information and adding it as an associated link to your course syllabus or on the course home/welcome page. In addition, consider using an audio file with each unit of instruction that describes expectations and tips for successful completion. It is also helpful for students new to distance learning to listen to instructions on how to navigate the course, as well as where to find important information such as the assignment list, due dates, and how to submit assignments. Contemplate providing the same information in text format as well as audio. (Note: To comply with Americans with Disabilities Act requirements, any information provided via audio must also be available in print format.)

Using Audio to Support Content.

Finally, since many students are auditory learners, providing an audio overview of main topics or concepts can be an excellent way to focus student attention on specific areas or to explain difficult concepts. Again, one audio file can be created for the entire course or created for each unit of instruction. Bratina et al. (2001) consider the use of audio for academic explanation as the best application of audio for distance learning courses, offering the suggestion to ask questions in the audio that stimulate students' thoughts and consideration of the topic.

In most face-to-face courses, instructors use class time to present content (lecture), while students take notes and ask clarifying questions. Audio files can be used as digital lectures. When published in MP3 format, students can download the lectures to their iPods for 24/7 access.

Audio Software and Pre-recorded Sound Files

Today's technology makes the process of creating audio for distance learning courses not only easy, but inexpensive. All anyone needs to create an audio file is a microphone that plugs into the computer and a sound program. There are a variety of programs, including open-source programs that will accommodate most audio needs, from the simple to the complex. A brief description of three audio programs is offered in Table 3.3.

In many cases, it is desirable for instructors to create custom audio files for digital lectures or PowerPoint narration. However, the burden of creating audio files to support content does not have to rest with the instructor alone. Another strategy for incorporating audio into online teaching as a subject-based resource is the location of web sites that include recorded music, speeches, presentations, or lectures. Take a moment to conduct an Internet search to find a multitude of excellent quality sources for audio content. A brief list of web sites that contain audio files appropriate for educational use is displayed in Table 3.4. Note that prior to downloading sound files it is important to first verify that the files are not copyrighted. Copyrighted files cannot be downloaded and injected into presentations or uploaded to a learning management system (LMS). However, copyrighted files can be accessed directly via the web site by inserting a hyperlink into a PowerPoint presentation or on a page in the learning management system.

TABLE 3.3   Audio Programs

Audacity

Audacity is free, open source software for recording and editing sounds and narration. It has compatible versions for Mac OS X, Microsoft Windows, GNU/Linux, and other operating systems. Audacity files can be published in MP3 format for easy downloading to iPods. Information, downloading instructions, and tutorials for using Audacity are available at http://audacity.sourceforge.net/

Windows Sound Recorder (WSR)

WSR is a simple sound recorder utility that has been included with Microsoft Windows since 1995. WSR allows recording of .wav format files that can be used on the Web, in PowerPoint presentations, and in videos. WSR files cannot be published in MP3 format.

Adobe Audition

Audition is a premier, proprietary recording, mixing, and editing software that will create music, produce audio appropriate for Web, radio, video, and PowerPoint, as well as restore imperfect recordings. Access additional information about Audition at http://www.adobe.com.

TABLE 3.4 Internet Resources for Audio Files

Assorted Sound and Music Files:
  http://www.thefreesite.com/Free_Sounds/Free_WAVs/
  http://dir.yahoo.com/Computers_and_Internet/Multimedia/Audio/
  Archives/WAV/
  http://www.partnersinrhyme.com/
  http://www.reelwavs.com/mstop25/index.html
  http://www.freeplaymusic.com

Speeches:
  http://www.historychannel.com/broadband/home/
  http://www.lib.msu.edu/vincent/presidents/

Science and Health:
  http://www.ornl.gov/sci/techresources/Human_Genome/education/audio
  .shtml

National Public Radio:
  http://www.npr.org/templates/archives/rundown_archive_hub.php

PBS—Arts & Literature:
  http://www.pbs.org/teachersource/recommended/arts_lit/lk_music.shtm

Discovery Channel:
  http://search.discovery.com/

MERLOT (miscellaneous subjects):
  http://www.merlot.org/search/ArtifactList.po?keyword=audio
  http://www.apple.com/education/mobile-learning/
  http://www.ant.com/tags/education/audio

Poetry:
  http://laurable.com/

Audio Books:
  http://librivox.org/
  http://www.gutenberg.org/audio/

The Importance of Scripting for Audio Presentations

The importance of writing a script for an audio narration or lecture cannot be overemphasized. Is script-writing additional work? Yes, but well worth it, in terms of the time and frustration it will save in limiting errors and re-recording. Ernie Kovacs once said that television is a medium because it is neither rare nor well done; the same could be said for many audio presentations completed without an adequate investment of time and preparation. Spending a moment becoming familiar with the material, organizing the sequence, and preparing a script will better prepare individuals for recording. Knowing what needs to be said before recording will help to make the communication meaningful and convey the intended information.

Remember that most students will have a short attention span, so it is wise to keep audio recordings short. In addition, long recordings increase the media file size, requiring more time for downloading to the students' computers. Fifteen to twenty minutes should be the maximum length of any one audio presentation. In fact, it is preferable to "chunk," or divide presentation material into logical, discrete units. When narration is coordinated to a PowerPoint or other slide type presentation, the amount of time each slide should be visible to the audience is 15–30 seconds for an instruction type presentation, and as short as 4–8 seconds for a fast-moving impact type presentation.

A script does not have to be a lengthy, well-edited document. A sample script for a brief unit introduction is presented in Table 3.5. Additional sample scripts can be found throughout the remainder of this chapter.

Narrating a PowerPoint Presentation

We have discussed general strategies for creating audio as a stand-alone, or more preferably, to support text-based information. However, at times it may be advantageous to include audio as an enhancement to graphic presentation. The advantage of using only an audio track with no graphical elements is that the file size is smaller, so delivery and/or download time to the student is quicker. However, when content is such that learning would

---

TABLE 3.5 Sample Script

Hello, I am Dr. Smith, and I welcome you to Personal Decision Making! You may be encouraged to know that this course is all about you!

You will focus on learning more about yourself, as well as what is going on in the world of work, both present and future. Obviously, this is an online class . . . you will access and submit all of your assignments through the LMS. Assignments must be completed in Microsoft Word. All computers in the school's computer labs are loaded with MS Office. Please be aware that although online classes are a convenient and flexible way to access instruction, you must commit significant time to the class. Pay attention to due dates, which can be found in the course calendar. Check your mail at least once per week, and participate in the discussion board several times a week. New and important information will be posted as an announcement on the course homepage.

Once you have logged in and accessed the course homepage, click on the syllabus and read it thoroughly. Click on and read the assignment information and calendar dates.

Feel free to contact me through the course email if you have any questions.

Again, welcome to the course. I look forward to working with you.

Time: 1 min. 20 sec.

be more meaningful when presented via a visual medium, then adding audio enriches the instruction even further. This is typically accomplished by synchronizing an audio track with still images or presentation software. Microsoft PowerPoint is one of the most common presentation software programs used by educators at all levels. The authors believe it is important to focus on specific uses for narrated PowerPoint presentations in distance learning courses.

Creating a PowerPoint presentation for a traditional face-to-face course is usually done in support of a lecture. Customarily, the presentation contains a series of slides with bulleted text, still graphics, and perhaps a design template to add color and visual interest. While presenting, the instructor adds important, detailed information that is not included on the slide. Simply uploading this type of PowerPoint presentation into a distance learning course without the benefit of the additional information provided by the instructor would not be sufficient for students to gain the knowledge needed. Therefore, to transform a traditional PowerPoint presentation into an appropriate format for distance learning requires the use of recorded narration. Note that with PowerPoint, an audio file is added to each slide. Consider the following tips for narrating PowerPoint presentations:

1. Before you begin scripting the narration, organize the slides in the PowerPoint presentation.
2. Arrange the presentation slides in a logical sequence.
3. Review the slides for ideas on additional information that needs to be added for clarity or support of the slide content. (What is it that you usually "say" while you are delivering this PowerPoint presentation in the traditional classroom?) Write/type this additional information; you now have the basis for your script.
4. When writing the script, use comfortable language and terms. Avoid a stiff and formal delivery style.
5. A slide should not be on the screen for more than 30 seconds, with the ideal time being 15 seconds. Long, rambling presentations will lose the audience. Content that requires extensive explanation can be provided in a printable text document, or in an additional presentation.
6. Typically, a narrated presentation begins with an introductory statement or provocative question that stimulates thought and interest from the students. Record this information and include it with your title slide.

7. Next, provide an overview, followed by a slide and narrative containing additional detail. Record this information and include it with the slide that outlines the presentation topics.
8. Continue this process until you arrive at the first key issue.
9. When recording narration for the key issues, keep in mind that it should not repeat the text points on the slide. Instead, the audio should communicate information that is connected to, but not seen on the slide. Refer to the text point(s) and then expound.
10. The slides containing key issues should not have more than three or four bullet items. If they have more than four items, consider breaking the slides apart to create additional slides.

It is not necessary to use an external audio software program when narrating a PowerPoint presentation. Narration can be recorded from within PowerPoint itself. First, connect a microphone to the computer. Then, click the *Slide Show* menu, and select *Record Narration*. To create the narration, simply read the script while speaking into the microphone. PowerPoint provides the ability to record separate narration for each slide. Students will be able to listen to the narration while viewing the PowerPoint presentation. However, keep in mind that the file size of the presentation, including the narration, will be much larger than the size of the original presentation. This could potentially create problems for students trying to download the presentation, particularly those with slower Internet connections; hence the need for chunking content/presentations into small, manageable segments.

Creating a Podcast

Another popular audio technology to support teaching at a distance is podcasting. As an asynchronous tool, instructors utilize podcasting to provide students with lecture and supplemental course material that is not dependent on the Internet for usability. Instructors upload audio and video files to a designated Internet site, from which students download the podcasts to a mobile device, such as an MP3 player, iPod, or cell phone. Students can then view the podcasts anytime, anywhere, from their mobile player. Since podcasts can be comprised of audio, video, and graphic formats, the possibilities are awesome. A list of additional podcast resources is found in Table 3.6. An excellent web site containing exemplary examples of educational of podcasts created by instructors at the University of Wisconsin at Madison can be accessed at http://engage.wisc.edu/podcasting/examples/index.html.

TABLE 3.6   Podcast Resources

Education Podcast Network
   http://epnweb.org/
Education Podcast Directory
   http://podcastingnews.com/forum/link_6.htm
Podcasting Station
   http://www.podcasting-station.com/showrss.php?category=Educational
   %20Podcasts
University and College Podcasts – Free Educational Podcasts
   http://www.openculture.com/2006/10/university_podc.html
Podcast Alley
   http://www.podcastalley.com/podcast_genres.php?pod_genre_id=7
Podcasts for Educators, Schools, and Colleges
   http://recap.ltd.uk/podcasting/

The steps in producing a podcast are much the same as previously outlined for creating an audio file. Good planning is paramount; prepare a script, or at the very least, an outline, of what you need to cover. You will utilize a sound program (such as Audition or Audacity software), along with a microphone to record your podcast. After saving the recording as a project file, you will need to save the file in an MP3 format so that it will be compatible with various mobile devices. Finally, upload your podcast to the LMS, or a podcast hosting site, such as iTunes U.

Using Animation in Distance Learning Courses

Visual learners prefer information that is either presented or supported by images, graphs, schematics, animations, video, demonstration, or other visual effects. In developing distance learning courses, instructors must be cognizant of the opportunities to improve the presentation of content through the use of visual clues. A human condition of the eye, called persistence of vision, allows animation to trick the brain into believing a still picture has moved. When light is used in a certain way, the eye remembers an image in the way it has seen it for a split second. If the image is replaced quickly with one that is in a slightly different position, the image will appear to have moved. Animation can be a powerful tool for demonstration of abstract concepts or concrete tasks.

Instructors can create animated images or short animations to illustrate important points or data, and incorporate arrows, pointers, and/or text overlaid on the animation for additional clarification of a concept. Animations are especially useful in explaining or demonstrating process or procedure. Processes that take place over long periods of time can be illustrated effectively in animation, as can processes that are particularly complex, such as photosynthesis, with its many sub-sets of progression. Models, theories, or developments that involve qualities that are invisible, such as speed, density, temperature, attitude, emotion, efficacy, etcetera, can be defined well in animation.

Designing Effective Animations for Distance Learning

The purpose of animations should be to assist the learner in making connections between verbal and conceptual representations of a concept and a concrete form, to the end that the verbal/conceptual/concrete representations are integrated. The following suggestions, adapted from Carnegie Mellon's (2006) summary of research on best practices for teaching with technology, are focused on designing animations for effective instruction:

1. Focus the animation on information that is relevant to the desired learning outcome. Motion or objects that are irrelevant to the concept may distract the student from more important material. Use pointers or cues to direct attention to relevant concepts.
2. Narration should occur simultaneously with the appropriate animation. Narration that occurs prior to or after relevant animation diminishes learning. Eliminate action that is not connected to the narration.
3. Animations can be particularly useful in demonstrating the error of misconceptions, misinterpretations, and wrongly held perceptions of the relevant concept. Animations can correct sequence or causal errors.
4. Be careful in the use of color and sounds, so that they do not wrongly indicate importance, relationships, or differences that do not exist among objects or concepts. Use color to distinguish between objects; sound may be used to define or indicate beginnings or endings of processes.
5. Parsimonious use of text in animation should be the rule. Attention overload occurs when too much information is presented simultaneously, resulting in a negative impact on knowledge acquisition by learners. Create a pause in animation action if text is needed to label new objects entering the visual field.
6. Strive to create a balance between too much detail and too much abstraction in objects. It is important to maintain the relative and proportional relationships and distinctions between objects.

7. The use of metaphor and analogy can be useful for learners to establish understanding of unfamiliar processes by activating knowledge of familiar characteristics and concepts.
8. Allow learners the ability to control the speed and flow of the presentation by providing controls. Suggested controls include speed, reverse, repeat, play, and quit.
9. Make the end of the animation apparent. It is recommended that when the animation ends, the presentation be automatically returned to the beginning, or the learner be prompted to start over or quit. Students unfamiliar with online animations may not recognize the end of an animated presentation, and conclude that an error has occurred. Students might be interested in replaying an animation to further understanding.
10. Animations show benefit for preparing students to do well in assessments that measure (a) problem-solving or knowledge transfer type problems, (b) the ability to recreate a procedure or sequence of tasks to accomplish a specific objective, and (c) diagnostic type problems.

Animation Software and Pre-recorded Animations

There are a variety of programs, including free open-source programs that will accommodate most animation needs, from the simple to the complex. Several inexpensive programs provide adequate instruction for beginners to create simple, short animations. A brief description of just a few of the animation programs that are available is contained in Table 3.7.

As mentioned in the section on integrating audio into distance learning instruction, a plethora of animated teaching resources is available on the Internet. You may create a direct link to these resources from within your course and use them as part of required course activities and assignments or as supplemental content. A partial list of Internet-based animation resources is provided in Table 3.8.

A Word about MERLOT

One excellent online resource for multimedia content, including animations, is MERLOT (Multimedia Educational Resource for Learning and Online Teaching). MERLOT's repository of online resources approximates 4,000 objects, and is continuously growing. The learning materials, created by college faculty around the world in all subject areas, have been peer reviewed, and include resources for assignments, animations, simulations, and explanations for utilization. The MERLOT site offers search features

TABLE 3.7 Animation Programs

Program	Description	Web site
Macromedia Captivate	Captivate is a proprietary program that allows users to create simulations, software demonstrations, and scenario-based training with no programming skills required. With its screen capture capabilities, Captivate can produce interactive tutorials for software demonstrations, as well as demonstrations of interactive websites. Captivate can also create digital assessments that provide immediate feedback to students and to the instructor. Graphics and audio files can be added to Captivate to enhance animation effects.	http://www.adobe.com/products/captivate/
Viewlet Builder	A proprietary screen capture program similar to Captivate. Viewlet Builder does not have digital assessment capabilities.	http://www.qarbon.com/presentation-software/viewletbuilder/
Wink	An open source, freeware screen-capture program designed primarily for software demonstration.	http://www.debugmode.com/wink/
Raptivity	A proprietary animation program that allows you to create animated interactions for a multitude of educational purposes. Animation types include game shows, board games, 3D objects, virtual worlds, video animations, and simulations.	http://www.raptivity.com
SoftChalk	A proprietary authoring tool that allows you to create pop-up text annotations, self-assessment tests, and interactive learning games.	http://www.softchalk.com

TABLE 3.8 Animation Resources Available on the Internet

Topic	Website
Health/Medical	
Interactive Health Tutorials	http://www.nlm.nih.gov/medlineplus/tutorial.html
Data sets, worksheets, tutorials	http://www.geospiza.com/education/materials.html#tutorials
Biology animations and interactive tutorials	http://science.nhmccd.edu/biol/bio1int.htm
Flash Tutorials	http://www.webwasp.co.uk/
Business Technology	
Art and drawing programs	http://www.serif.com/store/serif/education/tutorials/drawPlus/drawPlusExamples.asp
Automotive	
Automotive oscilloscope guide—movies and animations	http://www.picotech.com/auto/automotive-oscilloscope-guide/
Automotive service career guide, animated tutorials on automotive systems, etcetera	http://www.khake.com/page12.html
Culinary	
Cooking technique demonstrations	http://www.foodnetwork.com/food/ck_demos
A variety of tutorials that include animation, video, text, and graphics	http://recipes.chef2chef.net/conversion/meat-techniques.htm

Art

Museum of Modern Art	http://www.sfmoma.org/

Miscellaneous

National Gallery of Art: click on *Education*	http://www.nga.gov/home.htm
Questacon educational site focused on science with a fun approach	http://www.questacon.edu.au/index_flash.asp
American Museum of Photography	http://www.photography-museum.com/
Tons of multimedia	http://guide.real.com/
San Francisco Museum of Modern Art	http://www.sfmoma.org/
NASA	http://www.nasa.gov/home/index.html?skipIntro=1
National Geographic	http://www.nationalgeographic.com/
The Virtual Solar System from National Geographic	http://www.nationalgeographic.com/solarsystem/splash.html
World Central	http://www.wordcentral.com/
Earth Watch	http://www.earthwatch.org/site/pp.asp?c=8nJELMNkGiF&b=1322375
Mad Scientist	http://www.madsci.org/
Museum of Modern Art	http://www.moma.org/
Smithsonian Institutes	http://www.si.edu/
Library of Congress	http://www.loc.gov/index.html
Digital Classroom from the National Archives	http://www.archives.gov/education/index.html
National Parks Service	http://www.cr.nps.gov/
National Aquarium in Baltimore	http://www.aqua.org/

to conduct keyword or subject area searches. MERLOT may be accessed at www.merlot.org/merlot/index.htm.

Using Video in Distance Learning Courses

The use of video can be a powerful instructional strategy, when utilized appropriately, to provide insight and enlightenment, rather than as a diversion or entertainment. Careful consideration should be given to how the video(s) will facilitate teaching/learning, how the video will engage students in learning important concepts, and what activities should be included to reinforce concepts presented in the video. The flexibility of placing video presentations online allows students to examine and study important course concepts when it is most convenient to them. The stimulation of sounds, images, simulations, and text inherent in video productions imparts the opportunity for students to understand topics from different perspectives. As the saying goes, "a picture is worth a thousand words," often transmitting ideas in a fashion that is more easily understood than verbal or textual explanations.

Advantages of Video and Effective Practices

Incorporating video into instruction offers several advantages, as identified by Denning (2003), including (1) providing a visual presentation of information that may be difficult to present via other methods; (2) providing a sense of "being there," in that students can visit distant places without leaving the classroom; (3) containing emotional aspects that may impact the students more than textual information; (4) allowing students to experience events in different contexts and dimensions of time; (5) providing a means of demonstrating specific physical tasks or processes; (6) providing a visual demonstration of experiments or tasks that would be too dangerous or too expensive; (7) simplifying complex ideas; (8) modeling positive behavior to motivate students; (9) offering a venue appropriate for introducing a topic, or reviewing material already studied; and (10) capturing the interest of those with high visual preference in learning style or intelligence type.

Video is an excellent medium in which to present problem-based learning, such as case studies and scenarios. The key to using video in these types of learning activities is to build in other distance learning tools, such as discussion forums and/or chat sessions for interaction, analysis, and group problem-solving. This type of activity, requiring students to engage in thinking and problem-solving, is more effective than showing a video or reading a textbook case that describes a problem and reveals the answer. One effective method for using custom-made instructor video with problem-based learning involves the following steps:

1. Supply a brief introductory video of the topic that includes specific learning objectives and instructions.
2. Establish a discussion or chat forum for students to (a) share information they have on the problem, (b) decide what information is still needed to solve the problem, and (c) strategize what methods they will utilize to collect the information.
3. Provide a video mid-stream to offer guidelines, encouragement, and feedback on progress. If appropriate, raise additional questions for further exploration or to guide students in the right direction.
4. Require students to utilize the discussion or chat forum for continued sharing of ideas and discoveries.
5. Once students have completed the activity and posted their final products, post a video that offers a summary and conclusion of the learning experience.
6. Consider requiring students to post a video, PowerPoint presentation, or written report for classmates to review.

Another effective practice is the use of video as responses to threaded discussion. (The effective use of discussion topics and specific discussion strategies are detailed in Chapter 4.) The general process is outlined in a few simple steps.

1. Students respond to a threaded discussion.
2. At the end of the week, the instructor records via a webcam or other program a summary of student responses, adding additional caveats and/or connections to the subject matter, as necessary.
3. The video is placed in the distance learning course as either a discussion attachment or link on a resource page. The video summary should be brief, no more than five minutes, maximum.

Although video has definite benefits, instructors should be aware of the equipment and resources students have available to them. One important consideration is the download time for students. Streaming video is popular, since the technology allows the video to begin playing while the information is being transferred from the Internet to the computer. Another important issue is the software the learner will need to view the video. Media players such as Quicktime, Flash Player, Windows Media Player, and others are all free media players and are available on the Internet. When using any multimedia file, it is recommended that a direct link to the free media player page(s) be provided. Since students will not have to conduct internet searches to locate all of the media players, providing direct links will save them time.

Planning Your Video

Effective videos are not a fluke. Video making that is successful usually involves careful and detailed planning. Asking the question, "What impression do I want to leave the viewer with?" is an excellent way to begin the preparation process.

What is it that the students should learn, know, or feel about the video topic? Set the process in motion by making a list of all the main points that need to be included in the video. Write a script and outline the remaining video details. The opening segment of the video should typically include some details of the video content, enough to give the student an idea of the total focus. The main body of information should follow, concluding with a summary, resolution of the initial problem or question, and/or encouragement for the student to seek additional information/answers.

Sound a little bit like a book or movie plot? Audiences expect a certain flow to media presentations. A sample video outline is presented in Table 3.9.

Note that the level of detail in Table 3.9 demonstrates the length of the video, the structure of the content, and a list of various media to support the video message. Also notice that the video is short; it is recommended

TABLE 3.9 Sample Video Outline of a Course Overview Video

Segment Length	Segment	Supporting media
10 sec	Opening and title slides	Title graphic, music
30 sec	Welcome and introduction message	Camera shot; graphics 1–4
45 sec	Explain course navigation	Screenshot graphics of course homepage and icons
35 sec	Interaction via discussion	Camera shot
10 sec	Text information	Graphic of text
30 sec	Assignment information	Camera shot, graphics 5–8
20 sec	Conclusion	Camera shot
8 sec	Closing title slide	Title slide, music
Total length of video: 3 min. 8 sec.		

that videos stay under five minutes. Longer videos create large file sizes that may be difficult for students to download. Additionally, longer videos may be boring to viewers; if five minutes is not sufficient time for the video, consider "chunking" or dividing the video into subtopics. Once the video outline is complete, list all the materials needed to support the content, such as graphics, photos, music, narration, other video demonstrations or interviews, text information, and closing credits. Create or collect the supporting materials.

Scripting: It's Not Just for Hollywood!

As with the previous section regarding audio, scripts are an essential component of video-making. If necessary, review the previous section before continuing. Note that each section below follows the sections included in Table 3.9 for the sample video outline.

Opening and Title Slide.   The opening and title slide should provide a clear idea of the video content. Graphical elements must relate to content, and if music is used, the style of music selected should set the correct tone. For example, it would be inappropriate to have upbeat, jazz-type background music playing against a video on the Holocaust.

Welcome and Introduction Message.   The welcome and introduction message should provide enough information to interest the student in the main body of information to follow. Intrigue the student with a question, or present an overview of the main points to be covered. A sample script for the welcome message portion of your video is offered in Table 3.10. Feel free to embellish and add to the example. After all, the video should be personalized so that the instructor is comfortable and natural when narrating and speaking to the camera.

Video Content—Main Points: Course Navigation, Discussion, Text, Assignment. The next segment(s) of your video will most likely contain the main content of the video topic(s). From the supporting materials that were previously

---

TABLE 3.10   Sample Script for Welcome Message

Hello, I am (Your Name), and I'd like to welcome you to (Course Name, Unit or Lesson Title, or Topic Name).

In this video, we will (choose one: *learn about, explore, discover, demonstrate, view how to*), (describe the main topic[s] or list goals and/or objectives of the video). It is my goal to provide you with a level of comfort in this (topic, course, etc.), and I am confident that you will find this video beneficial in gaining a better understanding of (topic, content, activity, etc.). So let's get started . . .

---

identified and collected, select the items that enhance understanding of the topic. But remember, the purpose of supporting materials is to illustrate the main points. Keep the supporting materials simple. When supporting media is overdone, it can confuse and/or distract students from the main message. It is important to know the audience in order to communicate at the appropriate level of understanding, utilizing terminology and vocabulary that is fitting. Keep it succinct. The average newscaster delivers a story in less than one minute. Be unambiguous and to-the-point in all video communication.

Conclusion. Provide a conclusion to the video that summarizes the message or encourages students to independently seek answers to the questions or problems presented. Consider providing a brief list of specific resources for students to access. In addition, make sure to include the next step that the students should take after viewing the video. For example, should they access a discussion topic and post a response, access an assignment, or read a text chapter? A sample conclusion script is provided in Table 3.11.

Closing Title Slide. It may not be necessary to create a specific script for the Closing Title Slide. However, it is important to pre-determine if the closing title will include a graphic and/or music to accompany specific text, such as closing credits. Finally, the closing slide should include information on where in the course students can go to access a print transcript of the video content. Remember, in order to be compliant with

---

TABLE 3.11   Sample Conclusion Script

Terry, a history instructor, created a video on the Supreme Court decision in favor of the Africans in the Amistad case that involved Spaniards transporting kidnapped Africans to slave owners. The video contained narrated still images, interspersed with interviews from a judge discussing the case, negro spiritual music files, and an interview with a relative of one of the Amistad victims. At the end of the video, Terry recorded the following summary:

> The horrendous conditions of the "middle passage" that the Africans had to bear were common practice on slave ships. During this time in our nation's history, few people expressed concern about the millions of African men, women, and children who were shipped across the ocean to build the economy of the New World with their labor. Consider this statement: "Slaves were more valuable than gold." For your presentation assignment, be sure to discuss the conditions aboard the Amistad that made a mutiny possible. If necessary, conduct additional research to discuss how and why Africans participated in their own enslavement. In addition to your text readings, be sure to visit the websites included in your assignment instructions for supplemental information. Consult the rubric for evaluation instructions.

---

the Americans with Disabilities Act, any multimedia content must also include a print transcript. Note that your pre-made scripts will suffice to meet this requirement.

Video Software and Pre-recorded Videos

As with the audio and animation software, a variety of tools exist, both proprietary and open-source, for creation of video. Several video applications are listed in Table 3.12. A list of Internet sources for video clips is provided in Table 3.13.

TABLE 3.12 Video Applications

Application	Description	Web site
Windows Movie Maker	WMV is available as a free download, compatible with Windows operating systems. Movie Maker allows you to create, edit, and share digital movies on the computer using graphics, text, music, narration, and other video files.	www.microsoft.com/ windowsxp/downloads/ updates/moviemaker2 .mspx
ULEAD Visual Studio	Visual Studio is a propriety program. Easy to use, VS video software is good for entry-level and intermediate users.	www.ulead.com/ runme.htm
Camtasia	Camtasia is a proprietary program that allows screen capture recording. When combined with a webcam and audio, Camtasia can be used to create video webcasts and podcasts. PowerPoint presentations can be digitized and converted to flash files as well.	www.techsmith.com/ camtasia.asp
Visual Communicator	Visual Communicator is a proprietary program that combines ready-made templates with graphics, music, narration, and video to create high-quality video presentations. VC includes a green-screen backdrop and can be used with an inexpensive webcam to include instructor input and interaction.	www.seriousmagic.com

---

TABLE 3.13 Video Resources Available on the Internet

Google Video
   http://video.google.com
Video and audio clips, lesson plans, photographs, from the Florida Memory Project
   http://www.floridamemory.com/OnlineClassroom/
Video and audio clips from the History Channel
   http://www.historychannel.com/broadband/home/index.jsp
Video from the Discovery Channel
   http://dsc.discovery.com/
CBS News videos online
   http://www.cbsnews.com/
MSNBC Multimedia
   http://www.msnbc.msn.com/id/4999736/
ABC News video and audio
   http://abcnews.go.com/Video/
CNN video
   http://www.cnn.com/video/
Videos online from PBS-NOVA
   http://www.pbs.org/wgbh/nova/teachers/video.html
Nature videos online from PBS
   http://www.pbs.org/wnet/nature/database.html
YouTube
   www.youtube.com
Hulu
   http://www.hulu.com/
TeacherTube
   http://www.teachertube.com/

Using PowerPoint with Animation and Video

The previous section regarding audio contained tips for narrating a PowerPoint presentation for use in a distance learning course. Even with audio elements, PowerPoint is often maligned as a stagnate form of communication. However, PowerPoint can be combined with animation and video to create interactive presentations containing text, graphics, audio, video, and animation elements. PowerPoint is considered by many to be a fully functional multimedia tool.

PowerPoint Strategies

PowerPoint software is a convenient tool for creating slide show type presentations, but is not a tool for building an entire distance learning course. However, among the advantages of using PowerPoint are the facts that students are often familiar with its format, and most students have access to PowerPoint software. Consider PowerPoint to be one tool in a "toolbox" for creating dynamic and interactive distance learning courses. Following are general strategies for utilizing PowerPoint as a teaching/learning tool.

Digital Lecture. In transforming a face-to-face course for distance delivery, instructors frequently re-create lecture content in a PowerPoint presentation. In a survey conducted by Lancaster University, 69 percent of respondents reported using PowerPoint to present lecture materials for blended learning courses. In addition, 35 percent use PowerPoint for distance learning courses (Lancaster University, 2004).

Tips for narrating a PowerPoint presentation to be used for lecture purposes were discussed in a previous section of this chapter. Consider embedding video files and/or animation files into narrated PowerPoint lectures to create more dynamic and engaging presentations. It is recommended that discussion questions and brief activities be included as part of a PowerPoint lecture to help maintain student focus and to promote critical thinking.

Additional Uses. There are a variety of other ways that PowerPoint can be utilized in a distance learning course. Consider using PowerPoint to (1) introduce a unit of study, (2) provide instructions and focus for assignments and learning activities, (3) offer supplemental information not found in course text or other resources, and (4) review unit material, and/or guide the student to appropriate conclusions and summary. Also, PowerPoint is an excellent tool for creating a tutorial or course orientation that includes navigation instructions, an overview of course organization, and tips for success.

Designing a presentation is a very important, but often overlooked part of the process. Just as placement and pace of course materials in a lecture are important considerations for ultimate impact on the audience, where text and graphics are placed on an individual slide, and where audio, video, and animated elements are inserted within the presentation are important decisions in designing a PowerPoint. The presentation should benefit the students, not distract them. The text color, size, and amount of text on a slide should enhance student understanding and engagement. Many instructors find it beneficial to storyboard the presentation first, either by making notes or by sketching an outline. Whatever the purpose of the PowerPoint presentation, effective presentations must be organized, flow logically, project enthusiasm for the topic, focus the learner, and provide clarity of content.

Comparing Multimedia Tools

Multimedia tools provide the opportunity to add rich and engaging elements to a distance learning course. Most students interact with multimedia content, via the Internet, on a regular basis, including the use of YouTube and social network sites. Used wisely, multimedia can improve student retention of course content, as well as provide motivation and maintain interest. A comparison of capabilities for the proprietary multimedia software programs discussed throughout this chapter is provided in Table 3.14. Each can be used effectively to create course content that actively engages students in the learning process.

As discussed throughout this chapter, many multimedia programs are available for instructors to use to design learning materials. However, instructors are often challenged by media selection, unsure if the media type selected effectively presents the content in a manner that allows students to achieve intended learning objectives. Specific course content or activities with the multimedia software programs described above are combined in Table 3.15.

End of Chapter Activities

The end of chapter activities provide opportunities for you to acquire new knowledge, gain skill, and apply principles and concepts. These activities are located on the Companion Website, and are divided into three subsections: Knowledge Building, Skill Building, and Practical Application.

TABLE 3.14   Comparison of Multimedia Software Programs

Characteristics	PowerPoint with Audio	Captivate	Visual Communicator	Camtasia	Raptivity	SoftChalk
Audio						
Audio narration recording	Yes	Yes	Yes	Yes	Yes	Yes
Audio quality editing options	Yes	Yes	Yes	Yes	No	No
Import sound or music files	Yes	Yes	Yes	Yes	Yes	Yes
Special Effects						
Hyperlinks	Yes	Yes	No	No	Yes	Yes
Text animations	Yes	Yes	Yes	Yes	Yes	Yes
Apply actions to slides	Yes	Yes	Yes	Yes	No	No
Balloons, Call-Outs, Caption boxes	Yes	Yes	No	Yes	Yes	Yes
Roll-overs; Hot spots	No	Yes	No	Yes	Yes	Yes
Animated pointers	No	Yes	No	Yes	Yes	No
Zoom & Pan	No	No	No	Yes	Yes	No
Special Features						
Teleprompter	No	No	Yes	No	No	No
Templates	Yes	No	Yes	No	Yes	Yes
Quizzing	Yes	Yes	No	Yes	Yes	Yes
Video						
Full motion recording	No	Frames	Yes	Yes	No	No
Screenshot recording	No	Yes	No	Yes	No	No
Mouse Tracking	No	Yes	No	Yes	No	No
Single Picture Recording	No	Yes	Yes	Yes	No	No
Import movie files	Yes	Yes	Yes	Yes	Yes	No
Animation						
Screen capture	No	Yes	No	Yes	No	No
Adding Audio files	Yes	Yes	Yes	Yes	Yes	Yes
Audio recording capabilities	Yes	Yes	Yes	Yes	Yes	Yes

TABLE 3.15   Multimedia Tools for Developing Course Content

Strategy	PowerPoint with Audio	Captivate	Visual Communicator	Camtasia	Raptivity	Soft Chalk
Online Quiz or Self-check for Knowledge: Questions structured as multiple choice, true/false, matching, essay, short-answer, open-ended, etcetera.	Yes	Yes	No	Yes	Yes	Yes
Online Lecture: Video or Audio presentation; If using a video presentation, it is recommended to provide graphics or pictures relevant to lecture topics to provide visual interest.	Yes	Yes	Yes	Yes	Yes	Yes
Unit Introduction: Introduce goals and objectives of unit; outline the items included in the unit (required readings, lectures, discussion forums, etc.); offer tips or strategies for how to prepare for unit and assignments; provide guidance on how to approach and/or structure time for completing complex or group-oriented projects; include suggestions for resources (text, online, community) relevant to unit and assignments.	Yes	Yes	Yes	Yes	Yes	Yes
Link to other websites, additional information: Provide links to handouts and supplemental documents; include links to online resources.	Yes	Yes	No	Yes	Yes	Yes
Software demo and tutorial: Provide instruction for students in software applications; include screen shots, text instructions via captions and animated pointers; include interactive components (students must make appropriate choices to advance tutorial).	No	Yes	No	Yes	No	No

References

Bratina, T., Bratina, T., and Bratina, A. (2001). *Listen up! Using audio files in the curriculum.* Retrieved May 15, 2006, from: http://www.newhorizons.org/strategies/technology/bratina.htm

Animation Research (no date). Carnegie-Mellon University. Retrieved May 15, 2006, from http://www.cmu.edu/teaching/technology/animationresearch.html

Denning, D. (2003). *Video in theory and practice: Issues for classroom use and teacher video evaluation.* Retrieved May 15, 2006, from http://ebiomedia.com/downloads/VidPM.pdf

Report on E-Learning Survey (2004). Lancaster University, Learning Technology Group. Retrieved May 19, 2006 from: http://luvle.lancs.ac.uk/CELT/LearnTech.nsf/list/C7ACEDF3657E18CF80256EC30050B283

Littlefield, J. (2009). *Multimedia learning in online classes: How to learn effectively with podcast classes, web conferencing, and more.* Retrieved June 11, 2009, from http://distancelearn.about.com/od/studyskills/a/multimedia.htm

Siemens, G. (2003). *Evaluating media characteristics: Using multimedia to achieve learning outcomes.* Retrieved June 11, 2009, from http://www.elearnspace.org/Articles/mediacharacteristics.htm

4

Communication is Key

The most important element in designing effective and interactive distance learning course activities is the inclusion of communication tools. The research discussed throughout this chapter indicates that interactive communication in distance learning courses is essential for student satisfaction and success. This chapter focuses on course communication and the benefits of and strategies for implementing interactive communication techniques into distance learning courses. Upon completion of Chapter 4, readers will be able to:

1. Identify a learning activity that utilizes each of the following communication tools: announcement, calendar, mail, discussion, chat
2. Select a collaborative communication strategy to enhance learning effectiveness
3. Create a course syllabus using the distance learning course syllabus template
4. Identify specific communication strategies and develop a plan for their use in course communications

Communication is Key

The quality of online courses must be comparable to those held in traditional classroom settings. Historic research of traditional education delivery re-

Fluency in Distance Learning, pages 127–173
Copyright © 2010 by Information Age Publishing
All rights of reproduction in any form reserved.

veals that classroom methodology and strategies are significant because they transmit subject matter that is the "heart of the educational format" (Houle, 1974). Effective communication techniques and practices are important for establishing a sense of community, as well as for fostering student–student interaction and dialogue between instructor and students. As mentioned previously, employing various communication tools in distance learning courses empowers instructors to meet the learning needs of students in a manner comparable to traditional course delivery.

A major aspect of distance learning is the relative independence of the learning experience. Using communication tools can alleviate the isolationism of online courses. Just as a one-strategy-fits-all approach will not work in traditional courses, it will also not work in distance learning. There are many specific strategies for instructors' utilization of communication tools in a manner that fosters both independence and collaboration. Communication tools provide faculty with a wealth of opportunities to differentiate instruction and build a repertoire of learning activities that are as varied as each student.

Asynchronous and Synchronous Communication

Most learning management systems (LMS systems) include tools for two categories of communication: asynchronous (anytime communication) and synchronous (real-time communication). Both types of tools add value and flexibility to your facilitation of the online learning experience. In addition, both types of communication provide options for students with different learning and communication preferences. It is important to note that simply offering the communication tool for use does not ensure participation; it is the careful analysis, planning, and structuring of activities that promotes student participation and accountability for success.

As mentioned in the text introduction, asynchronous tools allow communication between students and instructor to take place at different times and in different locations. This eliminates obstacles related to time and travel constraints that prevent learners from interacting with each other at the same time. Examples of asynchronous communication tools included in most learning management systems are discussion boards, email, announcements, calendars, and file sharing.

Among the several advantages of asynchronous communication are the opportunities for learners to engage in reflection prior to responding. Students and instructor are allowed to participate in communication when it is most appropriate for them, at times when there are little or no distractions, when thoughts are lucid and they are mentally prepared to contribute. Asynchronous communication affords each learner the opportunity to be heard; students that may be shy and reticent in a group can find their voice when given the opportunity to contemplate their thoughts before responding. The asynchronous environment is non-threatening to many students that otherwise are reluctant to speak up in traditional class discussions. Students are able to experience a sense of control over their environment, while being socially engaged. The opportunity to socially construct meaning of concepts from shared perspectives, observations, discoveries, and resources results in deep learning.

Synchronous communication occurs in real time. Students and instructor exchange information at the same time and, most likely, from different locations. Forms of synchronous tools involve text-based chats, instant messaging, audio and/or video conferencing, and virtual whiteboards.

There are some activities for which synchronous tools are the most effective. The feeling of isolation that, at times, may become pervasive in distance learning can be alleviated when learners are able to interact in real time with the instructor and with each other. Students who are strong in spontaneous communication appreciate synchronous activities as a form of social engagement. For the instructor, conducting a synchronous chat session for the purpose of assessing student understanding is a useful strategy for monitoring student progress. The immediate feedback available in synchronous interaction is valuable for both student and instructor.

Challenges Associated with Asynchronous and Synchronous Communication

There are several challenges associated with synchronous activities. Profiles of distance learning students indicate that most work and have other outside responsibilities. Participation in synchronous activities may present obstacles for students who prefer distance learning courses for the flexible qualities of access. Trying to schedule a time that is convenient for all students to convene online is often very difficult. In addition, technology failure, such as loss of connectivity, can impede successful interaction. Also, synchronous communication via chat rooms tends to favor those with proficient keyboarding skills and those who read and process information quickly. Students who lack technical proficiency and those who read and process at a slower pace are often left behind in the conversation, resulting in high levels of anxiety and frustration.

One primary challenge associated with asynchronous communication such as discussion forums is the slower pace of the discussion. "Conversations" on discussion forums usually occur over a period of several days. Thus, discussion forums require close monitoring by the instructor and students. It is imperative that the instructor immediately correct any misinformation that is posted so that few students have the opportunity to read it and respond.

The lack of nonverbal cues in both synchronous and asynchronous communication can make "talking" online tricky, and lead to misunderstandings. Providing structure and guidelines, such as rubrics, straight-forward expectations outlined in the course syllabus, and step-by-step instructions, is important to reduce student frustration and maintain participation levels.

Again, careful planning and analysis are important for designing learning activities and selecting corresponding communication tools appropriate for the desired learning outcomes. This chapter is focused on effectively utilizing common LMS communication tools in conjunction with specific communication strategies and activities, and provides concrete suggestions for utilizing both synchronous and asynchronous forms of communication.

Common Learning Management System Communication Tools

Following is a brief description of the common communication tools included with most LMS systems, along with a handful of general tips to guide you as you plan to use each tool. Please note that this section is meant to provide you only with a general overview of each tool. A later section, *Using Communication Tools in Distance Learning Reinforces Good Teaching Practice*, explores the communication tools in depth and provides specific strategies that reinforce each principle. The next section, *Tips and Guidelines for Using Communication Tools in Distance Learning*, offers more detailed information on each tool, while the following section, *Using Communication Tools to Facilitate Teaming Activities*, describes specific teaming strategies and provides step-by-step instructions for implementation.

Announcements

An often overlooked method of delivering messages to an entire class is the Announcement feature. Announcements appear on the main or home page of the distance learning course, and are an excellent way to address all students at once with general information. It is true that an email distribution list would serve the same purpose, but many students do not access their email prior to beginning coursework. An announcement on the course home page is effective since the home page is typically the first place students visit to access other parts of the course. Announcements may include any or all of the following: (1) reminders of dates, tasks, or policy/procedure; (2) important notifications; (3) beginning of term instructions; (4) information on additions to learning content; (5) notification of recently sent email; and (6) information about community events, television broadcasts, political occurrences, school meetings, or other activities related to content.

Syllabus

Students want to know what to expect in your class and how to do well. The syllabus is an important communication tool for conveying this information. In fact, it is often considered to be the foundation of the course, along with the "teaching and learning contract" that you have with your students. The syllabus is your opportunity to provide students with information on policy, procedure, resources, and tips to succeed. A poorly written syllabus can negatively affect student attitude and motivation, while a well-designed syllabus offers direction and incentive. This is true for face-to-face courses as well, but it is particularly important for distance learning courses to provide straightforward, unambiguous instructions. Provide ample information in a clear-cut, uncomplicated fashion; vague statements and instructions create confusion and frustration for students. At the very least, the syllabus should contain instructor contact information, a list of the course goals and objectives, an overview of course content, information about assignments, grading criteria, and any special requirements or materials.

Many institutions provide a syllabus template of recommended/required information. A syllabus for a distance learning course should include the institution's required components, but must also include items specific to students who do not frequent the campus. In addition, suggestions to help students navigate the online course, as well as technical requirements and technical support information, should be included.

Guidelines for building a distance learning course syllabus are offered in Table 4.1. In addition, Appendix B, located at the end of this chapter, provides a sample distance learning course syllabus. For your convenience, a syllabus template is provided on the Companion Website.

TABLE 4.1   Recommendations for Distance Learning Course Syllabus

Syllabus Feature	Description
Course Title and related information	State the name of the course and any related course or section numbers. List course beginning and ending dates.
Instructor Information	Provide name, title, and contact information, such as phone number, fax number, email, office location, and office hours (whether physical or virtual).
Communication Policy	Indicate the best way to contact you (phone, email, chat, etc.). Provide students with an estimate of your turnaround time for getting back to them (for example: students will receive a response by email within 24 hours, Monday through Friday. Let students know if you read emails or take phone calls on the weekends or evenings. It is good policy to schedule virtual office hours, specific days and times that you will be available for synchronous communication.
Course Description	Supply the official course description as listed in institutional or organizational documentation. Offer additional details that present an overview of what the course will cover. State the initial class meeting date or orientation and subsequent meeting dates (if applicable).
Prerequisites	List any prerequisite courses, certifications, skills, or abilities.
Course Learning Objectives	Write the objectives to express what students will be able to demonstrate after the end of course. How will students demonstrate the knowledge, skills, and abilities? For example: After completion of this course, students will be able to: 1. Demonstrate understanding of [concept] (through reflective discussion board responses). 2. Compare and contrast the theories presented in the readings with your personal experiences with [concept] (through written assignment). 3. Demonstrate competency in [software skill] (through completion of software project).
Required and Optional Course Materials	List required textbooks with the following information: title, author(s), and ISBN. State what computer systems, hardware (such as CD drive, printer, etc.), and software (example: Microsoft Office Word and PowerPoint) are necessary. Indicate if students will access multimedia files such as video or audio. Supply a list of websites containing free downloads to enable students to view documents or multimedia files.

Syllabus Feature	Description
Policies and Procedures	Be straightforward with instructions that will assist you in facilitating a smoothly running distance learning course. For example: When does the "course" week start? Sunday? Monday? Most distance learning students prefer to have the weekend to do their schoolwork. When are assignments due? Sundays at midnight? Mondays at noon? If you have students in different time zones, indicate the time zone that you are operating under. Let students know how they should title their assignments. Is there a naming convention for electronic files? Should assignment files include the student's name and assignment title? Designate which writing style students should utilize for written assignments (e.g., APA, Minnesota, Chicago).
Course Withdrawal Dates	Provide information on institutional policy and deadlines for course withdrawal.
Assessment/ Grading Policy	Give students information on how they will be assessed on their achievement of the learning objectives. What is the grading scale? Is the class pass/fail? List assignments and how each assignment contributes to the total grade. Supply students with a rubric to explain how students earn points for assignments and what constitutes excellent and good work versus poor or unacceptable work on a specific assignment. Do students earn a grade for incomplete assignments? State the policy for accepting and/or grading late assignments.
Course Participation	Assert expectations and policies for student participation in the course. How often should students login to the course? Offer guidance on the amount and length of postings if discussion postings are required and graded. Outline (rubrics are useful) how points are earned for discussion response. Provide examples of exceptional and poor discussion postings. State deadlines for postings; suggest a schedule for initial posting and follow-ups.
Timeline	Prepare a weekly schedule of topics to be covered, required readings and assignments per topic, due dates for assignments.
Assignment Information	Describe each assignment, its purpose, and its relation to course learning objectives. List specific elements of a multi-faceted assignment and the value of each element to the total assignment. Explain grading criteria. Provide instructions on how to submit assignment.

TABLE 4.1   Recommendations for Distance Learning Course Syllabus (continued)

Syllabus Feature	Description
Tests/Quizzes/ Final Exam	List test/quiz/exam dates. Indicate any mid-term or final exam requirements and/or special instructions. Will students take exams online? Or must students complete tests/exams in a testing center? Is there a time limit? If taking a test in an external test center environment, what do student need to bring with them (e.g., ID, paper, scantrons, #2 pencils, etc.). Describe the value of the test in relationship to the final grade (20%, 50%, etc.).
Lab Requirements	Indicate whether there is an associated lab requirement for course. Provide instructions on when/how students will complete lab requirements.
Academic Honesty Policy	Mention requirements for academic honesty. Provide a link to institution's policy on academic honesty. Provide a link to the American Library Association's information on copyright and plagiarism. Furnish examples of dishonesty.
Request for Accommodations	Request students needing special accommodation contact you and the institution's disabilities office to arrange appropriate accommodations.
Resources for Students	Supply a list of, and information on how to access, resources that are available to students, such as: library, advising, tutoring, veterans services, preparatory services, child care, financial aid, career center, etcetera.
Tips for Online Students	Offer suggestions for achieving success in distance learning courses, for example: setting up a schedule for going online and scheduling study time.
Frequently Asked Questions (FAQ)	Offer answers to questions that are often asked about the course, your syllabus, assignments, due dates, policies, and procedures.

Chat

The chat tool provides the opportunity for you and your students to communicate with each other in real time. The communication takes place via typed messages in a chat room. The use of synchronous chat actively engages students in the learning process and requires them to keep pace with the course and not fall behind.

The chat tool offers many benefits to you, the distance learning instructor. It is an excellent tool for building a sense of community in a distance learning course. Chat can be a forum for one-on-one communication or for group communication. Many students are familiar with using chat for recreational purposes, thus, the learning curve is short. In addition, chat rooms can be monitored, and there is a written record of the dialogue.

One disadvantage is that the chat tool requires rapid responses. It tends to favor verbal and social learners, quick typists, and those who are fluent English speakers. Even though online "chatting" may be familiar to many of your students, we recommend that you not use chat for the most vital course content. Instead, you may want to reserve whole-class chat sessions for final questions before a quiz or test. Tips and guidelines for using the chat tool include the following:

1. When facilitating an online chat session, ask students to use symbols such as "~" or "?" to indicate that they have a comment or question. This expedites the communication process. Once a student indicates that he/she has a question, use features within the chat tool to call on him/her, just as if in a face-to-face classroom. We recommend that instructors provide a chat glossary of appropriate symbols and their meanings for students to refer to during the chat sessions, especially if a variety of symbols and abbreviations are being used.

2. When the need arises to type long messages into a chat session, consider breaking the message into chunks.

3. We recommend that, prior to the chat session, instructors pre-compose and type questions or comments, and then cut and paste them into the chat session. Once the text is pasted into the chat message box, press <enter> on your computer keyboard. Again, this expedites the communication process and allows instructors to focus attention on what students are saying, instead of trying to type responses or new questions.

4. The chat tool is beneficial for facilitating group work, brainstorming sessions, and continuation of interesting discussion topics. When utilizing group activities in your course, we recommend that instructors establish a private chat room for each team. This provides a private forum for your students to conduct team "meetings." In addition, instructors can monitor team chats by viewing the chat log transcript.

5. Students who are logged-in to the chat session, but who are not actively participating are called "lurkers." Determine why they are not participating. Plan in advance how to deal with lurkers. One

strategy is to send non-participating students a private email to discuss this issue.

6. Prior to the chat session, assign a greeter to acknowledge each student as he/she enters the chat room. In addition, the greeter can highlight names of late-comers and post a private message to that person. (Note that the other chat participants cannot view private messages and the chat log will not record them.) Chat logs can be emailed or posted for those students who had an excused absence from the chat session.

7. Remind students that it is okay to disagree, but not to be disagreeable. Create a set of chat guidelines for your students. In addition, if chat sessions are a required part of the course, create a scoring rubric so that students will understand expectations for participation. A sample guideline for instructor expectations for student chat participation is provided in Table 4.2.

Mail

Mail is an asynchronous communication tool that allows you, your students, co-teachers, and teaching assistants to send, receive, reply, and forward mail messages within the course. With most LMS systems, you can also store drafts of mail messages, search mail messages, and add mail folders. It

---

TABLE 4.2   Instructor Expectations for Student Chat Participation

Communication Points

Use these guidelines to strengthen your contributions to the online chat:

1. Log-in to chat room on time.
2. Make your presence known with timely and relevant comments that add value to the conversation. Don't "lurk."
3. Contribute comments, ideas, observations, resources, information, opinions, etcetera, where appropriate, that add new content to the dialogue, rather than just a restatement or rehashing of previous conversation. Comments such as "I agree" or "I disagree" should be followed by a logical rationale for why you feel this way. Include citations from readings or web sites to provide support for your claims.
4. It is perfectly acceptable to disagree, but please do so with respect and tolerance. Statements such as "That's a stupid idea!" or "Only an idiot would suggest that!" are, of course, inappropriate. However, comments like "That is interesting, but I must disagree because..." show consideration for the other person, allow you to communicate another view, and offer more opportunity for class exploration and growth.
5. When leaving the chat room, please signal your departure.

is a critical tool, with regard to the communication aspect of distance learning. It encourages interaction between all course participants.

The mail tool allows you to give private, detailed feedback, and can also be an excellent resource to facilitate interaction and group work among students. When using the mail tool in an LMS, you will not have to worry about receiving unwanted messages from the outside world or keeping track of changing email addresses. It is important to remember that the mail tool within an LMS will usually not allow you to retract or recall a message once it has been sent.

Another benefit in using the mail tool is that it is a primary form of communication within and outside of the education environment. Most of your students will be quite familiar with electronic mail procedures. In addition, the mail tool allows you to deal with urgent problems, enables you to provide personalized reinforcement on progress, and assists you with providing individualized feedback on assignments. Finally, the mail tool gives you the ability to communicate sensitive information not appropriate for public forum. Tips for using the course mail tool are listed here.

1. It may be helpful to emphasize to students that the mail tool is used for private questions regarding grades and other private issues. The discussion tool, which will be described in the next section, is a better venue for course-related questions for which the answer may be relevant for all students in the class. (Consider providing this information in the course syllabus.)
2. There are several ways to manage course mail that make the task less cumbersome and time consuming. If you receive the same question several times through email, consider sending the answer to the question in an email that is addressed to the entire class. Likewise, if a student sends a relevant comment or question through email, email him/her back and request to put the comment on the discussion board or another public venue.
3. If you would like to respond to a mail message, but do not have the time, mark the message as "unread" to remind yourself to come back to it later. If typing a longer message in mail, you may save it as a draft to come back to later, or you may compose it using a word processor and cut and paste the finished text into the message box.
4. Use the search tool for help in organizing longer lists of mail messages.

Discussion
The discussion tool is the most commonly used asynchronous tool in distance learning courses. Discussion forum posts are in threaded format, which

allows students to respond directly to one another. Discussion posts are usually public. However, in some instances, discussion boards can be made private.

The discussion tool provides a forum to exchange ideas. It establishes a social environment that encourages participation, helps you monitor student participation, provides a means for students to self-pace, is a learner-controlled environment, and provides students with access to multiple perspectives. In addition, the discussion tool is accessible anytime and establishes a format for students to collaborate in small groups without requiring scheduled sessions. Tips for using the discussion tool are listed here.

1. To avoid confusing students, we recommend that a separate topic be created for each discussion activity and that students be required to post their discussion responses in the specified topic area. Allowing students to post responses in a general topic area, as opposed to specified areas, creates confusion since the number of posts can quickly become overwhelming and students will be unable to follow the conversations. In addition, using a general topic area will eventually become difficult for instructors to manage. Basic structure rules for students posting discussion topics and responses are provided in Table 4.3.

2. One of the primary purposes of using the discussion tool in a distance learning course is to assist the communication between students. Therefore, we recommend that, in some cases, instructors have a "quiet" voice in the discussion. Allow students to discuss issues back and forth, and only respond to a post when it is needed to get the discussion back on topic or when a student's question goes unanswered. When facilitating course discussion, it is important to balance between participating too little, which can discourage students' individual participation, and participating too much, which can discourage ongoing communication among students.

3. We recommend that instructors include participation in discussions as one aspect of the final grade for the course. By doing so, the importance of ongoing discussion will be emphasized, as well as the value of reflective thinking. In addition, evaluating the quality and/or quantity of a student's postings is an objective way to evaluate overall course participation. Keep students informed of their participation grade on an ongoing basis, and offer tips on how they can improve their grade.

4. Make certain that communication is clear, regarding expectations for student participation in class discussions. Be specific about how often students are expected to read and respond to their

classmates' posts, as well as how often they are required to post original responses. Also, let students know how often you will post to the discussion topics and whether or not you will respond to each of their posts.

5. Keep in mind that it is not necessary for instructors to reply publicly to a student's post. Another option is to respond privately via the email tool. Or, depending on the LMS, some offer the opportunity to post private responses directly to the discussion board.

6. It is common for students to sometimes disagree with each other. Provide examples of statements that can be used to indicate that they disagree, letting them know that it is okay to disagree with someone, but not okay to be disrespectful. Provide guidelines and/or examples of appropriate and inappropriate responses.

7. Student participation must be closely monitored. If participation begins to fade, or if specific students are minimally participating, send an email to the entire class offering encouragement, or email the specific students to try to ascertain why their participation is lacking.

8. For large class sizes, it is recommended that the class be divided into teams. In this case, students should post responses only within their team discussion board. Periodically shuffle the teams so that students can gain access to multiple perspectives.

9. As a means of encouraging participation the instructor may decide to implement the rule that no feedback will be provided to

---

TABLE 4.3   Structuring Discussion Board Topics and Responses

Posting Structure

Use these guidelines to strengthen your contributions to the online discussions:

1. Compose a new message or start a new thread when you introduce a new thought or idea to the discussion topic.

2. The subject line for a discussion posting is the clue to its message. Try to create a subject line that captures the attention of readers and provides an indication of the content.

3. When you reply to a posting, you may edit the subject line to articulate your contribution to the dialogue, but leave the "re:" portion of the subject line. This allows readers to quickly surmise the direction of the conversation within a thread without having to open each posting.

4. You are encouraged to reply to more people than required in the assignments. Just as dialogue is important in a traditional classroom environment, our exchange of ideas and information is important in advancing the knowledge and learning experience for everyone in the course.

5. Post early and post often!

---

a student's post until at least two other students have responded. This gives the students the opportunity to interact with each other and share ideas, and allows instructors to see the "flow" or direction of the discussion before posting a response.

10. As a means of communicating high expectations to students, the best two or three responses to a topic can be selected and profiled. Use email or post directly to the discussion forum, explaining to students why specific responses were selected.

Calendar

The calendar tool allows you to provide a quick overview of events within or related to your course. In many LMS systems, faculty and students may also utilize the calendar as a personal organizer by making private entries. Once faculty become familiar with the calendar, they find it useful in organizing the course, outlining daily activities, and directing or providing access to other documents located in the course or module. The calendar tool assists students with time management. Tips for using the calendar tool are listed here.

1. Post community events on the course calendar. Require students to attend at least one outside event and to write a reflective journal on how the experience is connected to the course, as well as how the event influenced (or did not influence) their opinions about course content.

2. Use the calendar consistently; otherwise, it will become ineffective. Define the role of the course calendar in the syllabus, and then be consistent in its use.

3. Ask students to examine the course calendar, and then to make personal entries on their study plans, project completions, etcetera, as a step toward good study habits. Some students may want to use the calendar tool as a personal organizer by making private entries that provide personal organization, appointments, and reminders.

4. Allowing students to make public entries facilitates communication regarding activities such as group meetings, sign-ups with an instructor, and scheduled chats. If students are allowed to make public entries, it is strongly recommended that guidelines be provided for the types of entries that are permissible.

Summary of Tips and Guidelines

A comparison of features and uses for the four primary communication tools just discussed is included in Table 4.4. These tools are commonly included in most LMS systems. Examine your learning objectives in order to determine which tool will work best with specific course activities.

TABLE 4.4 Learning Management System Communication Tools Comparison of Features and Uses

Characteristics	Mail	Discussion	Chat	Calendar
Is communication happening at the same time (synchronous) or at different times (asynchronous)?	Asynchronous	Asynchronous	Synchronous	Asynchronous
Is there a record of the conversation?	Yes, but the student must include you in the email.	Yes, discussions are recorded and posted publicly.	Yes, conversations are archived.	Yes, entries are recorded.
Is the conversation moderated?	No, mail messages are not moderated.	No, postings cannot be reviewed prior to being posted. But, the instructor can remove inappropriate postings.	No, postings are not moderated. But, participation by students can be controlled by the instructor. (Instructor can remove students from the chat room.)	No, postings are not moderated. But, the instructor can remove inappropriate posts.
Does the student have to retrieve messages or do the messages come automatically to the student?	Automatic	Retrieve: Students must actively check the discussion board for new messages.	Both: Students must actively log-in to the chat room at the appointed time. Once the chat begins, messages are received automatically.	Both: Students must access the calendar. Once accessed, posts are available automatically.
What are common uses for this communication tool in an online course?	Announcements Distribute general interest information Reply to frequently asked questions Offer encouragement to students	Encourage interaction among students Group discussions Provide feedback to individuals or groups Determine level of comprehension of course content	Real-time conversations for small groups Real-time office hours Whole-class lectures Combine with other communication tools	Due dates Class meeting dates Office hours Test dates Institution deadline dates

Communication Tools outside the Learning Management System

Although LMS systems contain a variety of communication tools, the advent of Web 2.0 tools has added an additional array of external sites that have special relevance to distance learning. The networking sites have different functions that allow for development of course spaces that may have private membership specific to a course, or be in the public domain. Detailed information on the primary Web 2.0 tools was offered in Chapter 2, focused on active learning strategies. Below is a brief review of some of the Web 2.0 tools discussed in Chapter 2, but now focused on using these tools as a form of communication.

Blogs

A blog is a series of reflective self-expressions published on the Internet in reverse chronological order. Many blogs resemble personal journals or diaries, and embrace self-expression, creativity, story-telling, and exposé. Blogs offer a forum for people to share reflections, opinions, commentaries, and ideas. Currently, blogs appear to be a more fluid form of online communication, as compared to listservs or group chats. It is important to note that, unless the learning management system offers a blogging tool, blogs are in the public domain, unlike the traditional communication tools that are included with most LMS systems. A list of blog sites for creating custom blogs was provided in Chapter 3.

One advantage of using blogs as a means of communication is the fact that multiple topics are available to be accessed throughout a blog, whereas discussion boards are usually threaded so that the reader is directed to comment on a specific topic or question. As a learning tool, blogs can be utilized for discussion since they resemble the free flow of face-to-face conversation. They can also be used as a publishing site for student work. However, instructors should caution students to carefully evaluate blog resources to ascertain the reliability and authenticity of the information contained therein.

Wikis

A wiki is an asynchronous collaborative structure that allows users to create and edit the web page content of the wiki using any Web browser. Chapter 2 provided specific strategies for the instructional use of wikis. The unique quality of the wiki is its dynamic ability to allow content contributed by readers to be edited by other users. For communication purposes, a wiki can serve as a discussion medium where students can share ideas and information. Probably the most well-known wiki is Wikipedia.

Web Conferencing

Once at the cutting edge, video conferencing has stepped aside for Web conferencing as a synchronous instructional delivery method. Whereas video conferencing required a physical space set up with special video, sound, and lighting connected to a broadcast system such as a television or satellite network, which was then linked to classrooms in other locations, web conferencing requires only the software and a computer with Internet.

A broad term, *Web conferencing* generally refers to the phone and Internet technology used to join people at a distance in synchronous collaboration. Web conferencing allows students to interact with instructors and coursemates in real time. Web conferencing can be used to replace class discussions or as a means to interact one-on-one with students to answer questions, offer success tips, and to provide support and motivation, as well as lecture presentation. There are various forms of Web conferences, but often students are able to see the instructor on their computer monitor and speak directly to them using a headset or telephone connection.

Depending on the various applications utilized to facilitate the Web conference, the visual interface might consist of text messages, text and video, documents, PowerPoint presentations, and other visual media. The obvious advantage of Web conferencing is the real-time communication that allows immediate and spontaneous feedback, whereas asynchronous email and discussion type forums involve lapses in communication time. Conversely, limitations of Web conferencing include the complexity of conducting synchronous sessions that coordinate with members' schedules, as well as ensuring that all users have downloaded appropriate software and plug-ins.

An assortment of Web conferencing options exist, enabling instructors and learners to connect with classes all over the globe to learn about each other's country, culture, reaction to current world affairs, or perceptions about historical events. Each option has its advantages; with Skype, students in the class can capture the conversation and create podcasts to share on a wiki, Facebook page, or iTunes. Conversations can also be continued on a blog or wiki. A list of some common Web conferencing tools and their corresponding websites is provided in Table 4.5.

Twitter

Twitter is an online communication phenomenon created in 2006, and whose popularity soared in 2008, making it one of the most popular web sites and social networks. Twitter allows users to deliver and/or restrict access to text-based messages, commonly known as *tweets*. The tweets are limited to 140 characters and are also referred to as micro-blogs or micro-text mes-

TABLE 4.5   Collaborative and Web Conferencing Tools

Name	Website	Cost
Adobe ConnectNow	http://ctl.byu.edu/adobe-connectnow/	Free
Adobe Connect Pro	http://tryit.adobe.com/us/connectpro/webconference/?sdid=DJZHD	Yes
Elluminate	http://www.elluminate.com/	Yes
E-Meeting	http://www.e-meeting.cn/	Yes
Google Video Chat	http://mail.google.com/videochat	Free
Horizon	http://www.horizonlive.com/	Yes
iChat	http://www.apple.com/macosx/what-is-macosx/ichat.html	Free
ooVoo	http://www.oovoo.com/	Free
Skype	http://ctl.byu.edu/skype/	Free
Windows Live Messenger	http://download.live.com/messenger	Free
Ygma	https://www.yugma.com/	Free

sages. Educational use of Twitter as a communication strategy is varied. Many instructors borrow from the Twitter model, using LMS tools to achieve the succinct communication goals accomplished in external Twitter sources.

A Word about Etiquette and Common Sense

Delving a bit further into distance learning communication guidelines, we must briefly mention *netiquette*, a term that stands for "network etiquette," which has been in use since 1988. Online communication is no different than traditional face-to-face communication. Common courtesy and socially acceptable behavior are standard fare for online communication environments. As mentioned above, it is important for you to establish written guidelines so that students clearly understand appropriate versus inappropriate communication. Inappropriate communication distracts all students from the learning process and greatly diminishes the learning value of online communication. If you would like to learn more about this topic, we recommend you read www.albion.com/netiquette/. This website provides a comprehensive list of netiquette guides, including: (1) never type in all upper case, (2) always include a subject in the subject field, (3) refrain from using colored text or backgrounds, (4) do not respond to inappropriate posts, (5) always proofread before you post, and (6) respond promptly to your classmates' posts.

With the advent of texting, blogging, and other forms of social communication, the guidelines have been extended to incorporate considerations for these new environments. A more extensive list of recommended guidelines for communication can be found at www.swref.com/story/20090705/the_rules_of_netiquette. Some new directives are listed below:

1. Keep postings on topic
2. Don't post private messages in a public forum
3. In regard to replying to another person's post, your response is added below the part of the message you are responding to— which is the opposite of email, where the response is on top
4. Cite the source of information
5. For real-time messages such as text or chat, it is acceptable to type in lower case and/or use IM (instant messaging) abbreviations
6. Again, for real-time messages such as text or chat, send short messages instead of lengthy ones

One final caveat is the unexpected consequences for users of blogs, wikis, twitter, and social network sites. It is important not to lose sight of the fact that these forums are in the public domain. Therefore, blogger beware! Contributing private, sensitive, or inflammatory information can have serious outcomes. Prior to hiring a new employee, savvy employers often peruse Facebook and MySpace to search for inflammatory information on job applicants. According to the National Association of Colleges and Employers (2009), over half of all employers utilize online sites to screen applicants, and some companies admonish current employees who write negative comments about their employer online. Instructors will want to encourage students to practice discretion and common sense when posting online, as well as utilizing rubric guidelines to explain what constitutes an acceptable online post.

Using Communication Tools in Distance Learning Reinforces Good Teaching Practice

The American Distance Education Consortium (ADEC, 1999) outlines several guiding principles for distance learning teaching. The first principle states, "The principles that lend themselves to quality face-to-face learning

environments are often similar to those found in web-based environments."
Widely accepted throughout higher education today, the seminal work of
Chickering and Gamson (1987), *The Seven Principles of Good Practice in Undergraduate Education*, identifies specific approaches and attitudes necessary
for effective teaching. The practices are:

1. Good practice encourages student–faculty contact.
2. Good practice encourages cooperation among students.
3. Good practice encourages active learning.
4. Good practice gives prompt feedback.
5. Good practice emphasizes time on task.
6. Good practice communicates high expectations.
7. Good practice respects diverse talents and ways of learning.

Obviously, new or altered strategies are needed to ensure that these
principles are practiced in a distance learning/teaching setting. The principles were revised in a later paper, *Implementing the Seven Principles: Technology as Lever* (Chickering and Ehrman, 1998), to address the unique aspects
of the distance learning environment, but the underlying premises of these
important guideposts remain. The Institute for Higher Education Policy, in
cooperation with the National Education Association, released its *Quality
on the Line* report in 2000. The report identified 45 specific benchmarks for
success in internet-based distance education, all of which support Chickering and Gamson principles, and several of which focus on effective communication strategies.

Best Practices

The previous section offered general tips for using communication tools.
The focus of this section is the seven principles of best practice identified
by Chickering and Gamson and the communications-related benchmarks
identified in the *Quality on the Line* (QotL) report. Each principle and corresponding QotL benchmark is listed in Tables 4.6, 4.7, 4.8, 4.9, 4.10, 4.11,
and 4.12, with specific suggestions for utilizing LMS system communication
tools and outside communication tools to facilitate practice and accomplishment of the principle, with the overarching goal of improving student
performance.

TABLE 4.6   Best Practice 1: Student–Instructor Interaction

Linked to:

C&G Principle 1: Good practice encourages student–faculty contact.

Quality on the Line Benchmark 14: Student interaction with faculty is facilitated through a variety of ways.

Quality on the Line Benchmark 17: Feedback to students is provided in a manner that is constructive and non-threatening.

Quality on the Line Benchmark 21: Class voice-mail and/or email systems are provided to encourage students to work with each other and their instructor(s).

There is a direct correlation between instructors that actively communicate with their students, as well as provide course materials in a variety of formats, and better course evaluations (New Jersey Institute of Technology, 2005).

Tool	Strategies and Tips for Utilizing the Communication Tool
Chat	Conduct an initial chat session during the first week of class as a "kick-off" or orientation to the course. Use the first chat session to emphasize your syllabus and other pertinent course information, as well as to set forth your expectations. Provide ample time for a Q&A session. As a follow-up to the initial chat session, have a scavenger hunt planned. Post questions about where to find information in your course, and require students to search, navigate, and learn the design and set-up of your course in order to respond with their answers.
	Hold virtual office hours so students can "visit" (schedule virtual office hours weekly).
	Use chat as an introduction (assessment of background knowledge) for a concept or topic. Call on students in the chat to share their experiences or to ask questions for clarification.
	Chat is beneficial as a follow-up or wrap-up on a unit or project. Ask students to reflect on the experience: (1) What do they know now that they did not before? (2) What is still unclear? (3) What would they like to know more about?
	Keep the course's and students' momentum flowing by having intermittent chat sessions several times during the semester. Find out what students are *really* attending to, learning, and finding interesting. Assess their comprehension of concepts that were covered a few weeks earlier. How are they tying it in to current learning? Please note that if you choose to use chat sessions in this manner, you need to make sure that scheduled chat dates and times are included in your course syllabus.

(continued)

TABLE 4.6   Best Practice 1: Student–Instructor Interaction (cont.)

Tool	Strategies and Tips for Utilizing the Communication Tool
Discussion	Use an Introduction topic to break the ice and get students familiar with posting to the discussion board, as well as "meeting" each other in cyberspace. Start by introducing yourself and, perhaps, post a picture. Then, have students post a picture of themselves and share information about their background, hobbies, interests, families, work, etcetera.
	Encourage students to use discussions to post questions about the course or assignment(s). Chances are that other students may have similar questions, as well. By using the discussion board, you only need to respond once instead of needing to respond to several emails asking the same question. You may want to create a special discussion area for these types of postings, such as a "Student Lounge."
	When using the discussion board, post a "starter" question or "prompt" regarding a specific topic. Provide feedback to students on their responses. How frequently you respond, and to what extent you guide the discussion is up to you.
	At the end of the period allowed for discussion responses, summarize the points, discoveries, and conclusions offered by students. Post a final summary to the discussion board and email students, letting them know that your final comments have been posted. Also, let them know that this information may be utilized in quizzes or other types of assessments or assignments.
Mail	The ways in which learners are assessed and evaluated powerfully affect the ways they study and learn. Provide private, extensive feedback on progress via the mail tool.
	When providing information regarding an assignment or course activity, include specific instructions, attachments to be used as additional resources, and links to other website resources in your emails.
	As mentioned above, the mail tool can be used to attach files to send to students. But for files that you want to make available to the entire class, consider posting them on the discussion board.
	You may decide to use the mail tool for students to submit assignments with written responses. Ask students to put the same subject in the subject line so that you may compile and download the assignments quickly.
	It may be helpful to emphasize to students that the mail tool is used for private questions regarding grades and other private issues, while the discussion board is a public forum.

Tool	Strategies and Tips for Utilizing the Communication Tool
Calendar	Many instructors use the calendar as a course organizer, outlining each day's activities and directing students to content documents located in a content module (Web Resources Staff, Georgia State University, 2002).
	Allowing students to make public entries can accommodate communication regarding activities such as group meetings, sign-ups with an instructor, and scheduled chats.
Wikis	Wikis are an excellent collaborative tool, enabling instructors to edit student posts, thereby providing constructive feedback. Especially useful in writing classes, a wiki can be used for students to post drafts that the instructor can edit and provide commentary on, following which the student can then make revisions based on the feedback.
	An instructor may find a wiki useful in group project management. Having students keep a log in the wiki of group work and completed tasks helps instructors chart the group progress in completing the project.
	Blog use is similar to discussion forum activities, with the added advantage of being more fluid and less structured, since discussion boards are usually threaded. Blogs can be used as an introductory activity to establish a level of comfort and familiarity with students. Start the blog with your own introduction, modeling how you expect students to contribute to the conversation. Share an interesting or amusing fact about yourself, and ask students to do the same.
Blogs	Blogs can serve as a "water cooler" or "student lounge" where learners can "hang out" and talk about topics of interest to them, in addition to course-related questions, suggestions, and tips. This type of communication helps build the community of learners so valuable in social learning.
	Like the discussion board, posting a question prompt helps students to get started. Be sure to provide prompt initial feedback. How frequently you respond, and to what extent you guide the discussion, is up to you.
	Blogs can serve as personal journals where students can post their reactions to course material, progress in attaining skill and competency, and relate current learning to prior knowledge. Instructors can choose to make personal commentary on individual student contributions.
	This form of synchronous communication is particularly effective as virtual office hours.

(continued)

TABLE 4.6   Best Practice 1: Student–Instructor Interaction (cont.)

Tool	Strategies and Tips for Utilizing the Communication Tool
Web Conferencing	Web conferencing is an excellent mode for providing mentoring and/or tutoring to struggling students.
	Instructors can utilize Web conferencing tools to work with student groups as they progress through a group collaborative project.
	Students post topic drafts, tentative ideas, and hypotheses, and receive immediate feedback from instructor.
Twitter	Twitter can be used as a "One Minute Paper" for students to state their perception/understanding of the main ideas of a concept, lecture, reading, etcetera; instructors provide feedback to confirm or correct student comprehension.
	Borrowing from the "Muddiest Point" strategy, students succinctly state what they are confused about or need more information on; instructor provides clarifying feedback.

TABLE 4.7   Best Practice 2: Student–Student Interaction

Linked to:

C&G Principle 2: Good practice encourages cooperation among students.

Quality on the Line Benchmark 15: Student interaction with other students is facilitated through a variety of ways.

Quality on the Line Benchmark 21: Class voice-mail and/or email systems are provided to encourage students to work with each other and their instructor(s).

Quality on the Line Benchmark 22: Courses are designed to require students to work in groups, utilizing problem-solving activities in order to develop topic understanding.

Quality on the Line Benchmark 23: Course materials promote collaboration among students.

Just as important as interaction between teachers and learners in promoting learning and achievement is interaction among learners. The isolatory nature of online learning makes dialogue between students in online courses particularly significant. Additionally, students benefit from the experiences and knowledge of their classmates.

Tool	Strategies and Tips for Communication Tool Utilization
Chat	The chat tool can be used to facilitate online group work by allowing student teams to conduct "brainstorming" sessions in real time, as well as to plan future sessions and prepare final projects.

Tool	Strategies and Tips for Communication Tool Utilization
	Use chat for group or class projects to enable real-time discussion of topics, crafting of group goals, division of labor, and assignment of tasks.
Discussion	If a discussion question requires an "in favor" response or an "against" response, divide the class in half and ask each half to post a response that favors one side or the other. Then ask students to post responses to other students that defend their positions.
	Role-playing or assigning roles to students often makes for interesting discussion. Ask students to respond to a discussion question or statement from a particular perspective by taking on a persona that is not their own. This will require them to step into the shoes of others and will help them gain insight into multiple perspectives.
	When utilizing the discussion board with large classes, divide students into teams and have the requirement that students post and respond to only the topic for their team. Periodically throughout the semester, rotate teams so that each student has the benefit of perspectives from many course participants.
	By creating private discussion areas for students working collaboratively on a project, they are provided a space for team discussions that are not restricted by time (not in real time).
	Encourage students to use discussions to post questions about the course or assignment(s). Chances are that other students will have similar questions. By using the discussion board, you only need to respond once, instead of needing to respond to several emails asking the same question. You may want to create a special discussion area for these types of postings, such as a "Student Lounge."
	One of the main purposes for using the discussion board is to assist communication between students. In light of this, you may want to choose to have a passive role in the discussions by posting a response to students only when you need to re-focus their attention back to the discussion topic or when a student question goes unanswered.
	When using the discussion board in your course, post a "starter" question regarding a course topic. Design discussion questions that are open-ended (who, what, when, where, how), relevant to the course content, and of interest to students.
	Appoint students, individually or in pairs, to facilitate different discussion topics. Have each student/team post a summary of the messages once the discussion topic is closed.

(continued)

TABLE 4.7 Best Practice 2: Student–Student Interaction (cont.)

Tool	Strategies and Tips for Communication Tool Utilization
	The discussion tool can be used to attach files for the entire class to view, or to post a website that you want every student to read.
Mail	Mail is an excellent communication tool for student group work. Students can keep each other informed, pass along ideas, communicate progress, ask questions, and arrange group meetings.
Wikis	Students can contribute ideas and post media files to a wiki, with the goal of producing a storyboard that culminates in a completed media project, such as a video or animation.
	Working in teams, students tackle components of a research question or case study and post their individual findings to the wiki; through further collaboration via the wiki, students refine their writings and make decisions on what the final report should look like and the information it will contain.
	In small groups or as a whole-class project, students participate in the contribution, review, and editing of the needs assessment survey, analysis of results, and formulation of plan based on analysis; students participate to input information that contributes to the understanding and application of the shared information in producing a holistic marketing plan.
	Wikis are excellent sounding boards for solving math problems or puzzles. Students can try out various theories and solutions in the wiki, where trial and error remains visible and traceable.
Blogs	The free-flow style of blogging, which resembles face-to-face conversation, is useful in connecting students for introductory course activities, reflective sharing, and group projects. Students can also use blogs as a self-publishing site and invite critique from their peers.
Twitter	Students use tweets to send out questions and/or observations to group on assigned readings.
	Students can post and analyze tweets to communicate and compare events and perspectives with peers across the world.
Web Conferencing	Similar to the chat tool, Web conferencing allows real-time brainstorming for group projects so that student teams can plan and discuss project tasks.
	Web conferencing is dynamic for facilitating synchronous student discussion of lecture topics and quiz/test reviews.
Social Networking	Social networking is another option for student collaboration enhancing understanding of important course concepts. Students can share ideas, creations, and receive feedback from their peers. It can be useful for group projects and media presentations.

TABLE 4.8   Best Practice 3: Using Active Learning Strategies

Linked to:

C&G Principle 3: Good practice encourages active learning.

Quality on the Line Benchmark 9: During course development, the various learning styles of students are considered.

Quality on the Line Benchmark 10: Assessment instruments are used to ascertain the specific learning styles of students, which then determine the type of course delivery.

Quality on the Line Benchmark 20: Each module/segment requires students to engage themselves in analysis, synthesis, and evaluation as part of their course assignments.

Quality on the Line Benchmark 22: Courses are designed to require students to work in groups utilizing problem-solving activities in order to develop topic understanding.

Quality on the Line Benchmark 23: Course materials promote collaboration among students.

Quality on the Line Benchmark 28: Students are instructed in the proper methods of effective research, including assessment of resource validity.

Learning is not a passive activity. Students need to have opportunities to activate prior knowledge, connect learning to themselves and the outside world, and reflect on the learning experience through talking and writing about the learning.

Tool	Strategies and Tips for Communication Tool Utilization
Chat	The chat tool provides a vehicle for students to provide rapid feedback to the instructor. Students who may be initially uncomfortable with the online learning platform will be more at ease, since online "chatting" is something that many students do outside of the educational environment. In addition, it promotes active learning by allowing students to reflect on their own learning.
	Although the chat tool favors verbal and social learners and fast typists with good English skills, chat also may be beneficial to shy or withdrawn students who would normally not participate in a traditional class, but feel safe offering opinions in cyberspace
	Use the chat tool to provide a platform for guest speakers. If you use the chat tool for guest speakers, make sure that students prepare their questions in advance.
Discussion	Utilize the discussion to facilitate an online debate; pose a question and ask students to take sides posting their arguments for or against. Require students to cite sources in their arguments.

(continued)

TABLE 4.8   Best Practice 3: Using Active Learning Strategies (cont.)

Tool	Strategies and Tips for Communication Tool Utilization
	Have students post a summary of their work in discussion and attach their paper, PowerPoint, project, etcetera for class critique/response.
	Divide the class into learning groups and create separate discussion sections for each group.
Mail	Students can utilize mail as a journal by emailing reflective pieces to themselves and copying the instructor.
	Encourage students to utilize mail for group problem solving.
Wikis	Students build an FAQ for the next group of students taking the class.
	Divide the class into learning groups with assignments to create step-by-step instructions for a specific process or application; student contributions in the wiki build an online tutorial.
	Ask students to contribute important terms with definitions to the wiki, with the goal of creating a glossary.
Blogs	Improve literacy skills by having students read an article each week and then contribute their opinion in a blog, connecting the article to course concepts.
	Post a beginning to a story, and then ask students to create additional plot concepts and details, with the goal of creating a class story.
Twitter	Students can follow industry and media leaders to stay up-to-date on news, current affairs, and latest trends and developments.
	Compare events and perspectives with peers across the world.
	Students analyze tweets to assess opinion, examine consensus, determine patterns of thought, and find outlying ideas.
Social Networking	Ask students to create a MySpace or Facebook profile on a historical or literary figure.
	Use a social network to market a product.

TABLE 4.9   Best Practice 4: Prompt Feedback

Linked to:

C&G Principle 4: Good practice gives prompt feedback.

Quality on the Line Benchmark 16: Feedback to student assignments and questions is provided in a timely manner.

Quality on the Line Benchmark 26: Faculty members are required to grade and return all assignments within a certain time period.

The ways in which learners are assessed and evaluated powerfully affect the ways they study and learn. The chat, mail, and discussion tools each provide unique mediums for rich feedback that is frequent and timely.

Tool	Strategies and Tips for Communication Tool Utilization
Chat	Praise students publicly on outstanding observations and information shared in a chat session or discussion posting.
Discussion	Praise students publicly on outstanding observations and information shared in a chat session or discussion posting.
Mail	Offer words of encouragement to students that are struggling. Contact students early on to correct or re-direct their efforts.
Wikis	The editing features of wikis allow instructors to provide specific feedback to student posts.
Blogs	As in discussion, use the blog to comment on students' accomplishments; public praise is highly motivating.
Twitter	Succinctly offer specific commentary to students.
Social Networking	Provide media files or links to articles and websites that might helpful or of interest to specific students.

TABLE 4.10   Best Practice 5: Emphasis on Time on Task

Linked to:

C&G Principle 5: Good practice emphasizes time on task.

Quality on the Line Benchmark 19: The modules/segments are of varying lengths determined by the complexity of learning outcomes.

Quality on the Line Benchmark 25: Specific expectations are set for students with respect to a minimum amount of time per week for study and homework assignments.

Helping students stay organized can positively impact their learning. The calendar tool provides a format for organization, and can help students reduce the overall time they spend searching for information. As such, students have more time to devote to course assignments.

Tool	Strategies and Tips for Communication Tool Utilization
Calendar	Use the calendar as a course organizer, outlining each day's activities and directing students to content documents located in a content module (Web Resources Staff, Georgia State University, 2002).
	Some students may want to use the calendar tool as a personal organizer by making private entries that provide personal organization, appointments, and reminders.
	Allowing students to make public entries can accommodate communication regarding activities such as group meetings, sign-ups with an instructor, and scheduled chats.
	Use the calendar consistently; otherwise, it will become ineffective. Define the role of the calendar in the course to students and then be consistent in its use.

(continued)

TABLE 4.10   Best Practice 5: Emphasis on Time on Task (cont.)

Tool	Strategies and Tips for Communication Tool Utilization
Web 2.0 Tools (i.e., blog, Twitter, wiki)	All of the Web 2.0 tools encourage students to engage in self-directed learning. When participation in blogging, tweeting, or building a wiki is required, the instructor should provide a rubric that communicates expectations for specific levels of participation.

TABLE 4.11   Best Practice 6: Communication of High Expectations

Linked to:

C&G Principle 6: Good practice communicates high expectations.

Quality on the Line Benchmark 18: Courses are separated into self-contained segments that can be used to assess student mastery before moving forward in the course or program.

Quality on the Line Benchmark 25: Specific expectations are set for students with respect to a minimum amount of time per week for study and homework assignments.

Quality on the Line Benchmark 28: Students are instructed in the proper methods of effective research, including assessment of resource validity.

Quality on the Line Benchmark 29: Before starting the program, students are advised about the program to determine if they have the self-motivation and commitment to learn at a distance.

Just as knowledge of course/assignment goals are important to students' ability to achieve desired learning objectives, instructor standards must be communicated for students to understand the level of effort required for success. Use the chat, mail, and discussion tools to communicate goals, expectations, and to answer students' questions.

Tool	Strategies and Tips for Communication Tool Utilization
Chat	Conduct a chat session at the beginning of the semester to share expectations, clarify policies, and answer questions. Provide chat guidelines for the purpose of reminding students that the same "rules" that apply to in-class discussions (respect, appropriate language, etc.) also apply to online discussion.
Mail	Email learning contracts to students. Require students to email you at certain points in the semester to share how they feel they are progressing in the course. Provide specific feedback on assignments—what was exemplary or what needs improvement.

Tool	Strategies and Tips for Communication Tool Utilization
Discussion	Provide examples of high-quality work as attachments, and explain why you feel the work is exceptional.
	Celebrate students' successes by publicly praising them (or the group). Be specific about what the accomplishment is.
	Expect students to participate. Make participation part of their grade. Provide a rubric that outlines how they will earn points through discussion.
	Include Web addresses or information on supplemental readings to support course material.
Calendar	Include assignment due dates on calendar.
	Post benchmarks on the calendar, such as where students should be with course readings, content, or projects at a certain point in time.
Blog	Use the blog at the beginning of the semester to share expectations, clarify policies, and answer questions.
	Expect students to participate. Make participation part of their grade. Provide a rubric that outlines how they will earn points through blogging.
	Specific feedback can be provided that pinpoints what was exemplary or needs improvement.
	Provide links to examples of high-quality work with explanations of why the work is exceptional.
	Celebrate students' successes by publicly praising them (or the group). Be specific about what the accomplishment is.
Wiki	Expect students to participate. Make participation part of their grade. Provide a rubric that outlines how they will earn points with their wiki contributions. Demonstrate what are, and are not, acceptable wiki contributions.
	Edit student work in the wiki, making specific note of how the contribution was not accurate, and or what was exceptionally good about the contribution.

TABLE 4.12   Best Practice 7: Respects Diversity

Linked to:

C&G Principle 7: Good practice respects diverse talents and ways of knowing.

Quality on the Line Benchmark 9: During course development, the various learning styles of students are considered.

Quality on the Line Benchmark 10: Assessment instruments are used to ascertain the specific learning styles of students, which then determine the type of course delivery.

(continued)

TABLE 4.12   Best Practice 7: Respects Diversity (cont.)

Allowing students to access and utilize a variety of communication tools supports various learning styles and intelligence types. To accommodate the different learning styles and intelligence types, it is important for instructors to provide a variety of ways for students to demonstrate their learning. It is easy to recognize that communication tools can be used for a variety of assessment activities.

Tool	Strategies and Tips for Communication Tool Utilization
Chat	Oral exams benefit those with auditory learning styles and strong verbal/interpersonal intelligence types.
	Utilizing guest speakers exposes students to different presentation styles.
Mail	Oral exams.
	Reflective posting provides students with the opportunity to internalize the course content.
	Including attachments of media files in various formats serves to accommodate the different learning styles and intelligence types of students.
Discussion	Reflective posting provides students with the opportunity to internalize the course content.
	Including attachments of media files in various formats serves to accommodate the different learning styles and intelligence types of students.
	Utilizing guest speakers exposes students to different presentation styles.
	Shy students benefit from asynchronous discussion.
	Reflective learners have the opportunity to compose their thoughts, think about what they have written, edit, and refine their ideas and opinions before sharing with the group.
Web Conferencing	Utilizing guest speakers exposes students to different presentation styles.
	Synchronous discussions are compatible with auditory and interpersonal learning preferences.
Blogs	Blogging appeals to learners with a strong verbal/linguistic style.
	Shy students benefit from asynchronous blogging activities.
	The self-reflective style of blogging is encouraging for students with a strong intrapersonal style.
Twitter	Students who are naturally kinesthetic and/or analytic may enjoy the analysis of ideas and observations that accompanies the activity of frequent tweeting.
Social Networking	Because of the variety of tools and functions available, including multimedia options, social networking has wide appeal to all learning style preferences.

Using Communication Tools to Facilitate Collaborative
Learning Activities

Current research indicates that all students need the opportunity to share their ideas, questions, and comments in small groups and in whole-class discussions. These types of communication allow students to (1) share knowledge, (2) compare their thoughts to those of their classmates, (3) reflect on ideas, (4) provide feedback to each other, (5) internalize the course content, (6) clarify questions, (7) positively interact with classmates and instructor, and (8) have their interest in course topics stimulated. Communication tools are essential for providing interactive opportunities for students.

Collaborative learning is important in distance learning courses, and most LMS systems provide the tools needed to facilitate collaborative activities. As previously stated, discussion boards, chat rooms, and email are the most common tools used to facilitate online communication. Today, communication outside of the LMS is common in many distance learning courses. Many instructors are choosing to use external blogs, wikis, Twitter, video conferencing, audio conferencing, and social networking sites as a means to deliver course content and assess student learning. All of these tools are effective for student collaboration.

The following provides information regarding specific online collaborative communication strategies that can be used with any of the communication tools included in or external to the LMS. Step-by-step instructions are provided with each strategy, and the strategies are listed from the most simple to facilitate, to the most complex. We encourage instructors to use different tools to communicate. Most of the strategies below utilize a combination of communication tools. Note that some of the activities below require scheduled online "chat" sessions. It is important to plan carefully, so that you can include all scheduled chat sessions in your syllabus. It would be unfair to surprise students with an impromptu chat date and time, as they may have work and family schedules that prevent them from participating.

Talking Text

The purpose of *Talking Text* is to provide opportunities for students to ask clarifying questions directly to the instructor regarding the text or other assigned readings. The *Talking Text* strategy can be used with chat rooms, discussion forums, blogs, or Twitter.

1. Chat Room: Instructors may wish to schedule several *Talking Text* chat sessions during the course.
   a. Create a *Talking Text* chat room.

     b. Use email to remind students of the scheduled date(s) and time(s) of the *Talking Text* chat session(s).

     c. Conduct the chat session(s) and post the chat log to those with an excused absence.

  2. Discussion Forum

     a. Create a *Talking Text* discussion forum topic.

     b. Use email or announcements to ask a specific question regarding the required reading(s).

     c. Monitor the discussion forum and provide feedback to student responses.

  3. Create a *Talking Text* blog. (A user-friendly blog site is Blogger, located at www.blogger.com.)

     a. Post a specific question regarding the required reading(s) to the blog. Attach a rubric to guide students in their responses.

     b. Monitor the blog and provide feedback to student responses.

  4. Twitter

     a. It is not necessary to create an account on Twitter.com in order to use the "twitter" strategy in your course. (However, feel free to do so and encourage your students to do so.) Instead, use the discussion forum to facilitate the twitter activity. The twitter strategy allows instructors to evaluate their students' ability to succinctly summarize or respond to a specific topic and to determine student understanding of the main concept.

     b. Post a specific question regarding the required reading(s) to the discussion forum.

     c. Provide specific instructions for student responses, allowing students to respond to the question with a maximum of 146 characters.

     d. Since the responses are short, ask students to read all posts and to select the best three and include justifications for their selections. (Students can email their votes to the instructor.)

     e. Post the names of winners in the discussion forum or via email.

Peering In

    Peering In provides a forum for students to share their work and ideas in order to receive feedback/suggestions from their peers. The *Peering In* strategy can be used with discussion forums or blogs.

  1. Discussion Forum

     a. Create a *Peering In* discussion board category/topic for the specific assignment.

    b. Via email, or as part of the assignment instructions, require students to post "first drafts" of their work in order to receive feedback/suggestions from their peers.

    c. Provide a rubric for students to use to evaluate the work of their peers.

    d. Use email or post an announcement to request that students review the work of their classmates and to offer suggestions based on the rubric criteria.

    e. *Note.* Most of the feedback should come from other students, not the instructor.

2. Blog

    a. Create a *Peering In* blog category/topic for the specific assignment.

    b. Via email, or as part of the assignment instructions, require students to post "first drafts" of their work in order to receive feedback/suggestions from their peers.

    c. Provide a rubric for students to use to evaluate the work of their peers.

    d. Use email or post an announcement to request that students review the work of their classmates and to offer suggestions based on the rubric criteria.

    e. *Note.* Most of the feedback should come from other students, not the instructor.

TEST: It doesn't have to be a Four-letter Word

TEST: It doesn't have to be a Four-letter Word provides opportunities for students to receive extra practice in skills needed in a course, or to receive study assistance for an upcoming exam or quiz. The *TEST* strategy can be used with chat rooms, discussion forums, blogs, video conferencing, or audio conferencing. Below are instructions for using *TEST* with three of the tools.

1. Chat Room

    a. Create a *Test* chat room (for synchronous communication).

    b. Use email to remind students of the scheduled test review chat session.

    c. Use the session to answer student questions and to provide study tips.

    d. Be prepared to pose questions to the students as a means to focus their attention to certain topics.

2. Web Conference

    a. Schedule an optional video conference session. (*Note:* Include in the course syllabus that optional video conferences will be made available to students as a means to review for a test.)

   b. Use email and post an announcement to provide students with the conference date and time.
   c. Use the conference session to answer student questions and to provide study tips.
   d. Be prepared to pose questions to the students as a means of focusing their attention on certain topics.
3. Discussion Forum
   a. Create a Test Review discussion board (for asynchronous communication).
   b. Prior to a test, use email to remind students to post their questions regarding the content to be included on the test.
   c. Ask that questions be posted at least 48 hours in advance of the test, so that timely responses can be provided.

FAQ—What's on Your Mind?

If your goal is to provide a forum for students to post questions and to receive responses/answers from classmates, then *FAQ* is the perfect activity. The *FAQ* strategy can be used for any course content. The instructor should monitor the forum in order to correct any incorrect information that may be given. Note that specific instructions should be provided to students regarding appropriate uses for *FAQ*. The *FAQ* strategy can be used with discussion forums, wikis, or blogs.

1. Discussion Forum
   a. Create a FAQ discussion forum.
   b. Group students into teams of four, and use email to notify students of whom they are teamed with. Or, depending on the institution's LMS, use a group management tool to allow students to sign up for teams.
   c. Each team is assigned a specific week to monitor the FAQ discussion forum and to post responses to questions. For example, Team 1 can monitor the board during week 1. Team 2 can monitor the board during week 2, and so on.
   d. Students can post questions regarding required readings, assignments, due dates, or any other course content, policies, or procedures deemed appropriate.
   e. By the end of the semester, each team should have the opportunity to monitor the FAQ board three or four times.
2. Wiki
   a. Create a FAQ wiki. (An open-source wiki site is www.wetpaint. com.)

b. Group students into teams of four, and use email to notify students of whom they are teamed with. Or, depending on the institution's LMS, use a group management tool to allow students to sign up for teams.

c. Each team is assigned a specific week to monitor the FAQ wiki and to post responses to questions. For example, Team 1 can monitor the wiki during week 1. Team 2 can monitor the board during week 2, and so on.

d. The team that is monitoring the wiki will be required to respond to classmates' questions posted on the wiki. Each team member will be required to respond to each question and must be required to post an original comment, building upon the comments previously posted by team members.

e. Students can post questions regarding required readings, assignments, due dates, or any other course content, policies, or procedures deemed appropriate.

f. By the end of the semester, each team should have the opportunity to monitor the FAQ wiki three or four times.

3. Blog

a. Create a FAQ blog.

b. Group students into teams of four, and use email to notify students of whom they are teamed with. Or, depending on the institution's LMS, use a group management tool to allow students to sign up for teams.

c. Each team is assigned a specific week to monitor the FAQ blog and to post responses to questions. For example, Team 1 can monitor the wiki during week 1. Team 2 can monitor the board during week 2, and so on.

d. The team that is monitoring the blog will be required to respond to classmates' questions posted on the blog. Each team member will take turns posting responses to questions until their week is finished.

e. Students can post questions regarding required readings, assignments, due dates, or any other course content, policies, or procedures deemed appropriate.

f. By the end of the semester, each team should have the opportunity to monitor the FAQ blog three or four times.

Partner Interviews

The purpose of *Partner Interviews* is to provide opportunities for students to exchange ideas/knowledge with each other. This activity provides the option for students to use email, discussion, or chat. Or, the entire activity can be done in wiki format.

1. Email, Discussion, Chat
   a. Pair students and use email to notify them of the newly formed partnerships.
   b. Create an Interview discussion board and an Interview chat room.
   c. Provide the class with a topic.
   d. Ask students to use the communication tool of their choice (email, discussion board, or chat) to communicate with their partner.
   e. Partner #1 interviews partner #2 by asking two questions about the topic and makes note of the responses.
   f. Partner #2 interviews partner #1 by asking two additional questions about the topic and makes note of the responses.
   g. Each partnership uses the discussion board to share a summary of their discussion with the class.
   h. The instructor uses the discussion board or email to provide to the class a summary of all of the partnership responses. At this time, the instructor corrects any misinformation and, if necessary, posts a follow-up question.
2. Wiki
   a. Pair students and use email to notify them of the newly formed partnerships.
   b. Create an Interview discussion board and an Interview wiki.
   c. Provide the class with a topic and pose a specific question or questions regarding the topic.
   d. Ask students to use the discussion forum to communicate with their partner. (Each partnership can post a new thread.)
   e. Partners discuss and formulate a response to the question or questions.
   f. Partners post their agreed upon response(s) to the wiki.
   g. Each partnership must contribute an original thought, comment, or researched information regarding the topic/question.
   h. The activity ends when information regarding the question/topic has been exhausted.
   i. Students will quickly see the benefit in posting early; this will encourage participation.
   j. The instructor uses the discussion board or email to provide to the class a summary of all of the partnership responses. At this

time, the instructor corrects any misinformation and, if necessary, posts a follow-up question.

Four Heads Are Better than One

Four Heads are Better than One enables you to confirm that all students in the class understand course content. This activity provides options for using email, discussion forum, blog, and chat.

1. Use email to notify students that teams have been established. Establish teams of four and assign each team member a number from 1 to 4. (Or, depending on the institution's LMS, use the group management tool to allow students to sign up for teams.)
2. Create a discussion forum titled *Four Heads are Better than One.*
3. Post a question to the *Four Heads* discussion forum. The question should be factual in nature, but also require higher-order thinking skills.
4. Ask students to use the communication tool of their choice (email, discussion board, blog, or chat) to communicate with their team members. (Note: The instructor will need to create blog or chat sites if these team options are made available.)
5. Using the communication tool of their choice, each team discusses the question and formulates a response, making sure that every group member knows the agreed-upon answer.
6. Create a *Four Heads* class chat room and use email to remind students of the scheduled chat date and time. (You will want to provide the date and time in your syllabus prior to the beginning of the course.)
7. During the chat, call out a specific number, and each student with that number will act as team spokesperson and provide the team answer to the class. (The benefit of this tactic is that each member of the team will need to be prepared with the answer, which better ensures active participation by all.)
8. A whole-class chat session follows to clarify conflicting answers.

That's Debatable

The purpose of *That's Debatable* is to provide students with opportunities to conduct research regarding a specific topic, take a position on the topic, and defend their position. There are a number of methods you can use to facilitate online debate. In this section, we will focus on two methods: single person and small group.

1. Method One: Single Person
   a. Create a "Pro" discussion board and a "Con" discussion board.
   b. Identify a specific issue that relates to a current course topic.
   c. Identify two students. Assign one student to be "Pro" and the other student to be "Con." You can use the email tool to provide students with this information.
   d. By a specified deadline, the "Pro" student must post his/her argument to the "Pro" discussion board. The "Con" student must post her/his argument to the "Con" discussion board. Each must cite references from the text and/or from outside research that supports his/her position.
   e. The remaining students must read both posts and respond to each by stating agreement or disagreement with the position, as well as why they agree or disagree. Again, the students must cite references from the text and/or outside research that supports their agreement or disagreement.
   f. The two individual debaters are given an opportunity to respond to those who disagree. They must cite additional references to support their positions.
   g. Once the discussion is complete, each student emails the instructor with his/her vote for the debate winner.
   h. Based on the votes received, the instructor emails the class to announce the debate winner. At this time, it is appropriate for the instructor to summarize the main points of both arguments.
   i. Depending on the size and length of the course, if you use this strategy, it is recommended that each student be given the opportunity to participate as the "Pro" or "Con." In addition, it is recommended that the details of this activity be outlined in your course syllabus so that students understand the expectations.
2. Method Two: Small Group
   a. Select two teams of 3–5 students each.
   b. Follow the steps above to complete the debate.
   c. Again, depending on the size and length of the course, each student should be given the opportunity to participate on a debating team.

Picking up the Pieces (online version of Jigsaw)

By using the *Picking up the Pieces* strategy you are able to confirm that students have read and understand important concepts from the text. Notice that in this activity all of the most common LMS communication tools are used.

1. Divide a text chapter into equal sections. The number of sections is equal to the number of teams that you will form in the next step.
2. Group students into home teams of 4 (Team A, Team B, etc.) and assign each student in the team a number (1–4). You can use email to notify students of their team and number.
3. Create a Discussion Board for the 1's, the 2's, etcetera, and create a chat room for each home team: Team A, Team B, etcetera.
4. Use email to notify the students that everyone with the number 1 is assigned to read the first section of the chapter (e.g., pages 64–69). Everyone with the number 2 is assigned to read the second section, and so on. Each student will read his/her assigned pages.
5. After completing the reading, every student with the number 1 will use the *1's discussion board* to identify the main points included in their section. Every student with the number 2 will use the *2's discussion board* to identify the main points included in their section, and so on.
6. Once each member of each group has identified and understands the main points in their section of the reading, they "meet" with their home team in the designated chat room and "teach" their section of the reading to their home team members. During the chat sessions, students have the opportunity to ask questions to each other. (We recommend that you provide an instructor-monitored discussion board for students to post all unanswered questions.)
7. The instructor emails a summary of the main points from the chapter, and also provides answers to the unanswered student questions.

End of Chapter Activities

The end of chapter activities provide opportunities for you to acquire new knowledge, gain skill, and apply principles and concepts. These activities are located on the Companion Website, and are divided into three subsections: Knowledge Building, Skill Building, and Practical Application.

Appendix C

Sample Distance Learning Course Syllabus

Topics in Education – EDU 3110 – Section 53530

The Future: Gaining insight and perspective

Instructor Information

Name: Dr. Chris Smith
Email: csmith@school.edu
Office: Education Building EDU 304
Office Hours: Mon. & Tues. 9–11 am EST (office hours)
                 Mon. & Tues. 7–9 pm EST (virtual chat and email)
Phone: xxx-xxx-xxxx

Getting in touch with me

The quickest way to get my attention is to contact me via the course management system email. I commit to you that I will provide a 24-hour turnaround time (Monday–Friday) on your email questions. I have provided my school email for emergency purposes only (in case the course management system is unavailable). You can also take advantage of my in-office hours or virtual office hours; I will be online in the chat room on Monday and Tuesday evenings from 7 to 9 pm to answer questions and offer additional information on the weekly lessons and assignments via mini-lectures.

Course Description

The Future: Gaining Insight and Perspective

In this course, we review the ways in which we live, work, and learn, and how each are being transformed—from the Internet to biotech, from wireless and nanotech to robotics, from globalization to cultural isolationism. You will explore and discover what trends and issues impact the future of education and society. First mandatory class meeting is on Tuesday, August 29 at 5:30 pm. Other voluntary meetings by appointment; contact me via course email or by phone at xxx-xxxx to schedule an appointment.

Prerequisites

Prior to registration, students must have completed 45 credit hours.

Course Objectives

1. Students will demonstrate their ability to think critically
2. Students will analyze information, reports, and readings to compare, contrast, evaluate, and synthesize information sources

3. Students will demonstrate their ability to express themselves clearly in written and oral communication
4. Students will communicate understanding via an electronic portfolio, discussion, and written reports
5. Students will demonstrate their understanding of global political, social, economic, and historical perspectives
6. Students will utilize critical thinking skills to communicate their findings on historical/futuristic issues
7. Students will demonstrate their ability to use technology to access retrieve, process, and communicate information
8. Students will utilize the Internet to locate information on generational issues, communicate opinions/ideas/information through email and discussion board, and produce an e-portfolio of findings

Required Materials

Textbook: *The Crystal Ball*, 2nd Edition. I.M. Fortunetelling. ISBN 9456789012

This course is multi-modal, with a combination of mandatory class meetings and coursework completed via the course management system. Students will need to have access to a computers with Internet access and Microsoft Office software (Word and PowerPoint). Computers with Microsoft Office are available in the school's open computer labs to communicate and complete coursework through the course management system.

The class is delivered via a course management system. You will take all of your tests through the course management system and send all assignments to your instructor via the course management system. Specific instructions are provided below in the Assignment section. This is a totally paperless class. You will not need to print any assignments. To receive credit for an assignment, it must be turned in through the course management system, as instructed below.

If you have a computer and Internet connection at home, you will be able to access your grades and other data. This site is password protected. Your instructor will provide you with the URL and your username and password. Your instructor will demonstrate how to use this program. If you do not have a computer with Internet access at home, you will need to use computers in one of the computer labs.

Several of the assignments involve multimedia files; you will need to have Quicktime and Real Player on your computer. If you do not have them on your computer, you will need to download them. These are free downloads. Instructions are provided in the START HERE section of the course homepage.

Policies and Procedures

- The "course" week begins on a Monday
- Assignments are due by midnight (eastern standard time) on Sunday
- All assignments should be saved as follows: Studentname_assignmentname
- Written reports should be completed in APA style (American Psychological Association)

Course Withdrawal

You must take the Attendance Survey (click on Surveys on the course Homepage) by September 13 to avoid being withdrawn by the instructor for non-attendance.

Last day to withdraw from class and receive a full refund is **September 8**, or to receive a withdrawal grade of W is **September 29**.

It is your responsibility to turn drop forms in to the Admissions, Registration, and Records (AR&R) Office by the deadline date. A withdrawal from a course may affect your athletic eligibility, financial aid, veterans' benefits, as well as benefits received from other federal agencies.

If you do not officially withdraw by the deadline date, a letter grade other than a "W" must be assigned to the grade report by the instructor. This will affect your grade point average (GPA). If you decide to stop attending class, do yourself a favor and officially withdraw from the course.

Assignments and Projects

There are a variety of assignments. Detailed information about each assignment can be found on the course homepage under Assignments. Assignments are as follows:

Discussions: 1 @ 10 points; 2 @ 20 points each	50 points
E-portfolio: a collection of the following:	50 points
written report, PowerPoint, timeline, flyer,	
and Bibliography (annotated list of references)	
Attendance Survey	5 points
Course Survey	5 points
Total Points	*110 points*

Rubric for Grading E-portfolio:

Written report of future topic (list of topics to be provided;	
Minimum 1200 words, plus references)	20 points

PowerPoint (6 slide minimum, contains at least three
   Graphics and/or photos, contains at least one sound or
   music file)   10 points

Timeline (issue related to research topic)   10 points

Flyer (produced in Word or Publisher; captures
   the salient research points and includes photo
   or graphic)   5 points
Annotated bibliography of resources   5 points

Grading Scale
Pass/Fail

To achieve a passing grade, you must acquire points in each component (Discussion, Written Report, PowerPoint, Timeline, Flyer, Bibliography, Presentation, Surveys) and earn at least 70 points.

Course Participation

- Participation is a strong component of the course. It is in the sharing of discovery, opinion, and experiences that we learn much from each other. Students should login to the course several times per week.
- Discussion postings are part of the course grade. Guidance on the amount and length of postings and examples of appropriate postings are provided in Assignments on the course homepage.
- A grading rubric for discussions showing how points are earned for discussion responses is available in Assignments on the course homepage.
- It is recommended that the initial posting for the week's discussion be made by Wednesday, with follow-ups every other day thereafter.

Timeline
A detailed timeline is available in Assignments located on the course homepage.

Week One	Introduction and initial discussion posting
Week Two–Four	Module One: Read chap 1–4 in text; discussion
	Module Two: Read chapters 5 & 6 in text; PowerPoint, Flyer assignments
Week Nine–Eleven	Module Three: Read chapter 7 in text
Week Twelve	Module Four: Written report, bibliography, discussion

Tests
This is a project-based course; no tests/exams required.

Academic Honesty
The institution's Academic Dishonesty Policy applies to this course. Please see the Student Handbook if you have questions.

Request for Accommodations
If, to participate in this course, you require an accommodation due to a physical or learning impairment, you must contact the Office of Services to Students with Disabilities. The office is located in the Student Services Building DSTU 208. You may also reach the office by phone at (xxx) xxx-xxxx or by fax at (xxx) xxx-xxxx.

Additional Resources

- The Academic Support Center (ASC) provides comprehensive academic programs and service to help every student reach their academic potential. Programs include tutoring, mentoring, career services, disability services, and veteran services.
- Computing Services supports a wide range of computing services for faculty, staff, and students.
- The library is a gateway of information containing databases, books, journals, and other research materials.

FAQs
Q1   Who can I contact to ask for computer support, report problems, or send comments and suggestions?

A1   Contact the Help Desk, as follows: (Put web address or phone information here.)

Q2   Do I have to attend any on-site class sessions?

A2   (Provide information on required or voluntary class meetings.)

References

American Distance Education Consortium. (1999). *Guiding principles for distance learning*. Retrieved August, 31, 2006. Retrieved July 18, 2006, from http://www.adec.edu/admin/papers/distance-learning_principles.html

Chickering, A.W., and Gamson, Z.F. (1987). Seven principles of good practice in undergraduate education. *Faculty Inventory*. Racine, WI: The Johnson

Foundation, Inc. Retrieved June 19, 2007, from http://learningcommons.evergreed.edu/pdf/fall1987.pdf

Chickering, A.W., and Ehrman, S.C. (1998). *Implementing the seven principles: Technology as lever*, American Association for Higher Education . Retrieved Jun 19, 2007 from http://www.tltgroup.org/programs/seven.html

Houle, C.O. (1974). *The design of education*. San Francisco, CA: Jossey Bass Publishers.

National Association of Colleges and Employers (2009). *Employer interest in social networking grows*. Retrieved July 28, 2009, from http://www.naceweb.org/

National Education Association (2002). *Quality on the line report*. Retrieved May 14, 2007, from www2.nea.org/he/abouthe/images/Quality.pdf

New Jersey Institute of Technology (2005, February). *Online classroom*. Madison, WI: Magna Publications.

The Ultimate WebCT Handbook (2002). Web Resources Staff, Georgia State University. Retrieved October 9, 2006 from http://www.webct.com/communities/viewpage?name=ask_drc_ultimate_webct_handbook

5

Assessment Doesn't Have to be a Four Letter Word: TEST!

Numerous studies have demonstrated the importance of formative assessment and frequent and timely feedback in the learning process. Throughout this chapter, a myriad of assessment strategies is explored. Some of these approaches you will recognize as common practices in the traditional classroom, while other methods of alternative assessment may be less well known. The overriding goal of Chapter 5 is to provide solid explanations of a variety of assessment activities that help students and instructors benefit from the teaching/learning experience. Upon completion of Chapter 5, readers will be able to:

1. Define assessment, evaluation, feedback, summative assessment, and formative assessment
2. Describe the assessment process
3. Discuss the importance of utilizing rubrics
4. Design a rubric to assess student achievement of learning goals on a specific assignment
5. Select an alternative assessment strategy to use as part of a unit of instruction
6. Revise a lesson plan to include at least two assessment strategies from Chapter 5
7. Use the Course Planning and Delivery Guide to identify strengths and weaknesses

Fluency in Distance Learning, pages 175–212
Copyright © 2010 by Information Age Publishing
All rights of reproduction in any form reserved.

Assessment Doesn't Have to be a Four-Letter Word . . . TEST!

For most students *and* faculty, assessment is not taken lightly. Instructors are frequently frustrated when they realize—often while grading a major test or final exam—that what they thought they were teaching is not what the student learned. Historically, as Angelo (1991) explains, the assessment of student learning is valuable for both students and instructors:

> The purpose of classroom assessment is to provide faculty and students with information and insights needed to improve teaching effectiveness and learning quality. . . . [I]nstructors use feedback gleaned through classroom assessment to make informed adjustments in their teaching. Faculty also share feedback with students, using it to help them improve their learning strategies and study habits in order to become more independent [and] successful. . . . [C]lassroom assessment is one method of inquiry within the framework of classroom research, a broader approach to improving teaching and learning. (p. 28)

The focus on assessment and accountability of education is not new. Criticism on the gap between what educational institutions teach and the larger world has been a topic of debate for decades. In the first half of the 20th century, education was revered as the centerpiece of democracy. The "how" and "why" of education began to be scrutinized in the early 1970's. While deliberations continue amongst lawmakers as to the appropriate means and systems for conducting educational accountability, instructors must be able to design and employ effective assessment techniques to provide useful information and feedback on classroom instruction and learning outcomes. As the title of the chapter suggests, assessment must not be an infrequent or isolated class experience. Effective assessment is embedded in instruction and used to gather information and insight about students and their learning. DiGesu (no date) characterized six principles of assessment:

1. The primary purpose of assessment is to improve student learning.
2. Assessment practices must be fair and equitable for all students.
3. Communication about assessment is ongoing, clear, and meaningful.
4. Professional development and collaboration support assessment.
5. Students must be actively involved in the assessment process.
6. Assessment practices must be regularly reviewed and refined.

DiGesu explains that the primary purpose of assessment is for students to receive multiple attempts to practice and to demonstrate understanding of content and to develop skills by receiving specific and timely feedback by the instructor in order to improve achievement. With regard to the instructor, the primary purpose of assessment is to analyze student progress for the purpose of modifying and refining the teaching/learning cycle to better meet student needs. The American Association of Higher Education (1992) identified nine principles of quality practice for assessing learning that are still relevant for today's students:

1. The assessment of student learning begins with educational values.
2. Assessment is most effective when it reflects an understanding of learning as multidimensional, integrated, and revealed in performance over time.
3. Assessment works best when the programs it seeks to improve have clear, explicitly stated purposes.
4. Assessment requires attention to outcomes, but also, and equally, to the experiences that lead to those outcomes.
5. Assessment works best when it is ongoing, not episodic.
6. Assessment fosters wider improvement when representatives from across the educational community are involved.
7. Assessment makes a difference when it begins with issues of use and illuminates questions that people really care about.
8. Assessment is most likely to lead to improvement when it is part of a larger set of conditions that promote change.
9. Through assessment, educators meet responsibilities to students and to the public.

The Assessment Process

The assessment process is circular in nature and is continuous. These steps apply, regardless of the type of assessment being used. Assessment can and should be done at various times throughout a course or program, and a comprehensive assessment plan will include all types of assessment. The basic steps in the classroom assessment process are listed below and graphically represented in Figure 5.1.

1. Choose a learning goal to assess.
2. Choose an assessment technique.
3. Implement assessment technique with students.
4. Analyze the data and share the results with students.
5. Adjust instruction based on assessment data.

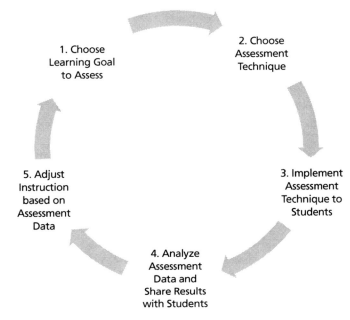

Figure 5.1 The assessment process.

Types of Assessments: Diagnostic, Formative, and Summative

There are three types of assessment. Each type is distinguished by the kinds of questions that it answers. With the exception of some very simple diagnostic tools, the same contexts, methods, and tools can be used to collect date for each of the three types: diagnostic, formative, and summative.

Diagnostic Assessment

Diagnostic assessment occurs at the beginning of the learning cycle. It provides instructors with an understanding of the prior knowledge and skills a student brings to the unit of instruction, as well as the strengths and specific learning needs of an individual or groups of students in relation to performance expectations. Data gathered via diagnostic assessment should not be used for reporting purposes. However, the results can be shared with students.

Formative Assessment

Formative assessment is a learning experience that provides immediate information regarding the student's understanding and/or the ability to apply course concepts. Formative assessments have inherent learning value and rarely involve grading. They are, instead, a tool for instructors to use to modify curricula. DiGesu (no date) characterizes the purposes of formative assessment as helping to keep the instructor and students focused on the purpose of the unit/activity/program, providing information to the instructor and students about progress being made, and determining the effectiveness of instruction in helping students to achieve the purpose. Critical elements of formative assessments include:

1. Specific learning goals and student outcomes
2. Criteria for meeting the learning goals and outcomes
3. Timely feedback from the course instructor
4. Frequent interaction/communication between student and instructor
5. Active learning strategies
6. The willingness of instructors to modify curricula and teaching/learning strategies as needed

Summative Assessment

Although it provides some measure of accountability, some would argue that summative assessment does not necessarily have specific learning value. Summative assessments are cumulative in nature, and usually occur at the end of a topic, unit, or program for the purpose of generating a grade. Traditionally, types of summative assessments include (1) fixed-choice tests (multiple choice, true/false), (2) short answer, and (3) essays. However, recently, and specifically in distance learning courses, alternative forms of summative assessment have been used, including performance tasks, reflective writing, and portfolios. We will explore these alternative types of summative assessments later in this chapter.

The Importance of Rubrics

Regardless of the types and variety of assessments chosen, it is important that students be absolutely clear regarding what they are being evaluated on, expectations for performance, and the format of the evaluation. Research suggests that students who have access to instructional rubrics have more knowledge of the expectations for an assignment and of the criteria by which they will be evaluated, resulting in greater achievement (Goodrich, 1997). A *rubric* is defined as a set of scoring guidelines for evaluation of student work. You will remember that a number of examples were presented in Chapters Three and Four. Basic questions answered by rubrics are:

1. By what criteria will my performance be judged?
2. What are the different levels of quality?

3. How are the levels of quality described?
4. How are the levels of quality quantified?
5. How are they different from each other?

Rubrics are assessment tools that focus on performance of a task or behavior that leads to a final product or learning outcome. Rubrics use objective, specific criteria as a basis for evaluating student achievement. The criteria are provided to students in narrative descriptions separated into possible levels of accomplishment for a given task or behavior. Most rubrics contain a scale of possible points that may be earned by the student. The points are on a continuum of quality, with the highest scores assigned to the best quality work. Each level of performance (i.e., number of points) contains a description of quality required to attain or qualify for that level of points. Scores or ratings can be numerical, such as a point value; qualitative, as in "good" or "poor"; or a combination.

A rubric may apply to a broad category of performance, or specific tasks. For example, the general category of communication may be assessed through a rubric, broken down into specific tasks such as written essay, oral presentation, journal activity, etcetera. Likewise, each specific task can be analyzed and scored via a rubric.

The benefits of using rubrics as an assessment tool are not confined to students. Many instructors consider rubrics to be an objective method of evaluating student performance, often eliminating confusion and questions centered on why a student earned a specific grade. An instructor may choose to create an original rubric that is specific to the task assigned. How-

---

TABLE 5.1 Key Elements of a Rubric

1. Levels of mastery: achievement of learning goals is described in terms such as excellent, good, needs improvement, and unacceptable
2. Dimensions of quality: assessment can address a variety of intellectual or knowledge competencies that target a specific academic discipline or involve multiple disciplines
3. Organizational groupings: students are assessed for their demonstration of multidimensional skills such as teamwork, problem solving, communication, etcetera.
4. Commentaries: a detailed description of the essential elements that should be found in the student's work
5. Descriptions of consequences: a rubric feature that provides students with insight into various lessons regarding their performance in a real-life setting (i.e., professionalism)

ever, a variety of rubric templates and builders exist on the Internet, many of which can be customized to meet the needs of students. Whether using an original rubric or a template, Huba & Freed (2000) suggest that a rubric should contain five key elements, as shown in Table 5.1.

It is important to emphasize that even though many rubrics use points as a means for assessing performance, rubrics are appropriate to use for graded and un-graded assessments. The points system used in the rubric does not necessarily need to translate into points for a grade. Instead, the points can simply be a measure of competency to help students identify areas of strength and areas that require further inquiry.

Subsequent sections within this chapter will outline specific assessment and evaluation strategies appropriate for distance learning courses. Sample rubrics are provided for each of these specific assessment types. In addition, information on the use of rubrics is listed in Table 5.2.

The Value of Providing Feedback: Un-graded Diagnostic and Formative Assessment

The previous section distinguished between diagnostic, formative, and summative assessments. However, additional distinctions are needed to include the differences between assessment, evaluation, and feedback. These distinctions may seem fuzzy at first. To clarify, assessment is a continuous process aimed at improving student learning. In the context of student learning, assessment (a test or assignment) is aimed at improving student learning on explicit tasks or concepts. Evaluation attaches a value (grade) to whatever is being examined, and may use assessment results in drawing conclusions in what is typically a summative appraisal. Evaluation ascribes meaning to whatever was assessed. Feedback is focused on providing infor-

TABLE 5.2 Website Sources for Rubrics

Website	Description
http://school.discovery.com/schrockguide/ assess.html	Variety of rubric templates, rubric builders
http://rubistar.4teachers.org/index.php	Rubistar, free rubric tool
http://www.uwstout.edu/soe/profdev/ rubrics.shtml	Rubrics from the University of Wisconsin
http://rubrics.kon.org/	Rubric samples for higher education
http://condor.depaul.edu/~tla/html/ assessment_resources.html#rubrics	Rubric examples from DePaul University

mation about progress on achieving the goals and objectives attached to specific understanding, application, and/or accomplishment. Most feedback is un-graded; the concept of value or judgment is not part of the feedback process.

Providing feedback is one of the most important responsibilities an instructor has to students. Giving effective and timely feedback is critical in enhancing student learning. Students that receive timely feedback learn and perform better than those that do not receive feedback (University of New South Wales, 2004). Furthermore, students appreciate feedback and identify it as one of the most important qualities of a good instructor. Feedback helps students evaluate their own learning, assisting them to see what they have performed well on and what they need to spend time learning and improving. The benefits of feedback are supported by research; specific, corrective feedback can significantly increase student learning (Lysakowski and Walberg, 1981, 1982; Walberg, 1999; Tennenbaum and Goldring, 1989; Boettcher, 2006).

Many instructors have found that in providing feedback it is important to keep the assessment activity simple. Explain to students the purpose of the assessment activity, and let them know how the information collected from the assessment activity will help them. Once students have completed the assessment, it is good practice to immediately sort and analyze the student responses. More than likely, student responses will fall into distinct categories. Check for patterns. What is the most common student response; how common is it? What information was gathered that you did not already know? Did you have any suspicions that were confirmed? What will be the instructional response to these responses? After the responses are analyzed, provide feedback to students. What was expected? What was not expected? How will the specific assessment activity impact students' future experiences as learners?

Instructors report that students benefit from understanding that the information provided by the assessment activity will be used by the instructor to make future course revisions. In addition, and perhaps more importantly, students want to understand how they, themselves, can use the results to improve their learning (University of Tennessee, 2006).

When providing feedback, it is important to focus comments and suggestions on specific facets of student work. Comments should be precise, detailed, and instructive. Consider the difference between "good work" and "good use of graphics to enhance Web message; amount of text does not overwhelm the reader; consider using bullets to help organize text information" as feedback on a student webpage assignment. Specific feedback eliminates ambiguity and allows for continued instruction by reinforcing learning and offering suggestions for improvement.

Distance learning instructors face some unique challenges and will find that utilizing multiple methods of feedback eliminates confusion and appeals to different needs and learning styles of students. Offer virtual office hours, telephone office hours, and physical office hours to accommodate your student's schedules. For instance, if most students work from 9:00 am to 5:00 pm, having all daytime office hours, virtual or otherwise, will not meet their needs. Acknowledge or instruct students on how they may ascertain that their submitted responses to course activities were received, when they can expect to receive feedback, and in what form the feedback will be provided to them, such as via the mail tool within the learning management system (LMS). Remember to provide detailed comments and suggestions, referring students to additional sources of information, readings, tutorials, etcetera. Written assignments produced in Microsoft Word can be edited electronically to provide feedback by inserting comments, highlighting and color-coding errors, and using the "track changes" feature, enabling students to see the progress of their work. Simply download the students' assignments, use the Microsoft Word features to provide feedback, and then email the assignments back to each student as an attached file. In addition, include with the email motivational messages, study tips, and references for additional resources.

Are you a CAT Person? (Classroom Assessment Techniques)

As previously stated, to make classroom assessment effective, the instructor must first define specific goals and objectives, as well as have a specific understanding of the purpose of the assessment and a vision for the expected student outcomes. Remember, assessment of student learning does not always have to be a TEST. The most basic type of assessment was just discussed—feedback. However, assessing student performance can take many forms that culminate in an abundant variety of teaching and learning activities. In their seminal work, *Classroom Assessment Techniques: A Handbook for College Teachers*, Angelo and Cross (1993) describe a number of strategies that faculty have successfully utilized to answer the fundamental questions "What are students learning?" and "How effective is your teaching?" Classroom assessment is defined by Cross and Steadman (1996) as "small-scale assessments conducted continually . . . to determine what students are learning in that class (p. 8)."

Classroom Assessment Techniques (CATs) are formative, focused on awareness of student learning and the comprehension and application of what is being taught. One primary premise of CATs advocated by Angelo and Cross is that instruction be learner-centered. CATs are usually simple, non-graded, sometimes anonymous activities, offering valuable feedback for teachers and students on the teaching–learning process. Because CATs are directed at course improvement as well as at improving student learning, they differ from tests and other forms of assessment. The information collected is not used for grading, but rather to facilitate dialogue between students and instructor on the quality and success of the teaching–learning process, and how to improve it. The three fundamental questions CATs address are:

1. What are the essential skills and knowledge I am trying to teach?
2. How can I find out whether students are learning them?
3. How can I help students learn better?

As Angelo and Cross advocate, the CAT process assumes that students need to receive feedback early and often, and that this feedback is central to improving the quality of instruction. Furthermore, they contend that students must have opportunities to evaluate their own learning. CATs provide instructors with a "menu" of evaluation tools that can be used to answer each of the above questions, as well as to meet the demands outlined by Angelo and Cross. By using CAT strategies, you can:

1. Check for student background knowledge
2. Identify areas of confusion
3. Enable students to self-assess their learning level
4. Determine students' learning styles
5. Target and build specific skills

CATs and Distance Learning Instruction
This section provides several examples with step-by-step instructions for providing formative feedback to students. Several CATs from the Angelo and Cross (1993) research, the Teaching and Learning Center at Penn State (2006), and the University of Tennessee at Chattanooga Teaching Resource (2006) are compiled and adapted for use in a distance learning format and are listed in Table 5.3. The CATs are categorized by assessment and feedback goals, including assessing prior knowledge, recall, and understanding of information; synthesis and critical thinking; problem solving; and application and performance. Note that many of these strategies are identical to those provided in the chapter on active learning. The purpose here, however, is to provide instructors with the rationale for using this

TABLE 5.3 Feedback Techniques for Distance Learning Courses

Assessment Type	Description	Objective	Strategy + Online Tool
Measuring Prior Knowledge, Recall, and Understanding			
Background Knowledge Probe	Short surveys to use at beginning of course, beginning of a new unit, or prior to introducing a new concept	Determine most effective starting point for lesson and appropriate level to begin new instruction	Brief online quiz or survey to check for knowledge Discussion board, email, blog, wiki
Focused Listening	Focus students' attention on single term or concept from unit; direct students' awareness to information that is closely related to the "focus" of the unit	Determine what learners recall as the most important points of the lesson	Guided reflective posts Live chat, online white board
Misconception/ Pre-conception Check	Gather information on prior knowledge or beliefs	Uncover knowledge or beliefs that might prevent learning	Brief responses submitted via online tool Live chat, discussion board, blog, twitter, Web conference
Empty Outlines	Provide students with empty or partially completed outline of class lecture, presentation, or homework	Ascertain how well the important points were captured by students	Document provided to students online for their completion and online submission or response Live chat, attachment to discussion board, email, blog, wiki, Web conference, or white board presentation

(continued)

TABLE 5.3   Feedback Techniques for Distance Learning Courses (continued)

Assessment Type	Description	Objective	Strategy + Online Tool
Memory Matrix	A rectangle divided into rows and columns to organize information and to provide a visual illustration of relationships	Assess recall of course content and skill at organizing and categorization	Document provided to students online for their completion and online submission or response Attachment to discussion board, email, blog, wiki, or live chat; Web conference or white board presentation
Minute paper	Ask students to respond in two or three minutes to either of these questions: "What was the most important thing you learned during this session/unit?" or "What questions do you have that remain unanswered?"	Simple and quick way to collect written feedback on student learning	Require students to be online at a specific time (synchronous) if spontaneous response is goal; or submit online (asynchronous) if reflective response is goal Synchronous: live chat, web conference or white board presentation Asynchronous: Discussion, Email, online submission of paper, blog, wiki, twitter
Muddiest point	Ask students to respond to the question: "What is your muddiest point in . . . ?"	Reveals what students find least clear or most confusing about a particular lesson	Same as Minute Paper
Assessing Skill in Syntheses and Critical Thinking			
One-sentence Summary	Students answer investigative questions such as: "Who does what to whom, when, where, how,	Assess student skill level in synthesizing information and thinking critically	Require students to be online at a specific time (synchronous) if spontaneous response is goal; or

	and why?" Student responses must be written in one sentence		submit online (asynchronous) if reflective response is goal Synchronous: live chat, Web conference, or white board presentation Asynchronous: discussion, email, online submission of paper, blog, wiki, twitter
Word Journal	Ask students to summarize a short text in a single word, and then to write a paragraph on why that word was chosen	Assists student to read carefully, and improves skill at explaining and defending with brevity	Written response Online paper submission; discussion, email, blog, wiki
Approximate Analogies	Have student complete second half of analogy	Determine understanding of relationship between concepts or terms	Written response Online paper submission; discussion, email, blog, wiki
Concept Map	Provide drawings or diagrams (visuals) of mental connections that should be made between a major concept and other learned concepts	Provides an observable graphic record of students' conceptual schema, and associations made in relation to a given focal concept	Document provided to students online for their completion and online submission (asynchronous) OR interactive lecture and discussion (synchronous) Asynchronous: discussion, email, online submission of paper, blog, wiki, twitter Synchronous: live chat, Web conference, or white board presentation

(continued)

TABLE 5.3   Feedback Techniques for Distance Learning Courses (continued)

Assessment Type	Description	Objective	Strategy + Online Tool
Invented Dialogues	Ask students to synthesize knowledge of issues, persons, or events into a structured and illustrated conversation	Reveals ability to capture essence of other personalities and expression styles, theories, controversies, and opinions	Verbal or written response Live Chat, white board, discussion board, blog, wiki, video
Annotated portfolios	Ask student to compile selected examples of student's work and provide written commentary	Assess synthesis, critical thinking, communication skill, and progressive achievement	Digital compilation of accomplishment and progress Discussion board, blog, wiki, or social network site PLUS attachments (video, images, illustrations, sound files, text, webpages)
Assessing Skill in Problem Solving			
Problem Recognition Tasks	Provide examples of common problems; direct students to determine the specific type of problem for each example given	Assess recognition of problem types (which is critical for solving the problem)	Verbal or written response Live chat, white board, Web conference, discussion board, blog, wiki, video, social network site
What's the Principle?	Provide examples of problems and ask students to state the primary principle that best applies to each problem.	Determine students' ability to connect specific problems with specific solution principles	Verbal or written response Live chat, white board, Web conference, discussion board, blog, wiki, video, social network site
Documented Problem Solutions	Require students to document step-by-step the tasks completed to solve a problem	Assess how students solve problems; how well they understand/ describe problem solving methods	Verbal or written response Live chat, white board, Web conference, discussion board, blog, wiki, video, social network site

Audio- and Videotaped Protocols	Record students working through problem-solving process	Able to analyze problem-solving in detail	Student-produced narrated PowerPoint or video file uploaded to white board, discussion board, blog, wiki, social network site

Assessing Skill in Application and Performance

Directed Paraphrasing	Identify a specific purpose and target audience and have students paraphrase (in their own words) part of a unit/topic.	Assess understanding and internalization of learning; provide feedback on ability	Verbal or written response Live chat, white board, Web conference, discussion board, blog, wiki, video, social network site
Application Cards	Students describe real-world/workplace applications for the important principle, theory, or process that they just learned	Depicts whether or not the student clearly understands the concept and applications	Verbal or written response Live chat, white board, Web conference, discussion board, blog, wiki, video, social network site
Students Create Test Questions	Students develop test questions from course materials such as textbook, online discussions, group chat sessions, instructor feedback, etcetera	Reveals what students remember, what they consider to be most important	Written response Discussion board, email, blog, wiki, twitter
Prospectus for a Paper or Project	Students prepare a prospectus which can be a brief first-draft or plan for a research paper or course project	Helps students to organize their thinking, outline the steps needed to complete the task, and focus on the product to be created	Written or video response Submitted paper, white board, discussion board, blog, wiki, video, social network site

strategy as an assessment of student learning, as well as providing tips for facilitating the assessment.

You may find it useful to study Table 5.3 and reflect on which are the most beneficial feedback strategies for the distance learning course(s) you are or will be teaching. Tables 5.4, 5.5, and 5.6 offer examples of rubrics for three of the CAT strategies listed in Table 5.3. While examining these tables, ask the following questions:

1. Why should a specific strategy be used?
2. What might the student learn by using the strategy?
3. What might I learn from using the strategy?
4. How valuable will the feedback be?

TABLE 5.4   Example 1: Yes–No Rubric

Word Journal

1. Chosen word adequately reflects the content of the text.	Yes	No
2. The paragraph response provides ample justification for the word that was chosen.	Yes	No
3. The paragraph response was written using appropriate grammar and spelling.	Yes	No
4. The student completed the activity by the assigned due date.	Yes	No

---

TABLE 5.5   Example 2: Scoring Rubric

Annotated Portfolio

5 = Superior, 4 = Above Average, 3 = Adequate, 2 = Below Average,
1 = Unacceptable, 0 = did not submit

1. The portfolio contained examples of student work from each major content area.	5	4	3	2	1	0
2. The examples of student work presented in the portfolio represent a variety of formats (written, multimedia, product, etc.).	5	4	3	2	1	0
3. The examples of student work presented in the portfolio represent a progression of student achievement.	5	4	3	2	1	0
4. The annotations included with the examples succinctly summarized the assignment goal(s) and ways in which the student's response met the goal(s).	5	4	3	2	1	0
5. The annotations were written using proper grammar and spelling.	5	4	3	2	1	0

**TABLE 5.6   Example 3: Self-Assessment Checklist
(for the student to complete)**

Students Create Test Questions

1. I thoroughly reviewed all of the materials   Date completed:
   associated with this unit of instruction (textbook,
   handouts, class notes, etc.).

2. I created one test question for each major topic   Date completed:
   associated with this unit.

3. I created a variety of question types (multiple   Date completed:
   choice, true-false, short answer, short essay, etc.).

4. I provided my test questions to another course   Date completed:
   participant for review and revision.

5. I submitted my test questions to the instructor by   Date completed:
   the due date.

Evaluation and Graded Assessments

CATs are simple, un-graded assessments that are easy to implement, respond to, and modify. With the increase in distance learning courses offered by educational institutions at all levels, there is heightened interest in how evaluation of learning can be conducted for distance learning students. One of the prickliest issues in online teaching is the subject of *graded* assessment.

One of the most pervasive issues that exist with graded assessments in distance learning courses is academic dishonesty. And while this is an age-old issue, faced by instructors long before distance learning courses were available, there are new dimensions to academic dishonesty in distance learning courses. Olt (2002) identifies four major disadvantages in online evaluations. We will address these disadvantages throughout the next several sections of this chapter.

1. The instructor's inability to identify if the student is actually the person completing the evaluation instrument
2. The instructor's inability to control the students' use of unauthorized materials while completing the evaluation (e.g., textbook)
3. The possibility of student collaboration
4. Technical difficulties (computer "crashes," LMS issues, etc.)

Quizzes, Tests, and Exams

To cheat or not to cheat.... If that is the question some students ask, *To catch a cheat* is the concern of many an online educator. "How do I know that the test submitted by the student was really completed by the student?" is a frequent query by concerned faculty. This remains one of the principal oppositions to distance learning by educators wary of online delivery of instruction. The Higher Education Act mandates that distance learning institutions must authenticate the identities of students taking tests online in a credit-generating course. Hence, the industry has developed several anti-cheating technology solutions. The various solutions include webcam snapshots, thumbprint scants, palm vein scanners, randomized security questions, student ID scans, analysis of keystroke rhythm, and biometrics that authenticate a test-taker by using fingerprint, face, and iris authentication.

Most educational institutions do not have the high-tech solutions described above. So, as you might expect, some instructors are concerned about the possibility of not being able to insure that cheating is minimized or, better yet, eliminated. One of the more popular alternatives to online testing is to require students to visit a remote testing center where tests are proctored. However, this is labor-intensive, costly for educational institutions, as well as inconvenient for students, and compromises the concept of distance learning.

Instructors often opt to use the quiz/test tools within the LMS. Many LMS systems include features that provide some control in online testing, especially when using fixed-choice tests (multiple-choice, true/false, and matching). The control features include timed quizzes and tests. A time limit can be assigned to each question, to the entire quiz or test, or to both. Another prominent control feature is the randomization of test questions, so that no two students receive the questions in the exact same order. A few tricks of the trade for delivering online fixed-choice quizzes, tests, and exams include:

1. Release the exam on a specified day and within a specific time period.
2. If the LMS system allows, when creating the quiz/test within the system, assign a specific time limit to each question as well as a time limit to complete the entire exam. By doing so, students will automatically be taken to the next question when the time expires.
3. Allow only one attempt to answer each question.
4. When creating the quiz/test within the LMS, structure it so that students are allowed to move forward to the next question, but are not able to move back to a previous question.
5. Randomize the presentation of questions, so that each student gets the same questions, but in different order.

6. Within your LMS, create a large database of questions so that the questions can be randomly selected for the quiz, resulting in every student receiving a different version of the quiz.

Alternative Assessments

There are a multitude of other evaluation methods that you can use as a graded measure of student learning. Popularly known as "alternative assessments," these strategies minimize the opportunities for cheating and promote active learning. Following is a variety of alternative assessment strategies appropriate for distance learning courses.

Team Projects/Group Work. The use of group work and team projects as active learning strategies in distance learning courses was included in Chapter 2. Sample group activities, grouping strategies, and tips for facilitating group work were all discussed in detail. In this chapter, we will provide a variety of sample rubrics. The rubric contained in Table 5.7 can be used for students to evaluate the overall effectiveness of their team once the team assignment is completed. Consider modifying this rubric for students to use as an ongoing evaluation of their progress. Or, change it to include a points rating system.

The rubric displayed in Table 5.8 can be used for teams to monitor their ongoing progress. Provide the rubric to students in advance and ask them to submit the completed rubric to you both at the mid-point of the

---

TABLE 5.7 Rubric Example: Group Effectiveness

Group Effectiveness Survey

Please plot your level of agreement on the continuum below each statement. This instrument will be used as a guide to reflect on the effectiveness of the team's work.

1. All team members contributed equally.
   Disagree ——————————————————————————— Agree

2. Team members were cooperative, patient, and respectful with each other.
   Disagree ——————————————————————————— Agree

3. We did a better job together than we each could have done alone.
   Disagree ——————————————————————————— Agree

4. Team members offered encouragement to each other and shared ideas openly.
   Disagree ——————————————————————————— Agree

5. I am pleased with the overall effectiveness of my team.
   Disagree ——————————————————————————— Agree

TABLE 5.8 Rubric Example: Guiding and Evaluating Progress of Group Work

Categories for Evaluation	Excellent Progress 4	Adequate Progress 3	Average Progress 2	Poor Progress 1	No Progress 0
Group Objectives	Defined and established as part of the group plan	Discussed and defined; group plan still needs work	Discussed but not well-defined; little or no overall group plan	Some discussion; little or no overall group plan	No evidence
Group Roles	Defined and assigned to all group members	Defined but not assigned	Discussed at length, but still needs clarification and/or agreement	Some discussion on group roles	No evidence
Group Tasks	Defined and established as part of the group plan; assigned to group members	Defined and established as part of the group plan; not assigned	Discussed, but still needs clarification	Some discussion	No evidence
Resources	Resources identified, located, analyzed	Identified and located, but not analyzed	Identified but not all located; little or no analysis	Not all resources identified	No evidence
Timelines and/or benchmarks	All task completion on time per timeline; some tasks ahead of schedule	Task completion on time per timeline	Some work late but completed in time to be included in the finished product	Some work never completed and project in danger	No evidence
Mid-point					No evidence
Near completion date					No evidence

TABLE 5.9 Rubric Example: Drafting Activity

Drafting
Read a minimum of two of your coursemates' drafts and use this
  rubric to evaluate each and provide feedback.

1. All major topics are included	Yes	No
2. There is adequate support information for each topic.	Yes	No
3. The draft was written using appropriate grammar and spelling.	Yes	No
4. The content is organized coherently and there is a logical flow.	Yes	No
5. There is evidence from the course text and other course materials.	Yes	No

---

project and upon completion. Also, you may want to provide students the opportunity to critique themselves and each other by utilizing the rubric.

Peer evaluation of students' drafts of written assignments is a common practice throughout all levels of education. In itself, this is not a team activity. However, it requires interaction and communication among students. The rubric presented in Table 5.9 can be used for students to provide feedback to their peers. Or, ask students to provide you with the evaluation criteria, and create a rubric based on their input.

Student Presentations.   At first glance, student presentations may appear to be an impossible event for distance learning courses. However, not only are they possible, they are very much a desired learning activity for students. Implementing student presentations as an active learning strategy was discussed in Chapter 2, along with examples of the types of presentations that are appropriate for distance courses. A rubric in a checklist format that can be used to score student presentations is found in Table 5.10.

Another form of student presentation is allowing students to lead synchronous chat sessions. The rubric supplied in Table 5.11 can be provided to students to guide them in their preparation for the session. Note that this rubric does not contain points or any type of measurement. It simply serves as an advanced organizer to help students successfully complete the activity. The rubric may or may not be used as part of the student's grade.

Written Reflection, Synthesis, and Application.   Evaluating student learning and assigning a grade based on the student's ability to critically reflect on, synthesize, and apply information includes asking students to (1) reflect on interesting and/or significant points, (2) summarize important concepts, and (3) connect or apply concepts to the real world or to current events. These written evaluation strategies can take the form of reflective journals, research reports, or written responses to specific questions posted in a blog,

---

TABLE 5.10 Rubric Example: Student Presentations Scoring Checklist

5 = fully complete, 3 = partially complete, 1 = minimally complete,
0 = not complete

_____ Presentation contained all required information in a thorough manner.

_____ Presentation contained all required information in an accurate manner.

_____ An outline of the presentation was submitted by the outline due date.

_____ A draft of the presentation was submitted by the draft due date.

_____ The presentation included an introduction.

_____ The presentation content was organized in a coherent manner with logical flow.

_____ The presentation included a summary.

_____ The presentation included proper grammar and spelling.

_____ The presentation content shows evidence of additional research outside of the text and class materials.

_____ The presentation was submitted by the due date.

TABLE 5.11 Rubric Example: Synchronous Chat Preparation

Synchronous Chat

You have been chosen as one of three facilitators to lead a synchronous chat session on the following topic: (put topic here). Use this rubric to guide your preparation.

1. I have reviewed all of the course content for this topic.   Date completed:

2. I have prepared two discussion points that I plan to facilitate.   Date completed:

3. I have created a list of questions that I anticipate receiving.   Date completed:

4. I have pre-typed my responses to the above questions so that I can quickly copy/paste my responses to keep the session flowing smoothly.   Date completed:

5. I have contacted the other two facilitators to coordinate our discussion.   Date completed:

---

wiki, twitter, or social networking site. Use the rubric example offered in Table 5.12 to evaluate and assign points to your students' written work.

The rubric contained in Table 5.13 is a self-assessment checklist for students to use when completing a written assignment or reflective journal activity. Ask students to submit the completed checklist when they submit the assignment. With simple modification, this rubric can also be used as a means for peers to evaluate each other.

TABLE 5.12   Rubric Example: Written Evaluations

Research Report Scoring Checklist

5 = Superior, 4 = Above Average, 3 = Average, 2 = Below Average,
1 = Unacceptable, 0 = No evidence

____ The report topic is relevant to the course content and approved by the instructor.

____ A report outline was submitted by the outline due date.

____ A report draft was submitted by the draft due date.

____ The report includes a thorough introduction.

____ The report content is written in a logical sequence and organized coherently.

____ The report includes an effective summary.

____ The report includes the student's thoughts, ideas, reflections, etc.

____ The report includes information derived from sources other than the course text and course materials.

____ The report demonstrates proper grammar and spelling.

____ The report was submitted by the report due date.

____ TOTAL POINTS (50 possible)

TABLE 5.13   Rubric Example: Self-assessment of Written Assignment

Written Reflection: Self-assessment Checklist (to be completed by the student)
Please initial next to each item once the item is completed.

1. I completed the required readings and reviewed all appropriate course material prior to writing my reflection. _____
2. I used "spell check" and "grammar check" and made corrections. _____
3. I included reflection on all major topics included in the unit. _____
4. I read my written reflection prior to submitting it to the instructor. _____
5. One of my coursemates peer-reviewed my reflection and provided feedback. _____
6. I submitted my written reflection by the assigned due date. _____

The scoring rubric displayed in Table 5.14 is intended to be used to evaluate students' research reports. Again, it is important to provide this rubric to students in advance so that they are clear on the criteria for success. In addition, consider posting an exemplary report for students to use as a model.

Student Portfolios (Constructivism and Authentic Learning).   Constructivist theory is the foundation of many distance learning courses. The dynamic nature of distance learning is compatible with the tenets of constructivism. Learning as a personal event is central to Constructivist learning theory.

TABLE 5.14   Rubric Example: Research Report

Categories for Evaluation	Outstanding Evidence 4	Adequate Evidence 3	Average Evidence 2	Poor Evidence 1	No Evidence 0
Research Question	Introduction asks a clear question and explains its importance	Introduction asks a clear question but importance not explained	Introduction asks a clear question but the topic and relevance is not important	Introduction does not include a clear question	Topic question is not included
Understanding of topic and related issues evidenced throughout paper	Topic and related issues thoroughly explored and explained	Topic and related issues discussed at length, but still needs clarification	Topic and related issues defined but not explained thoroughly	Some exploration and explanation of topic and significant related issues but thorough understanding not demonstrated	Little or no exploration or explanation of topic and related issues
Accuracy of information	Information accurate, specific, and complete	Most information accurate, specific, and complete	Some information accurate and specific, but vital pieces of information missing	Some information accurate and specific; vital pieces of information missing,	Inaccurate information presented; vital pieces of information missing

Analysis	Student analyzes information logically, makes appropriate contrasts and comparisons, and adds new observations and insights	Student analyzes information logically and makes appropriate contrasts and comparisons	Student analyzes information logically, makes adequate contrasts and comparisons, but overlooks some important points	Student analyzes information with some lapses in logic; many comparisons and contrasts overlooked; inaccurate information presented	Little or no logical analysis; few or no comparisons or contrasts
Sources	Appropriate scope and number of sources correctly cited	Appropriate number of sources correctly cited	Appropriate number of sources but incorrectly cited	Inappropriate number of sources	No sources cited
Format	Format model followed; no spelling and grammar errors	Format model followed; some spelling and/or grammar errors	Format model followed with few exceptions; some spelling and/or grammar errors	Format model followed with some exceptions; several spelling and/or grammar errors	Format model not followed; several spelling and/or grammar errors
Points					

Constructivist theory speculates that effective learning takes place when learned information is applied to experiences and situations relevant to the learner. Application of learning requires the individual to amend existing knowledge or create new information. It is preferable that learning take place in real-world venues that are pertinent to learners' experiences. When learning takes place in settings that are significant and relevant to learners' needs and circumstances, it is said that "authentic learning" has taken place.

Authentic learning as an instructional strategy is grounded in reality and, like the real world, encourages social interaction to facilitate understanding and creation of knowledge by providing opportunities for reflection, collaboration, and construction of meaning. Authentic learning celebrates the unique prior knowledge, experience, and beliefs that students bring to the learning situation. Accommodation, assimilation, or rejection to construct new conceptual structures and meaningful representations are part of the learning process. Distance learning courses have the ability to provide a variety of dynamic activities, such as websites, online readings and activities, videos, tutorials, games, and simulations—activities that are an integral part of the learning experience and part of the real world. Surrounded by an infinite variety of images, ideas, information, and other sensory stimulation, students are challenged to extract information that matches their existing understanding, with the goal that new knowledge will be constructed in multiple ways, through a variety of tools, resources, experiences, and contexts available within the course. Activities should be designed so that learning will occur in a variety of ways, keeping the students engaged through active and reflective learning.

Authentic assessment refers to the evaluation of students based on examination of their work or production of a product, rather than standardized test scores. Student learning is assessed through projects, products, and portfolios with specific criteria established by a rubric. Portfolio assessment is quickly becoming a popular form of authentic, workplace-style assessment. As a rule, both the instructor and students determine the types of items to be included in the portfolio, as well as the evaluation criteria used to determine if the items submitted by the students meet performance objectives. Items that may be included in student portfolios could include problem-based essays, collaborative group work, class discussion activities, reflective writings, case study analysis, service-learning projects, annotated bibliographies, and Web resources. Evaluated as a whole, the above items provide a foundation for summative assessment that documents evidence of meeting course objectives. In addition, the abundance of current software programs makes the creation of electronic portfolios easier than ever. Electronic portfolios may be uploaded to the course using a variety of tools included in most LMS systems. Or the portfolios may be added to a blog, wiki, or social network site.

Please note that a sample rubric for an annotated portfolio was provided earlier in this chapter. Additional portfolio rubrics are included on the Companion Website.

Rubrics for Standard Communication Using LMS Tools

Discussion forums and synchronous chat sessions are common strategies found in most distance learning courses. As with any course activity, students need to be completely clear as to how they are being evaluated. The rubrics displayed in Table 5.15 and Table 5.16 are useful for evaluating

TABLE 5.15 Rubric Example: Chat Session Participation and Contribution (1)

Points	Chat behavior
7–10	Student logs in to chat room on time and posts relevant comments with appropriate timing that contribute to the overall conversation; makes no attempt to dominate conversation
4–6	Student's chat contributions are generally timely and relevant; may need occasional prompting to contribute and/or may tend to dominate conversation
2–3	Student is not consistent with participation; comments may not be relevant and/or are very short; limited initiative
0–1	Student rarely participates; remarks are not timely and are irrelevant

TABLE 5.16 Rubric Example: Chat Session Participation and Contribution (2)

Points	Chat Behavior
5	Posts demonstrated deep understanding of the topic; contained ample evidence of information from all required readings and course activities
4	Posts demonstrated adequate understanding of the topic; contained some evidence of information from required readings and course activities
3	Posts demonstrated nominal understanding of the topic; limited evidence of information from required readings and course activities
2	Posts demonstrated little understanding of the topic; minimal evidence of information from required readings and course activities
1	Posts demonstrated no understanding of the topic; no evidence of information from required readings and course activities
0	Student did not participate in the chat session and did not have an excused absence

participation and contributions in chat sessions, while rubrics specific to discussion activities are contained in Tables 5.17 and 5.18.

Rubrics for Web 2.0 Strategies

Web 2.0 strategies have been discussed throughout this book. Many instructors express concern that the casual nature of conversation that transpires outside of the classroom via these tools makes it difficult to use them for educational purposes. Actually, the contrary is true. Using tools that students are comfortable with and motivated by allows them to spend more time focusing on course content and learning goals. The simple answer for instructors is to provide students with a rubric that clearly details expectations and requirements. Rubrics that can be used with a variety of Web 2.0 tools are presented in Tables 5.19, 5.20, 5.21, and 5.22.

TABLE 5.17   Rubric Example: Discussion Forum Posts (1)

Discussion Board Rubric
(Each Discussion Board posting is valued at 10 points)
The primary objective of the discussion board is to provide a forum for students to interact substantially with each other and share thoughts, opinions, and feelings. With regard to online discussions, contributing to the learning community is not only posting original messages, but replying to those of others in the class.

0 Points
You will get 0 points if your entries do not add to the discussion in any substantial manner. These are typically entries that simply agree with what someone else said or just restate what someone else said. Original postings that do not answer the assignment question also fall in this category.

3–5 Points
You will receive 3–5 points if your entry contributes some original thinking to the discussion but (a) are still somewhat superficial in thought, or (b) do not use the knowledge gained and information provided by the readings and material of the course, or (c) if you simply reply to another posting and do not enter an original posting of your own.

5–7 Points
You will receive 5–7 points if your entry contributes substantially to the discussion and uses the knowledge gained and information provided by the readings and material of the course, but you do not reply/respond to classmates when asked to do so.

10 points
You will receive 10 points if your entry contributes substantially to the discussion and uses the knowledge gained and information provided by the readings and material of the course, and you reply/respond to your classmates in a thorough and thoughtful manner.

TABLE 5.18   Sample Rubric: Discussion Forum Posts (2)

Category	4	3	2	1
Timeliness	Responds to posts in less than 24 hours; demonstrates initiative	Responds to most posts within 24 hours; requires occasional prompting	Responds to most posts, but several days after initial discussion; very little initiative	Responds to few posts; requires constant prompting
Writing skills	Grammatically correct with only an occasional misspelling	Few grammatical errors or spelling errors	Spelling and grammar errors in several posts	Very poor spelling and grammar in most/all posts
Expression of Ideas	Original ideas and opinions are written in a clear and concise manner and are focused on the topic	Original ideas and opinions are written clearly; sometimes drifts from topic	Few original ideas and opinions are expressed; minimal connection to the topic	Ideas and opinions are not expressed in a clear manner; no focus on the topic
Relatedness	Posts are always related to the discussion topic; sometimes cites additional resources/Web sites in the discussion post	Posts are frequently related to the discussion topic; ideas and opinions prompt further discussion	Posts are sometimes off topic; minimal in length and do not further the discussion	Posts are not related to the discussion topic; posts are short and appear hurried
Sense of Community Team-building	Often motivates the group discussion; responds to classmates' posts in a manner that fosters good team-building relationships; displays an excellent sense of community	Sometimes attempts to motivate the group discussion; responds to classmates' posts in a manner that sometimes fosters good team-building relationships; displays a good sense of community	Displays little sense of community; rarely acts as a motivator or attempts to foster good team-building relationships	Displays no sense of community; never attempts to motivate the class discussion

TABLE 5.19   Rubric Example: Twitter Activities (Tweets)

Rubric criteria

Knowledge 1 point	Comprehension 2 points	Application 3 points	Analysis 4 points	Synthesis 5 points	Evaluation 6 points
Restates facts; lists already-stated facts	Describes, discusses, or explains concept	Applies concept to new or unique setting	Conducts comparison or contrast of concepts; performs calculations; tests hypothesis	Constructs new model; creates process; designs a system; organizes event; prepares a plan	Assesses facts and opinions; argues for or against; makes predictions; provides supportive information; chooses from options and provides justification; validates position

TABLE 5.20 Rubric Example: Wiki Posts

Criteria	Evidenced 1 point	No Evidence 0 points
Information contributed		
Contribution adds new information to wiki (not a restatement of previous information)		
Contribution presented in a variety of formats (text, pictures, Web links, video, audio)		
Contribution is supported by facts with references provided		
Contribution poses a new question to stimulate further knowledge building		
TOTAL		

TABLE 5.21 Rubric Example: Reflective Blog Post

Posts	There is at least one blog post for each week of the course (min. 400 words)	Above Average (2 pts) Average (1 pt) Needs Improvement (0 pt)	_____
Participation	Responded to at least three coursemates' blogs (min. 100 words)	Above Average (2 pts) Average (1 pt) Needs Improvement (0 pt)	_____
Content	Posts and comments offer personal connections to class content and discussion	Above Average (2 pts) Average (1 pt) Needs Improvement (0 pt)	_____
Writing Standards	Ideas, observations, discoveries, and suggestions are communicated clearly and coherently. Spelling and grammar is correct.	Above Average (2 pts) Average (1 pt) Needs Improvement (0 pt)	_____
Total Points			

Rubrics for Other Types of Assessment

Various other forms of assessment are important for distance learning courses. Adult learners need to have opportunities to evaluate each other via peer assessment, or to evaluate themselves via self-assessment tools. Also, students need to be able to provide feedback to the instructor; this is usually accomplished via course surveys.

TABLE 5.22 Rubric Example: Analytical Blog Post

Criteria	3 points	2 points	1 point	0 points
Participation	Blog posts made throughout the week prior to deadline	Blog posts made within the deadline	Blog posts often respect deadline, but some posts made after deadline	Very few blog posts
Contribution of new knowledge	Blog posts reveal extensive reading and research external to course content	Blog posts shows some evidence of external readings	Very few blog posts that provide information external to course content	No new information offered in blog posts
Demonstration of Learning	Blog posts indicate student is able to relate course concepts to different and new situations	Blog posts indicate student attempts to connect course concepts to new situations	Blog posts allude to course concepts student has learned through course content	Blog posts make no reference to course concepts
Vocabulary	Consistent use of new vocabulary; blog posts contain new expressions and details used appropriately	New vocabulary is used occasionally and in appropriate context	Vocabulary use is poor and often used inappropriately	No development of new vocabulary evidenced

Total Points

Peer Assessment

The predominant view of assessment has been that it is the instructor's responsibility. However, research findings support peer assessment as an effective alternative assessment strategy. Peer assessment involves students in an interactive process of review, assessment, and feedback to fellow students for the purpose of enhancing their own and their peers' learning and achievement. The benefits of peer assessment include (1) learning in a non-threatening environment, (2) diminishing the perceived power struggle between student and teacher, and (3) involvement of student in assessment process (Topping, 1998). In addition, peer assessment meets the needs of diverse learning styles by allowing students to model appropriate cognitive behavior, which reinforces student learning. The strategy also involves students in acquiring alternative perspectives on issues, and encourages self-assessment and reflection (Cowan, 1999; Moon, 1999). Instructors find benefit in a reduction of time spent providing feedback and commentary on individual assignments.

Preparing students for participation in peer assessment is crucial for the success of this strategy. The preparation includes providing guidance for students in understanding and developing assessment criteria, and how to objectively evaluate peer work. Instructors find that it is advisable to let students know in the syllabus that peer assessment is a part of the course requirements. Students should also be provided with a set of written instructions on how to conduct a peer assessment, along with a rubric to guide their assessment. In addition, most students will need training in how to effectively communicate feedback. You may want to consider providing students with concrete examples of appropriate and inappropriate feedback. Written texts, videos, or audio files demonstrating appropriate and inappropriate feedback can be posted within your distance learning course. An example of a peer assessment rubric that can be used for students to evaluate each other's performance as part of group activities is offered in Table 5.23.

Instead of providing students with a peer assessment rubric, some instructors involve students in constructing the peer assessment criteria. This strategy strengthens their understanding and engagement in the experience. Students benefit from instruction by example in how to question, support, re-assure, and encourage their peers, and they take ownership in the peer evaluation experience, since they were partially responsible for its creation. A sample activity that you can use that allows your students to create peer assessment criteria is displayed in Table 5.24.

As a final exercise in peer assessment, students should be encouraged to reflect on the experience paying particular attention to their own learn-

TABLE 5.23 Rubric Example: Peer Assessment

Instructions: Complete Sections 1 and 2. Then email the completed assessment to your instructor.

Your Name: _____

Section 1: Rate EACH of your team members on their performance for all group activities included as part of this course. Assign a point value (up to 20 points) using the assessment criteria below. If you are rating a team member with a score of 14 or below, please provide additional details explaining the reason for the score.

Name of Team Member	Points Given	Possible Points	Criteria
		18–20	Participated in ALL team activities in a timely manner and frequently interacted with members of the team. Met all team deadlines.
		14–17	Participated in MOST team activities in a timely manner and occasionally interacted with members of the team. Met most team deadlines.
		10–13	Participated in MOST team activities, but sometimes not in a timely manner. Seldom interacted with members of the team. Met some team deadlines.
		5–9	Participated minimally in team activities and had little interaction with team members.
		0–4	Did not participate in team activities or have any contact with team members.

Section 2:
Write a brief paragraph summarizing your thoughts, opinions, and/or feelings regarding your team experiences. Include any information that may help your instructor improve the course OR monitor the team process in the future.

TABLE 5.24   Rubric Example: Devising Peer Assessment Criteria

Work in your previously identified teams to create a rubric to assess discussion
performance for the assignment outlined below. Each team is to construct
a rubric with four criteria by which the posts are to be assessed and graded.
Each team must share their completed rubric by posting it in the student
presentation section. Then, each student must review all of the rubrics and vote
for the one that you think is best. Email your vote to your instructor no later
than (date). The rubric receiving the most votes will be used to evaluate the
assignment topic.

Assignment Topic:
Brainstorm how technology has changed society, in general, and education, in
particular. Identify and list the ways in which computers and software have
had an impact. Then determine five ways in which they are likely to change
society and education in the future. Post your initial response to the class
discussion board titled Technology and Society. Once you have posted your
initial response, review the responses of at least five of your fellow coursemates
and provide peer feedback to a minimum of three. Use the rubric as a means to
evaluate and respond to your coursemates' posts.

---

ing, progress, and achievement. Consider conducting a de-briefing session
via discussion or chat that introduces questions to trigger contemplation,
analysis, and summation of learning. Other reflective exercises include
reflective journaling, written summary, and individual or group presentation. The asynchronous tools (discussion board, blogs, wikis, social network
sites) facilitate peer assessment well.

Self-Assessment

Another alternative assessment strategy gaining in popularity, particularly
in distance learning, is self-assessment. Self-assessment requires students to
critically reflect on the learning, paying particular attention to their progress in
achieving pre-determined learning goals. An ongoing process, self-assessment
compels students to continuously monitor their understanding and growth,
document progress, and note where extra time and attention to learning may
be required. In self-assessment, students may have the opportunity to create
learning contracts and suggest grades for their accomplishments.

Guidelines and instructions are necessary to focus students in appropriate ways for self-assessment. Targeted questions help to engage students in
reflecting on the level of their performance. Such questions may include:

1. What makes this your best work?
2. How did you go about completing this work?

3. What problems did you encounter and how did you go about solving them?
4. What were your learning goals for this work?
5. What efforts did you put forth to accomplish them?
6. What was the least effective part of this work? Why is this so?
7. What could you have done differently to improve your work?

Self-assessment often motivates students to stay actively engaged in the course and to sustain their efforts in areas they may be weak in. Self-reflection and assessment enhances awareness of what they have learned and how it will be applied in the context of the real world. The strategy of self-reflection allows instructors to focus their professional development in meaningful directions, while self-grading provides insight for the instructor as to the level of learning that is taking place.

To allow students to comment on their own participation and performance, use the Peer Assessment in Table 5.23 and include the opportunity for students to evaluate their own performance. Ask students to provide a score for themselves and then write an explanation for the score. Blogs and social network sites are exceptionally well-suited for self-reflection and self-assessment.

Please note that the incorporation of peer or self-assessment strategies does not abolish instructor involvement. The instructor still maintains responsibility for assessment, feedback, final grading, and reporting.

Surveys in Distance Learning Courses

Careful planning of distance learning courses helps to insure maximum learning value as well as the smooth flow of the course. However, even after thorough planning, it sometimes becomes evident that certain activities and/or course content do not lead to the outcome(s) that we expected. Surveys can be used as a means to receive feedback from students regarding course content, organization of materials, clarity of instructions, and overall facilitation. The purpose of surveys is to provide you with information that you can use to make changes in curriculum, learning activities, and teaching strategies. In addition, as previously stated, giving students a voice in the teaching–learning process improves student motivation and overall student achievement.

An example of a survey that can be used to evaluate a unit of instruction is presented in Table 5.25. You can modify this survey to evaluate specific course assignments, projects, and facilitation strategies, such as the use of communication tools. In addition, we recommend that, once the course

---

TABLE 5.25   Survey Example: Unit of Instruction

Unit 3 Survey

Please complete the following survey regarding Unit 3. The results will be used to modify the curriculum for future offerings of this course.

5 = strongly agree, 4 = agree, 3 = neutral, 2 = disagree, 1 = strongly disagree, 0 = no opinion

1. The content of this unit was aligned with course objectives.	5 4 3 2 1 0
2. The learning goals for this unit were clearly stated.	5 4 3 2 1 0
3. The activities included in this unit enhanced my learning.	5 4 3 2 1 0
4. All instructions were clear.	5 4 3 2 1 0
5. This unit provided me with the opportunity to interact with my coursemates.	5 4 3 2 1 0
6. This unit provided me with the opportunity to interact with my instructor.	5 4 3 2 1 0

Following are my recommendations for this unit, including changes that I would make as well as activities and materials I would keep:

---

is complete, you provide students with the opportunity to evaluate the entire course separately from other evaluation forms that may be utilized by your institution.

End of Chapter Activities

The end of chapter activities provide opportunities for you to acquire new knowledge, gain skill, and apply principles and concepts. These activities are located on the Companion Website, and are divided into three subsections: Knowledge Building, Skill Building, and Practical Application.

References

9 Principles of Good Practice for Assessing Student Learning (1992). American Association for Higher Education, Assessment Forum. Retrieved June 19, 2007 from http://www.fctel.uncc.edu/pedagogy/assessment/9Principles.html

Angelo, T.A., (1991). Ten easy pieces: Assessing higher learning in four dimensions. *Classroom research: Early lessons from success. New directions in teaching and learning.* (#46), Summer, 17–31.

Angelo, T. & Cross, P. (1993). *Classroom assessment techniques: A handbook for college teachers.* San Francisco, CA: Jossey Bass.

Boettcher, J. (2006). E-Coaching tip 19: Feedback on assignments: Being timely and efficient. *Designing for Learning.* Retrieved June 30, 2009, from http://www.designingforlearning.info/services/writing/ecoach/tips/tip19.html

Cowan, J. (1999). *A handbook of techniques for formative evaluation.* London: Kogan Page.

Cross, P., & Steadman, M. (1996). *Classroom research: Implementing the scholarship of teaching.* San Francisco, CA: Jossey Bass.

DiGesu, E. (no date). *The purpose of assessment.* Retrieved June 30, 2009, from http://www.gecdsb.on.ca/d&g/onlinepd/Assessment%20&%20Evaluation/Purpose.htm.

Goodrich, H. (1997). Thinking-centered assessment. In S. Veenema, L. Hetland, & K. Chalfen (Eds.), *The Project Zero classroom: new approaches to thinking and understanding.* Cambridge, MA: Project Zero, Harvard Graduate School of Education.

Huba, M. E. & Freed, J. E. (2000). *Learner-centered assessment on college campuses: Shifting the focus from teaching to learning.* Boston, MA: Allyn & Bacon.

Lysakowski, R. & Walberg, H. (1981). Classroom reinforcement in relation to learning: A quantitative analysis. *Journal of Educational Research, 75,* 69–77.

Lysakowski, R. & Walberg, H. (1982). Instructional effects of cues, participation, and corrective feedback: A quantitative synthesis. *American Educational Research Journal, 19*(4), 559–578.

Moon, J. (1999). *Reflection in learning and professional development: Theory and practice.* London: Kogan Page

Olt, M. R. (2002). Ethics and distance education: Strategies for minimizing academic dishonesty in online assessment. *Online Journal of Distance Learning Administration.* Volume V, Number III. State University of West Georgia, Distance Education Center.

Teaching and Learning Center at Penn State website (2006). Retrieved September 9, 2006, from: http://www.cl.psu.edu/ets/teaching_resources.htm#CATs

Tennenbaum, G. and Goldring, E. (1989). A meta-analysis of the effect of enhanced instruction: Cues, participation, reinforcement and feedback, and correctives on motor skill learning. *Journal of Research and Development in Education.* 22/3, 53–64.

Topping, K. (1998). Peer assessment between students in colleges and universities. *Review of Educational Research, 68,* 249–276.

University of Tennessee at Chattanooga Teaching Resource Center Webpage (2006). Retrieved September 9, 2006, from: http://www.utc.edu/Administration/WalkerTeachingResourceCenter/FacultyDevelopment/Assessment/assessment.html

University of New South Wales (2004). *Guidelines on learning that inform teaching at UNSW.* No. 16.

Walberg, H. J. (1999). Productive teaching. In H. C. Waxman & H. J. Walberg (Eds.), *New directions for teaching practice and research,* 75–104. Berkeley, CA: McCutchen Publishing Corporation.

6

Organizing and Designing Course Pages

Whether you realized it or not, the previous chapters and the Course Planning and Delivery Guide have taken you step-by-step through the instructional design process. Instructional design is all about what, why, and how you teach a course. The focus of this chapter is instructional design, including aesthetics and design principles that reinforce learning. Upon completion of Chapter 6, readers will be able to:

1. Explain the best practices for good page/course design
2. Utilize the lesson plans created throughout Chapters 1–5 and create two full units of instruction
3. Design a course home page (create a course home page if access to an LMS is available) that includes a *Start Here* folder

Aesthetic Considerations

We began a discussion of the importance of good instructional design in Chapter 1. Ralph Tyler (1949) developed the basic four-step model for instructional design with four questions:

1. What are the educational objectives?
2. What experiences will support the objectives?
3. How should the experiences be organized?

Fluency in Distance Learning, pages 213–223
Copyright © 2010 by Information Age Publishing
All rights of reproduction in any form reserved.

4. How should the experiences be evaluated for effectiveness in attaining the objectives?

Subsequent instructional design models incorporate Tyler's standard into their framework. In this chapter, we again revisit the instructional design process and take a closer look at the visible appearance and navigation of an online course and associated course materials.

The Importance of the Instructional Design Process

As a reminder, the first step in distance learning course design is defining the learning outcomes (what needs to be learned and/or accomplished by students), which, in turn, determine the learning objectives (the steps taken to achieve the learning outcomes). The learning outcomes and objectives drive the selection of content. The next step is to choose the teaching/learning activities most likely to help learners achieve the intended learning outcomes. Teaching and learning activities must be organized in a way that scaffolds learning. Finally, evaluation and assessment strategies are identified to determine what students have learned and to provide feedback to them for continuous learning.

In the meta-analysis conducted by the United States Department of Education (2009) showing an advantage for online learning, it is important to note that it was the combination of time spent on tasks, curriculum, pedagogy, and opportunities for collaboration, that most likely produced the observed learning advantages. In light of this recent evidence for the benefits of distance learning, an important aspect of employing instructional design is its focus on the quality of learning experience for students. When engaged in the process of instructional design, you consider what content should be taught, additionally making decisions about how the knowledge, skills, and attitudes embedded in the content will be communicated to students in a systematic way.

Sound instructional design not only focuses on the development of curriculum, which has been the focus of this book up to this point, but it also includes additional design principles such as content organization, page layout, the use of color and graphical enhancements, and so on. All distance learning courses should, at a minimum, have these basic features:

1. Course home page
2. Course introduction: can be included on the course home page or as a separate page linked from the home page
3. Syllabus with contact information, list of objectives, and requirements: can be included as a link from the course home page

4. Course schedule: can be included on the course home page, calendar tool, or as a separate page linked from the home page
5. Course content arranged into modules and including the use of communication tools and activities: a link to the course content needs to be included on the course home page
6. Communication and collaborative tools, such as chat, discussion, email, wiki, and blog (or links to these tools)
7. Assessments, both formative and summative, should be included with each unit of instruction
8. Glossary of terms used in the course
9. Resources page with links to useful external course related information
10. Course evaluation: use quiz or survey tool, email, discussion postings, or evaluation forms required by institution/organization

Including the above components helps create a learner-centered online course. Teemant, Smith, Pinnegar, and Egan (2005) determined through a review of the literature that learner-centered online instruction contains the following characteristics: (1) is clear and understandable, (2) is responsive to the ways in which students learn and communicate, (3) recognizes student interests and motivations, (4) respects the social nature of learning, (5) engages students, and (6) provides meaningful and timely feedback. We would like to add one more element to this list: *is easy to navigate.* Frustration that interferes with learning ensues when students must contend with a confusing home page, spending precious time and effort puzzled about where important course information and resources are located. The presentation of visually appealing course materials is an important element of course design, and is considered by researchers to influence student motivation and satisfaction in the distance learning experience. Chan (1988) believes that students are attuned to the aesthetic aspects of the learning environment, and that aesthetic perceptions can significantly impact their learning. Recognizing that courses that are visibly well-designed and attractive include interesting images, balanced layout, straightforward navigation, and creative content presentation, Hathaway (1984) also noted that students express more enthusiasm for these courses.

The remaining sections of this chapter will focus on instructional design from a visual perspective. You will learn basic design principles for creating course pages and course documents. By following these design principles, you enhance your students' learning and provide visual interest and motivation.

Universal Principles of Visual Design

Hathaway (1984) insists that distance learning students prefer visual elements that are typically associated with aesthetic visual design. These visual elements, derived from knowledge about visual arts, include the use of text, graphics, space, and color applied in an effective manner that allows an ease of use, clarity of understanding, and that facilitates positive response. We begin our discussion of visual design with basic principles relevant to both online course pages and course documents. These principles include the elements of balance, rhythm, and dominance.

Balance

Balance has to do with the equilibrium that is achieved through the arrangement of the objects on a course page or document. Are the elements on the page or document designed in a manner that enhances their visual appeal? This question asks for consideration of symmetrical and asymmetrical stability. Symmetrical stability occurs when the items on a page (text, graphics) are evenly distributed around a centralized vertical or horizontal axis. Asymmetrical stability occurs when the items on a page are not evenly distributed around a centralized axis, but is achieved because items of various sizes are arranged on a page so that they visually balance each other. The visual elements of symmetrical and asymmetrical balance are represented in Figure 6.1.

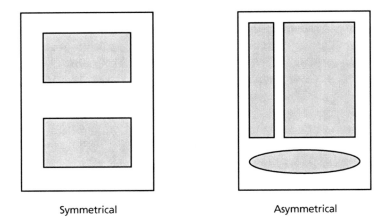

Symmetrical   Asymmetrical

Figure 6.1 Symmetrical and asymmetrical balance.

Rhythm

Visual *rhythm* is defined as the repetition or alternation of items that establishes a defined pattern, texture, or sense of movement. Regular rhythm occurs when the items have defined intervals between them, and the items themselves are the same size or length. Progressive rhythm depicts a sequence or hierarchy of items, such as a numbered list. The elements of rhythm are demonstrated in Figure 6.2.

Dominance

Dominance relates to the degree of emphasis placed on the item in the page or document. Giving dominance to an item impacts the visual weight of the entire page and often influences where your eye goes first when looking at the page. Elements may be dominant (the object that is given the most visual "weight"), sub-dominate (the element that receives secondary emphasis), and subordinate (the element that receives the least emphasis). The principles of dominance are represented in Figure 6.3.

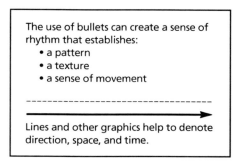

Figure 6.2 Demonstrations of rhythm.

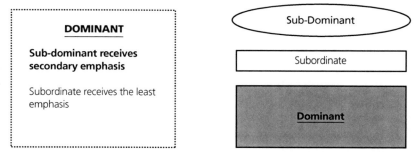

Figure 6.3 Principles of dominance.

Additional Course Design Principles

Sound instructional design not only focuses on the development of curriculum, but it also includes additional design principles such as content organization, page layout, the use of color and graphical enhancements, and course navigation. You must also consider the concept of *cognitive load* when designing your course pages. Of course, the most important page of your course is the home page. Specific strategies for designing the course home page are described in this section.

Cognitive Load

Cognitive Load is a psychology term referring to the burden placed on working memory during thinking, reasoning, and problem-solving processes. The greater the cognitive load, the harder it becomes to process information in working memory. Cognitive Load Theory (Sweller, 1988) states that "optimum learning occurs in humans when the load on working memory is kept to a minimum" (p. 266).

Three types of cognitive load have been identified: intrinsic, germane, and extraneous. Extraneous cognitive load, defined as the amount of unnecessary information provided, pertains specifically to the design of instructional materials and, therefore, will be our focus here. Based on this idea of extraneous cognitive load, page layout and design should be kept simple, with no unnecessary elements (links, graphics, text, etc.) on the course home page or other course pages. Only the most important elements should be included on the course home page, and course navigation must remain easy and consistent. In short, simplicity is the key to helping your students successfully maneuver through your course.

Cognitive Load Theory tells us that we must eliminate guesswork and frustration by making it simple for students to find information. To achieve simplicity, you will want to consider the "7 +/– 2" rule. This rule applies specifically to the course home page, but can also be used when designing other course pages. The course home page is valuable real estate and should not be overly cluttered with multiple links to other course resources. Simply stated, the 7 +/– 2 rule means that seven links from the course home page is considered to be the optimal use of home page space. However, you can use as few as five links, but no more than nine links, to achieve efficient and student-friendly course navigation. Hence, the 7 +/– 2 rule. Employing the 7 +/– 2 rule helps insure that there is plenty of "white space" on your course page, so as not to be cluttered and confusing to students.

The Course Home Page

Why all this fuss over the course home page? Students will form opinions about the visual appeal and organization of the home page in a few seconds, and first impressions count. First impressions can influence perceptions of credibility, user-friendliness, and value. As the introduction to your course, the home page is the initial page your students will visit when accessing the course; thus, it sets the stage for the rest of their experience.

The purpose of the course home page is to welcome students and provide a means for disseminating announcements and other information. A course home page usually contains links to the syllabus, course content, course resources, assessments, student grades, and communication tools such as a calendar, discussion board, email, and chat. The course home page provides structure and direction for students and helps to make the course come alive.

When developing your course home page, use straightforward instructions written in the active voice with easily understood buttons, icons, and labels. Overly complex designs with large graphic file sizes may be a barrier for students who connect to the Internet with low-bandwidth modems, or for disabled learners using special devices to interpret texts. In addition, avoid using animated graphics on your course home page, since they are often distracting for students.

Other Design Considerations for Your Course Home Page

The use of color on your course pages may seem like a simple task. However, the over-use of color can distract students away from the course content. It is recommended that you use no more than three colors for your course. And, once you have decided upon a color scheme for your course home page, keep the scheme consistent for all course pages. Make sure to use colors that complement each other. If your page has a dark background, use a light color for text; for a light background, choose a dark color for text.

Graphics can enhance your course home page, as well as other course pages and the presentation of course content. As previously mentioned, be mindful of file size, so that students using slower modems will not experience increased time for downloading pages. If you choose to use graphics, select graphics that relate specifically to the content of the page or unit.

When selecting your font type(s), keep the font choices simple. Some learning management systems (LMS systems) limit your font choices. Either way, use different fonts and font colors to create interest and organization, but do not go overboard. Limit choices to no more than two different fonts and colors. Black is easiest to read on a white background, so keep the body of your content in black, using a different color, such as red or dark blue, for headings and titles. Font styles are typically divided into two different categories: serif and sans serif. Serif fonts contain little curls at the end of the characters and are considered the easiest to read. Times New Roman, Bookman, and Garamond are popular serif fonts. Sans serif fonts, such as Arial, Helvetica, and Verdana, do not contain the curls and are often used for headings and titles in a larger size. It is recommended that font size be at least 12 point for easier readability.

Elements on the course home page should be visually connected; alignment of lines of text and images helps to organize and establish relationships between elements. The organization provided through alignment creates order and ultimately guides the student through navigating the page(s).

Applying Design Principles to Content Organization

The limited viewing nature of computer screens makes it cumbersome to read long passages of information. In addition, slow modems make it difficult for students to download large multimedia files. Therefore, it is better to deliver content in discrete chunks of information organized in a uniform format. Also, applying uniform design principles to the arrangement of content information allows students to efficiently navigate the course by effectively predicting location and access of course materials.

How course content should be structured and chunked must be guided by the nature of the content, which will direct in what ways it should be divided and organized. The chunked (sectioned) content should offer a reasonable amount of introduction and explanation of the subject. Base each section around specific objectives; identify them with titles and subtitles. Information that is not appropriate for chunking should be placed in a document available for students to download and/or print.

Sequencing

Course content can be arranged in a number of ways, depending upon the type of material and the context in which the material is presented. You may decide to sequence subject matter in chronological order, by topic, from concrete to abstract, by increasing level of proficiency, broad base of knowledge to specific focus, theory to practical application, or in many other ways appropriate to the content and learning objectives. Some considerations useful in guiding the logical sequence of material are (1) the relationship of the phenomena to the real world; (2) ways in which students use the information in educational, career, or personal situations; (3) the manner in which the major concepts and relationships are organized in the discipline; and (4) ways that knowledge has been created in the field.

Element Structure

The positioning of images, text, headings, video, and hyperlinks influences the visual appeal of the content presentation. Through the balanced grouping of these elements, visual organization is achieved. Controlling the amount of content that is presented helps students locate and retain information. Pomales-Garcia, Liu, and Lopes (2009) concluded that by commanding various dimensions of organization, structure, simplicity, and clarity, the attractiveness and aesthetic appeal of a distance learning course can be controlled through the following design elements: font, bullets, spacing, color, visuals, headings, borders, symmetry, balance, and navigation. Their study further determined that clarity is very important, with the use of text in a module the most important design element that influences all other design dimensions.

Course Navigation

Organizing the access of content for the end-user, the student, enhances the learning experience and makes life easier for the instructor. Carefully planned navigation provides a learning encounter that enables students to focus on learning, rather than experience stress about how to maneuver through the course. As mentioned in Chapter 1, having a "Start Here" or "Getting Started" section directs students to tasks that need to be completed at the beginning of the course, thus helping them to start the course on a positive note.

Examination of the Course Planning Guide will identify the main components of your course, which, in turn, may suggest appropriate links to important content areas and/or learning paths. Depending upon how the course is sequenced, the navigation may provide optional starting points or a linear step-by-step conduit to sequenced learning modules or units of study. Links will also be available to communication tools, such as email and discussion, as well as assignments, assessments, and other resources.

Design Principles for Handouts and Online Documents

Up to this point in the chapter, we have focused our attention on the design of course pages and the organization of course content. However, distance learning courses can and should include course content delivered via printable documents. As discussed in Chapter 3, the dynamic nature of distance learning is an excellent medium for conveying course concepts by utilizing rich multimedia resources that provide visual representation. The use of multimedia-based handouts (text with graphics) related to course curriculum provides imagery that helps students capture and share theories and assumptions about the content in a holistic way. Also, it must be noted that in order to be compliant with disabilities laws, any course content presented in multimedia format such as video, audio, or animation must include a printable transcript of the content.

Instructors often exert a lot of energy planning and creating handouts and documents to distribute to their students. It is particularly important for instructors of distance learning courses to pay close attention to the visual appearance of the document. Devoid of the face-to-face interaction of traditional courses, online documents must contain good layout and design to enhance the communication process. A paper/page that contains only pages and pages of text may have little appeal to today's students. To engage as well as instruct the learner, a well-designed document may include text, charts, and images arranged in a balanced and aesthetic way. The same color principles, font considerations, and alignment issues discussed for course pages also apply to printable documents. Remember, the first impression created by the appearance of a document can turn on or turn off the student's instincts to engage with the learning material.

Consistency

Provide unity in the document by utilizing the same design principle throughout the document. Using too many design styles makes the document hard to follow and may confuse the reader into thinking that it is not part of the same information. In addition, once you have created your document design, use the same design for subsequent documents.

Paragraph Spacing and Headings

Indenting or placing space between paragraphs helps readability. Another organizer is the use of headings and subheadings to break up long sections of text. It is easier to read and study sections of text than long, unbroken stretches of information.

Graphics

The use of graphics on course pages has been previously discussed. Using graphics for course documents/handouts as a means to provide visual imagery is valuable in explaining and making connections with content because graphics (1) provide alternatives to the constraints of language; (2) display relationships and dynamics that are difficult to represent through text; (3) appeal to intuitive, creative learners, as well as more logical, concrete learners; (4) make visual graphic connections to vague, theoretical, unusual, or esoteric descriptions and explanations; (5) stimulate imagination; (6) demonstrate interrelationships between different content; and (7) clarify complex processes.

Graphics, diagrams, charts, and tables should clarify the text. Sometimes graphics can actually be visual noise and detract from the message. Use visual media to focus learner attention to information that is critical to the understanding of concepts. Graphics are often an excellent way to help students make connections to complex concepts, or as a guide for processes, steps, or progressions.

End of Chapter Activities

The end of chapter activities provide opportunities for you to acquire new knowledge, gain skill, and apply principles and concepts. These activities are located on the Companion Website, and are divided into three subsections: Knowledge Building, Skill Building, and Practical Application.

References

Chan, T. C. (1988, January). The aesthetic environment and student learning. *School Business Affairs, 54*(1) 26–27.

Hathaway, M. D. (1984). Variables of computer screen display and how they affect learning. *Educational* Technology, 24(7), 7–11.

Pomales-Garcia, C., Liu, Y., Lopes, A. D. (2009, July). *Student perceptions on the importance of distance learning module design dimensions.* White paper presented at the 39th ASEE/IEEE Frontiers in Education Conference, San Antonio, TX.

Sweller, J. (1988) Cognitive load during problem solving: Effects on learning. *Cognitive Science,* 12(1): 257-285.

Teemant, A., Smith, M., Pinnegar, S., Egan, M.W. (2005). Modeling sociocultural pedagogy in distance education. *Teachers College Record, 107*(8). 1675–98.

Tyler, R. W. (1949) *Basic Principles of Curriculum and Instruction,* Chicago, IL: University of Chicago Press.

United States Department of Education, Office of Planning, Evaluation, and Policy Development. (2009). *Evaluation of evidence-based practices in online learning: A meta-analysis and review of online learning studies.* Washington, DC: U.S. Department of Education

7

The Future of Distance Learning

By now you have been provided with all of the necessary elements to create a dynamic and learner-centered distance learning course. From identifying the knowledge, skills, and attitudes necessary for effective distance learning facilitators, to incorporating specific active learning and communication strategies into your course, to designing multimedia-based content, to creating rubrics and providing instructions, to creating a variety of assessment types, to the physical/visual design of your course pages and documents—you are now ready to put all of the elements together to create your course. But before you begin, we ask that you reflect on the information provided in this chapter. Upon completion of Chapter 7, readers will be able to:

1. Discuss future trends in distance learning
2. Describe the possibilities that new technologies create for distance learning
3. Discuss the challenges facing distance learning instructors for the future

The Future of Distance Learning

Advances in technology and the pressure students feel to balance their busy lives with the help of distance courses has helped to fuel the exponential

Fluency in Distance Learning, pages 225–228
Copyright © 2010 by Information Age Publishing

growth of distance learning over the last ten years. With over 96% of institutions offering online courses, and almost 4 million students enrolled, it is doubtful that e-learning is a passing fad. History and technological progress is increasing the amount of information to be learned at an astounding rate. Today's students are exposed to more information in one year than their grandparents were during a lifetime. The nature of distance learning is conducive to helping students store, locate, research, analyze, and manipulate information on the Internet. Sustaining a competent workforce requires that employees continuously acquire new repertoires of knowledge, skills, and attitudes throughout their life. Business and industry, recognizing the efficiency and effectiveness of distance learning, have implemented e-learning for their professional development programs. But what does the future of distance learning look like? Which trends are influencing the path of distance learning? What issues should educators and students be concerned with? We offer the following observations for your reflection and consideration.

The World is a Classroom

The growing ubiquity of the Internet throughout the world has effectively shrunk our planet, creating a global society in which people collaborate in social and educational activities with others around the world in real time. The lack of geographic boundaries can dissolve cultural misunderstandings and biases, as faculty and students have opportunities to engage with others across the world. The evidence is clear that the Internet has revolutionized the way we deliver education.

Access to Information on Internet Empowers Learners to Assume Responsibility for Learning

Strained budgets will influence workplaces and educational institutions to offer more instruction online. The 24/7 access to information on the Internet is observed by several researchers as a positive influence on self-directed learning. Draves (2002) specified that learning at one's own pace, access to a large quantity of information, and ability to track personal progress are primary factors for cognitive learning occurring more effectively via the Internet than with in-person learning. Kerka (1997) notes the anytime, anywhere flexibility of the Internet in supporting self-directed learning. The stimulation of continuous access to information with no geographic boundaries or restrictions was acknowledged by Candy (2004).

Progress of Technology and Prevalence of Internet Encourages Innovative Web Resources

With millions of people online, and many more millions to come online in the near future, an increasing number of organizations, institutions, services, and resources will be housed online or have a component online. Museums, medical services, retail operations, government functions, and educational institutions already utilize the Internet and collaborative systems to connect with users. Today's students and faculty are able to interact synchronously and asynchronously with experts to access information and service. And technology will continue to progress, producing technologies much more advanced than those utilized today. Tomorrow's learners may engage with holographic images that depict historical battles, or consult virtually with their faculty as they work in a virtual 3-dimensional chemistry lab.

The Ability of Libelous and Threatening Postings on the Internet to Become Viral

The power to disseminate messages globally via blogs, twitter, and other Internet tools for discourse also has negative ramifications when people make false statements or claims in these forums that damage individual reputations. The Internet offers an environment where truth, opinion, satire, or libel can spread in viral fashion. What safeguards will companies and individuals take to protect their reputations against false salacious attacks? Educators will be faced with increasingly more difficult and complex cases of cyber-bullying.

Instructional Delivery gets Smaller and More Mobile

The ability to transmit audio, video, and other multimedia files to mobile devices has prompted development of an increasing number of applications. In the future, people may participate in real-time polls and voting, apply for jobs, chart real-time sales data, and perform synchronous collaborative presentations, all on an iPod, cell phone, or other mobile device. Moreover, an increasing number of educational institutions are venturing into the world of "mobile classrooms."

Final Thoughts

Many things will drive the future of distance learning. Certainly, Web and instructional technologies will serve as an infrastructure for online education in the coming years. The primary foundation, however, in the continued development and expansion of online learning will be the instructors who persist in facilitating creative thinking, reflective analysis, social responsibility, and collaborative decision-making through authentic learning activities that make for a valuable online learning experience. We hope that the information we have shared with you in this book has helped provide guidance and lay the groundwork for your participation in moving distance learning forward to meet the needs of learners.

References

Candy, P.C. (2004). Linking thinking—self-directed learning in the digital age. Canberra City, Australia: Department of Education, Science, and Training. Retrieved July 30, 2009, from http://www.dest.gov.au/sectors/training_skills/publications_resources_brochures/linking_thinking.htm

Draves, W. (2002, May). *How the Internet is changing how we learn.* Paper presented to the Seventh Annual Teaching on the Community Colleges Online Conference. Retrieved July 31, 2009, from http://kolea.kcc.hawaii.edu/tcc/tcon02/greetings/draves.html

Kerka, S. (1997). *Distance learning, the internet, and the world wide web.* Retrieved June 30, 2009, from http://www.ericdeigests.org/1997-1/distance.html

About the Authors

Celeste Fenton, Ph.D.

Holding a BA in Psychology, a M.Ed., and a Ph.D. in Education from the University of South Florida, Celeste has over 20 years experience as an educator in K–12 and higher education, and spent ten years in Human Resource management. In addition to directing the Center for Innovative Teaching and Technology Faculty Development department at Hillsborough Community College, she is an adjunct faculty member, teaching distance learning courses for Social Sciences. Celeste was selected as a consultant to the United States Agency for International Development (USAID) for international educational and workforce development. Other credentials include:

- Senior-level Advanced WebCT/Blackboard Certified Trainer status
- DACUM certified
- Finalist for the prestigious 2006 Bellwether Award from the Community College Futures Assembly for her work in online course development
- Contributor to many conference presentations including, most recently, the 2009 Innovations Conference sponsored by the League for Innovation
- 2008 Patricia Cross Fellowship Recipient; co-authored the 11th edition of the Cross Papers: *Learner-Centered Assessment: Real Strategies for Today's Students*

Fluency in Distance Learning, pages 229–231

- 2007 recipient of the United States Distance Learning Association Platinum Award for Online Teaching
- 2007 Innovation of the Year Award recipient from the League of Innovation for Community Colleges
- Finalist for the prestigious 2006 Bellwether Award from the Community
- Co-authored *Online Professional Development: A Community College and K–12 Partnership*, published by the League of Innovation for Community Colleges
- Co-authored *Teaching and Learning Strategies for 21st Century Workforce Education*
- Co-authored the *Occupational Education Distance Learning Policy Manual*
- Adjunct for University of South Florida (graduate courses) and Hillsborough Community College

Brenda Ward Watkins, M.A.

A full-time faculty member of the University of South Florida's College of Education for nine years, Brenda taught Business Technology Education courses and Diversity courses, both online and on-site. While at USF, she served on a committee that developed the first fully online M.A. program to be offered by the College of Education. For the past five years, her current position of Instructional Designer for Hillsborough Community College has allowed her to manage several major College initiatives, including the creation of online professional development for HCC faculty and staff, and the implementation of online professional development for Hillsborough County School District K–12 educators. Brenda's work experience includes finance work for a Fortune 500 company, as well as sales and marketing. She holds a B.S. in Finance, an M.A. in Business and Office Education, plus an additional 30 graduate hours in Higher Education Administration. Other credentials include:

- Adjunct faculty member for HCC's Educator Preparation Institute teaching the online Diversity course.
- Graduate level certification in Multi-media Instructional Design
- Contributor in many conference presentations including the WebCT Users Conference and, most recently, the 2009 Innovations Conference sponsored by the League for Innovation

- 2008 Patricia Cross Fellowship Recipient; co-authored the 11th edition of the Cross Papers: *Learner-Centered Assessment: Real Strategies for Today's Students*
- Finalist for the prestigious 2006 Bellwether Award from the Community College Futures Assembly for her work in online course development
- Co-authored *Online Professional Development: A Community College and K–12 Partnership*, published by the League of Innovation for Community Colleges
- WebCT Certified Trainer status
- Co-authored *Teaching and Learning Strategies for 21st Century Workforce Education*
- Co-authored *Occupational Education Distance Learning Policy Manual*

Glossary of Key Terms

Assessment

A continuous process aimed at improving student learning

Asynchronous

Instruction and/or communication takes place at different times, in different locations, eliminating obstacles related to time and travel constraints

Authentic assessment

Refers to the evaluation of students based on examination of their work or production of a product rather than standardized test scores

Authentic learning

Learning that takes place in settings that are significant and relevant to learners' needs and circumstances

Avatar

Allows students to create digital alter egos in a safe online environment

Balance

In reference to visual design, the equilibrium that is achieved through the arrangement of objects on a course page or document

Fluency in Distance Learning, pages 233–242
Copyright © 2010 by Information Age Publishing
All rights of reproduction in any form reserved.

233

Blended/Hybrid

Facilitation of course is a combination of online and face-to-face methods, with thirty to seventy-nine percent delivery conducted via online resources; examples of online activities include online discussions, posting and submission of assignments online, and multimedia lecture content available online (Allen & Seaman, 2008)

Blog

Commentaries published on the Internet in reverse chronological order; an asynchronous form of Internet discussion

Bloom's Taxonomy

Classification of levels of intellectual behavior important in learning; Bloom identified six levels within the cognitive domain, from the simple recall or recognition of facts as the lowest level (knowledge level), through increasingly more complex and abstract mental levels (comprehension, application, analysis, synthesis), to the highest order (evaluation level)

Case study

A specific situation or scenario that may be fact or fiction, where students explore solutions to the problem by asking "what if" questions which eventually leads students to solve the problem and/or form a conclusion

Chat

A synchronous communication tool included in many learning management systems that provides opportunity for real time collaboration

Classroom Assessment Techniques (CATs)

Formative assessments focused on awareness of student learning and the comprehension and application of what is being taught; strategies are learner-centered, simple, non-graded, sometimes anonymous activities, offering valuable feedback for teachers and students on the teaching–learning process

Cognitive load

A psychology term referring to the burden placed on working memory during thinking, reasoning, and problem-solving processes

Collaborative learning

A strategy that involves two or more students committed to and engaged in the sharing of ideas for construction of new learning

Computer Based Instruction (CBI)

A phrase also sometimes used to depict distance learning, but this is a less accurate term, as CBI can also involve students receiving instruction on a computer via CDs or DVDs without accessing instruction from a remote location

Constructivist learning theory

Speculates that effective learning takes place when learned information is applied to experiences and situations relevant to the learner

Copyright law

Provides authors and artists the right to deny others from copying and/or using their work without appropriate permission

Cyber classroom

One of the terms used to distinguish courses or degrees offered online through the Internet

Diagnostic assessment

Occurs at the beginning of the learning cycle; provides instructors with an understanding of the prior knowledge and skills a student brings to the unit of instruction as well as the strengths and specific learning needs of an individual or groups of student in relation to performance expectations

Digital generation

Learners that are not strangers to digital technology; today's students live in a media-rich, networked world of immediate information, and access.

Digital technology

Electronic technology that generates, stores, and processes data, primarily used in communications media such as satellite, fiber optics, computers, video, and audio

Discussion

An asynchronous tool that allows users to post messages and reply in a threaded forum

Distance learning

The acquisition of knowledge and skills through mediated information and instruction, encompassing all technologies and other forms of learning at a distance. (USDLA Glossary of Terms, 2009)

Dominance

In reference to visual design, relates to the degree of emphasis placed on the item in the page or document

E-Learning

One of the terms used to distinguish courses or degrees offered online through the Internet

Evaluation

Attaches a value (grade) to whatever is being examined, and may use assessment results in drawing conclusions in what is typically a summative appraisal

Fair Use Policy

Sets restraints to copyright protection, by allowing that limited use of a copyrighted work for certain purposes, particularly educational, is not an infringement

Feedback

Focused on providing information about progress on achieving the goals and objectives attached to specific understanding, application, and/or accomplishment; most feedback is un-graded; the concept of value or judgment is not part of the feedback process

Formative assessment

A learning experience that provides immediate information regarding the student's understanding and/or the ability to apply course concepts

Investigative inquiry

An active learning strategy that encourages students to explore and elucidate their findings based on their discoveries

Learning activity

What students do to learn the knowledge, skills, or attitudes necessary to demonstrate mastery of the learning objectives

Learning Management System (LMS)

Software that facilitates the delivery of distance learning content; anytime, anyplace, any pace access to instruction is a hallmark of LMS systems and is achieved through Web-based communication, and typically includes online tools that allow assessment, such as surveys and quizzes; communication tools, including email, discussion boards, and live chat; and content pages containing text documents and multimedia instruction

Learning objectives

Detailed statements that outline specifically what learners will know or be able to do at the conclusion of an activity, unit, course, or program, and the conditions and criteria that indicate the acceptable level of performance; expressed as knowledge, skills, or attitudes

Learning outcomes

Specify what the achieved results of student learning should be as the result of the instruction, that is, how the learning that took place will be evidenced

Learning styles

An approach to learning that recognizes that individuals attend to and process information in different ways

Mail

Common LMS asynchronous communication tool that allows users to send, receive, reply, and forward email messages within the course

MERLOT

The Multimedia Educational Resource for Learning and Online Teaching is an excellent online resource for multimedia content, including animations and other Web resources (www.merlot.org)

Mobile Technologies

Portable technology devices that facilitate the access and communication of information; examples of mobile devices include cell phone, iPod, MP3, personal digital assistants (PDA), laptop computers, and global positioning systems (GPS)

Multiple Intelligence Theory

Gardner's (1985, 1993) theory that suggests each individual has a unique pattern of strengths and weaknesses he deemed "intelligence types"

Online course delivery

The primary facilitation of the course is online, usually with no face-to-face meetings and eighty percent or greater of teaching and learning activities conducted online (Allen & Seaman, 2008)

Online learning

One of the terms used to distinguish courses or degrees offered through the Internet

Peer assessment

Involves students in an interactive process of review, assessment, and feedback to fellow students for the purpose of enhancing their own and their peers' learning and achievement

Podcasts

Distributes multimedia files over the Internet for playback on a computer or a mobile device, such as the iPod

Problem-based learning

The exploration by students of a problem within structured guidelines; students typically work collaboratively to define, conduct, and analyze a challenging real-world question or issue

Question bundle (QB)

A cluster of questions structured according to Bloom's Taxonomy that is beneficial in guiding students to think about a concept or topic in an organized way

Rhythm

In reference to visual design, the repetition or alternation of items that establishes a defined pattern, texture, or sense of movement; r*egular rhythm* occurs when the items have defined intervals between them, and the items themselves are the same size or length; p*rogressive rhythm* depicts a sequence or hierarchy of items, such as a numbered list

Rubric

Set of scoring guidelines for evaluation of student work

Self-assessment

Requires students to critically reflect on their learning, paying particular attention to their progress in achieving pre-determined learning goals

Service-learning

A strategy intended to promote academic enhancement, personal growth, and civic engagement by integrating academics with serving the community in ways that benefit both; students engage in meaningful service at a site within the community that supports course curriculum

Simulation

A specific real-world scenario is explored to answer specific questions and/or solve a problem

Skype

A free Internet-based communications software program that allows individuals to talk to each other all over the world for free through the Internet; a webcam can be used to send video

Social networking

Web 2.0 tools that engage users in reading, participating, commenting, contributing, and networking with each other; examples are wikis, blogs, YouTube, eBay, Amazon, Myspace, Facebook, and Twitter

Summative assessments

Cumulative in nature, and usually occur at the end of a topic, unit, or program for the purpose of generating a grade

Synchronous

Instruction and/or communication occurs in real time, whereby students and instructor exchange information at the same time and, most likely, from different locations

Traditional course delivery

Zero percent online technology resources utilized to deliver content or engage learners (Allen & Seaman, 2008)

Twitter

An online communication system that allows individuals to connect in real time via frequent and quick exchanges called *tweets* that are a maximum of 140 characters and can be thought of as micro-blogs or micro-text messages

Unit Content Guide

A tool for organizing thoughts, decisions, and the collection/creation of materials for your course in a sequential process

Virtual classroom

One of the terms used to distinguish courses or degrees offered through the Internet

Virtual fieldtrip

Websites that allow students to virtually journey to places they may not otherwise ever be able to visit and to make connections with course curriculum and the real world; many virtual fieldtrip sites allow students to ask questions of an expert, such as resident scientists, librarians, or historians, through email or phone

Virtual worlds

Can be used to create 3-dimensional learning environments that simulate various workplaces

Vodcast

Videos that are produced to be shown on cell phones and iPods

Web 1.0

Web technology tools engages users in reading content accessed from a website; content is static with little opportunity for student interaction

Web 2.0

Web technology allows learners to engage in peer-to-peer collaborative learning through tools such as blogs, wikis, webinars, multimedia, and social networks

Web 3.0

Technology based on intelligent Web applications with which users will be able to create new tools and applications through open-source software and systems

Web conferencing

Phone and Internet technology to join people at a distance in synchronous collaboration

Web-facilitated course delivery

Course is delivered primarily face-to-face, with one to twenty-nine percent usage of online technologies, such as utilizing a learning management system or website to present syllabus and assignment information (Allen & Seaman, 2008)

Web learning

One of the terms used to distinguish courses or degrees offered through the Internet

WebQuest

"An inquiry-oriented activity in which some or all of the information that learners interact with comes from resources on the Internet, optionally supplemented with videoconferencing" (Dodge, 1997); student-centered learning activities that present a question or problem centered around a topic or concept and challenge students to use Internet resources to obtain information on the topic

Wiki

A composition system that allows users to create and edit webpage content using any Web browser; for educational purposes, a wiki can serve as a discussion medium, a repository of ideas and contributions, and a tool for facilitating cooperative learning and collaboration

References

Allen, I. E. & Seaman, J. (2008). *Staying the course: Online education in the United States.* Sloan Consortium. Retrieved January, 2009 from http://www.sloan-c.org/publications/survey/pdf/staying_the_course.pdf

Dodge, B. (1997). *Some thoughts about WebQuests.* Retrieved June 9, 2007, from http://edweb.sdsu.edu/courses/edtec596/about_webquests.html

Gardner, H. (1993). *Frames of mind: The theory of multiple intelligences. Tenth anniversary edition with new introduction.* New York: Basic Books. (original work published 1985)

United States Distance Learning Association. (2009). *DL glossary.* Retrieved February 17, 2010, from http://www.usdla.org/html/resources/dictionary.htm

LaVergne, TN USA
14 September 2010

196874LV00001B/8/P